AMERICAN SOCIAL TRENDS

A M E R I C A N
S O C I A L
T R E N D S

Theodore Caplow
University of Virginia

Under the general editorship of
Robert K. Merton
Columbia University

Harcourt Brace Jovanovich College Publishers
Fort Worth   Philadelphia   San Diego
New York   Orlando   Austin   San Antonio
Toronto   Montreal   London   Sydney   Tokyo

Cover photo: HBJ Picture Library, San Diego, California. Photo courtesy of the United States Department of Agriculture.

ISBN: 0-15-502588-0

Library of Congress Catalog Card Number: 90-84049

Printed in the United States of America

PREFACE

This book is the result of my involvement during the past several years in two major studies of social change. Each was a collaborative effort that enlisted social scientists from several disciplines, and each pursued its elusive subject with a variety of methods. These studies provide interesting accounts of the collective American experience of recent decades.

One study was called the Middletown III project. Beginning in 1976, with generous support from the National Science Foundation, Howard M. Bahr, Bruce A. Chadwick, and I set out to reexamine the midwestern city that Robert and Helen Lynd selected in 1924 as a manageable specimen of American culture. The Lynds' first report, published in 1929 under the title of *Middletown*, became an instant classic. They went back to the same community in 1935 and meticulously described the changes wrought by the Great Depression.[1] These studies provide perhaps the best baselines we have for assessing continuity and change in American social institutions during this century. The Middletown III research team mined this extraordinary resource by matching thousands of items of information about contemporary Middletown with those collected by the Lynds many years before. My indebtedness to Howard Bahr and Bruce Chadwick, and to the many other scholars who joined the Middletown III team, is reflected on almost every page of this volume.

The findings of the Middletown III study, which centered on the major institutions of family, education, work, religion, leisure, and government, are not easy to summarize. We found innumerable changes but also much more continuity than we expected. Perhaps the most important change was the erosion of barriers between the business class and the working class. Although income and occupational advantage are as unevenly distributed in Middletown today as they were in 1924, education has been substantially equalized, and the living standards and cultural habits of blue-collar workers are no

[1]Robert S. Lynd and Helen Merrell Lynd, *Middletown: A Study in American Culture* (New York: Harcourt and Brace, 1929); *Middletown in Transition* (New York, Harcourt and Brace, 1937).

longer so very different from those of white-collar professionals. Middletown's two cultures have merged into a common culture.

The most striking continuities were found in the family, in religion, and in politics. The relationships between parents and adolescent children in 1978 were almost identical to those of 1924, except that parents and children spent more time together in 1978. The sermon topics of 1978 were indistinguishable from those of 1924, and the people we interviewed in 1978 described their private religious experiences in the same language their grandparents had used when interviewed by the Lynds in 1924.

Many of Middletown's family, religious, and political patterns had successfully resisted the pressures emanating from metropolitan centers, particularly the expanded local presence of the federal government and the influence of network television. The resistance was conscious and motivated. By and large, the Middletown people of 1978 were happy with their local and personal relationships but very uneasy about the nation's future. As we wrote in *Middletown Families*:

> With respect to the larger society, Middletown is gloomy indeed. What people of all ages see as they look into the future is nuclear war, environmental pollution, inflation, exhaustion of resources, and a general deterioration of the quality of life. Faced with these discouraging prospects, they avert their eyes and return to the felicities of family life, the comforts of religion and the wide range of private pleasures available to them. The alternative to catastrophe that they desire is not continued progress but a prolongation of the status quo.[2]

That finding forced us to ask whether Middletown's view of national trends was accurate or mythical, and it eventually led us into another team research project; begun in 1986, it is called the International Research Group for the Comparative Charting of Social Change in Advanced Industrial Societies. This project grew out of several years of informal collaboration between the Middletown III team and a group of scholars at the University of Paris, led by Henri Mendras and Jacques Lautman, who were involved in a very large interdisciplinary study called the Observation of Social Change. Mendras recruited a research team—they adopted the collective pseudonym of Louis Dirn—to examine the causal relations among

---

[2]Theodore Caplow, Howard M. Bahr, Bruce A. Chadwick et al., *Middletown Families: Fifty Years of Change and Continuity* (Minneapolis: University of Minnesota Press, 1982), 37.

French social trends and to develop methods for analyzing a matrix of related trends.[3]

The discovery that researchers at J. W. Goethe University in Frankfurt and at Laval University in Quebec were working along parallel lines led to the establishment in 1986 of the International Research Group, which was facilitated by a grant from the Council for European Studies. The group's activities have been coordinated in Germany by Wolfgang Glatzer, in Canada by Simon Langlois, in France by Henri Mendras, and in this country by this author. John Modell of Carnegie-Mellon University, Michel Forsé of the French OFCE, and Karl-Otto Hondrich of Goethe University have made particularly important contributions to the theoretical framework of the project.

At a conference in Paris in May 1987, the four national teams agreed on a list of 71 categories of trends that, taken together, might provide a standardized profile of social change for a modern national society. During the year that elapsed before the next conference at Bad Homburg in May 1988, the national teams prepared detailed reports on most of these trends in their own countries. At Bad Homburg, the number of trend categories was increased to 78 and their format was considerably refined. The 1989 conferences in Quebec City and in Nice and a 1990 conference in Madrid continued the work. At this writing, a complete set of trend reports has been published for each of the four societies, a second cycle of reporting has begun with the recruitment of teams from several other nations, and about a dozen comparative analyses involving international and interdisciplinary collaboration are in progress. I have drawn on this body of work for the present volume and on the U. S. trend reports prepared by Professors Bahr, Chadwick, and Modell, Dr. Achsah Carrier, and myself.[4]

The outline we follow here is quite different from that of the Comparative Charting Project. In a description of the Comparative Charting Project prepared for the Council for European Studies we summarized our common purpose as follows:

> As we compare our separate bodies of work, we have the impression of being surrounded by the bits and pieces of a new

[3]See Louis Dirn, "Pour un Tableau Tendanciel de la Société Française: Un Parti de Recherche," *Revue Française de Sociologie,* 26 (1985): 389–408.

[4]Theodore Caplow, Howard M. Bahr, Bruce A. Chadwick, and John Modell, *Recent Social Trends in the United States, 1960–1990* (Frankfurt: Campus Verlag and Ottawa: McGill University Press, 1990). Similar volumes, presenting English translations of the French, German, and Quebecois trend reports, will be published in the same series.

theoretical model waiting to be assembled, a model that does not require social change to continuous, cumulative, consistent, or irreversible, but that acknowledges the symbolic and subjective character of social reality.

The most important thing we know about this unbuilt model is that it treats the future of contemporary societies as open—not completely determined by the past, and not inevitable. With such a model, prediction does not consist of peering into a crystal ball to descry the ordained shape of things to come, but of specifying the available choices and the constraints that accompany them.[5]

In Act III of Bizet's *Carmen*, the gypsy girls ask the tarot cards to give them "news of the future," and Carmen draws the card that tells her she must soon die. She accepts her fate because—as she sings in a lovely aria—"the cards are sincere and will not lie." For Carmen the future is as unalterable as the past. This predestinarian view of the future is not restricted to gypsy fortune-tellers. Many theories of social change are predestinarian, telling us that some future condition of society is inevitable. This book takes the contrary position, assuming that past trends influence but do not determine future events. The choices we make as we go along are decisive, and social science research is one good way of exploring our options.

The trend reports produced by the Comparative Charting Project are all based on *time series*, which are tables or charts that display the changing values of some quantitative measure of a social phenomenon over time. To be admissible in one of the project's trend reports, a time series must cover a period of at least ten years, include information for at least three points of time, be subject to independent verification, and be replicable in other countries and in future years. To be useful for charting present tendencies, a series must extend close to the present, preferably to within two or three years. But how far back should it go? Initially, we thought that 1945 would be appropriate for most purposes, although we did not intend to disregard longer historical series when they were available. But as the work proceeded, it became increasingly clear that 1960 marked a point of inflection for western Europe and North American societies, with the completion of the postwar adjustment and the emergence of new tendencies. Our awareness of 1960 as a turning point was reinforced by the publication in 1988 of Henri Mendras'

---

[5]Theodore Caplow, "The Comparative Charting of Social Change in Advanced Industrial Societies," Council for European Studies, *European Studies Newsletter*, 17 (April 1988), 1–9.

brilliant analysis of recent social trends in France, *La Seconde Revolution Française, 1960–1985*,[6] which took 1960 as the starting point for a dramatic transformation of French society. That bloodless revolution resolved many of the traditional problems of French society—the lack of demographic vitality, the isolation of the peasantry, the stagnation of provincial cities, the excessive centralization of authority, the conflict between republicanism and clericalism, political instability, class conflict, and blocked mobility. It was an era of unalloyed triumph.

In the United States, too, 1960 seemed to usher in a new era, marked both by remarkable achievements and by extraordinary setbacks. We landed on the moon but we lost our industrial supremacy. We emancipated minorities but we created the most deprived underclass in the Western world. We were badly defeated in Vietnam but we won the cold war. We expanded the welfare state and we aggravated the problems of poverty, health care, crime, and education. We enacted political reforms and we got an unbroken string of political scandals. We enjoyed the longest economic boom in history and we incurred a mountain of debt.

These past three decades have been extraordinarily eventful for the United States. We stop with 1990 because we must, but the story continues.

I want to thank Louis Hicks for his invaluable assistance in the preparation of this book and the staff of Harcourt Brace Jovanovich: Jon Preimesberger, for his careful and sympathetic editing; Diana Parks, for the cover design; Jamie Fidler, for the interior book design; and David Hough, for production management.

---

[6]Henri Mendras, *La Seconde Revolution Française, 1960–1985* (Paris: Presses Universitaires de France, 1988).

CONTENTS

1

INTRODUCTION

This is a book about social change in the United States, focused on the 30 years from 1960 to 1990, a time of great excitement and mixed blessings. The major directions of change will be described by statistical trends. After the existence of a trend has been confirmed, anecdotal material may come into the discussion, but we will not speculate about any trend that is not based on apparently reliable numbers.

The reason for this self-imposed rule is that trends derived from anecdotal information, common knowledge, and personal observation often turn out to be imaginary. The casual observer of social change compares some observed present condition with a supposed past condition and concludes that marriage is going out of style, that colleges have deteriorated, that mental illness has become epidemic, that religion has lost its influence, that workers no longer take pride in their work, that everything costs more than it used to, that highways are more dangerous, crime more violent, and businesspeople more predatory than ever before, and so on and so forth. Many Americans take all of these trends for granted and view them with justifiable alarm, although on the available evidence, all of them are false.

Scholars are susceptible to similar errors when they reconstruct the past without numerical data. It was scholars who first told us about the isolation of the nuclear family, the alienation of the white-collar worker, the end of ideology, the managerial revolution, and many another trend that owed more to intuition than to evidence.

There are good reasons why intuitive descriptions of social change are so often mistaken. Nostalgia prettifies and improves the past. Personal experience is projected to the whole society. Things around us look different as we grow older. Intuitive observers are especially vulnerable to their own political biases; conservatives always perceive increasing welfare fraud, and liberals always count a growing number of hungry children.

The most serious defect of the intuitive approach to social change lies in the material rather than the observer. Social change is much less orderly than we intuitively expect it to be. The trends displayed by time series are inexplicably diverse. No one really knows why attendance at harness races fell so sharply in recent years while attendance at other horse races was rising. No one completely understands why Americans became more pious after World War II while religion was weakening throughout western Europe. The positive correlation between the divorce rate and marital happiness is not what most people would expect. Intuition tells us that social trends should march in step; the numbers tells us that they seldom do.

Throughout this volume, we will distrust intuition and try to follow the excellent maxim of Bernard de Fontenelle (1657–1757), a pioneer of the scientific method who said, "Before seeking the cause of a phenomenon it is prudent to ascertain that the phenomenon exists."

When we do find that a phenomenon exists, the question remains of where to look for its cause. Trends in collective behavior and social relationships may be traceable to social and technological inventions, the efforts of change agents, market transactions, the discovery and exhaustion of resources, the imitation of successful projects, or just to the oscillations of values and attitudes that occur spontaneously in every field of human activity.

The typical adaptation of a social system to a technological or social invention is rapid and discontinuous. The mode of utilization and the accompanying perceptions appear almost overnight and then persist for many years without much alteration. Almost everything the Lynds had to say about the social meaning of the automobile in Middletown in 1924,[1] when automobiles were new, is still valid today. The American pattern of television programming developed in the first three or four years of commercial telecasting and has remained essentially unchanged ever since. This sequence—rapid adaptation to a new invention followed by a long period of stability in the mode of utilization—has even been observed in bands of apes.

Modern societies are crowded with change agents—government agencies, political leaders, moral entrepreneurs, educators, experts, advertisers, gurus, consultants, lobbyists—who have innumerable designs for modifying the actions and sentiments of their fellow citizens. Many of these efforts induce measurable changes in collective behavior and social relations, always somewhat different from the changes that were sought.

Every social system operates under material constraints that reduce the immense number of projects that can be conceived to a much smaller number for which the necessary resources can be found. The boundary between the possible and the impossible keeps shifting as resources are discovered or exhausted and as the costs and benefits of projects are modified by fluctuations in various markets.

The repeated imitation of successful small-scale projects accounts for a great number of important social trends like international migration, urbanization and suburbanization, and the diffusion of new forms of leisure. It is not a social force, but it does the work.

The oscillation of values and attitudes in every field of human activity appears, on the evidence, to be partly cyclical and partly random. It is exemplified by such diverse phenomena as the rise and decline of scholarly theories, clothing fashions, fads and crazes, the fluctuation of party strength in two-party systems, changes in nutritional patterns, and shifts in public opinion. Such oscillations are never predictable in detail; they are produced by innumerable minor accidents.

In addition to seeking the causes of change, we must make room for the factors contributing to stability in social systems. There is a great deal of continuity in contemporary societies and change often fails to occur where it might be expected. Why, for instance, has the content of the American high school curriculum remained virtually the same since 1890, despite recurrent waves of educational reform? How can the content analyses of Protestant sermons show the same distribution of themes today as in the 1920s? Why are there no fashions to speak of in men's clothing? Why are occupational prestige scales more stable than the occupations to which they refer? Why is the division of household labor between husbands and wives so little affected when wives take paid jobs?

The reasons for such continuities must be sought in the transmission of roles between generations, the principle of limited possibilities, the inflexibility of linguistic and symbolic systems, the persistence of archaic elements in modern societies, and the deliberate conservation of real and synthetic traditions.

A large number of roles and expectations—especially those having to do with family relationships, childhood and adolescence, work, and religion—are acquired from the parental generation and transmitted to the filial generation without much change.

The principle of limited possibilities tells us that such relationships as marriage, friendship, apprenticeship, and rivalry do not have infinitely variable forms, so that any given form, once established, tends to persist.

The inflexibility of linguistic and symbolic systems is more easily demonstrated than explained. Despite large accretions of new vocabulary, the major languages of the Western world have shown very little grammatical evolution during the twentieth century. The same is true of many other symbolic systems, like the rules of chess, wedding customs, or the operatic repertory.

The survival of archaic elements is a ubiquitous feature of the modern era. Archaic occupations, work methods, organizations, artifacts, and attitudes survive in rural communities long after they have disappeared from metropolitan cities. But there are plenty of survivals in metropolitan culture too. Obsolete modes of transportation, for example, do not disappear but are converted to leisure use, so that contemporary urban-dwellers have large numbers of horses and canoes.

The social value attached to tradition imposes a certain stability on the rituals of repetitive occasions: festivals such as Christmas and Easter, political conventions and inaugurations, anniversaries and centennials, graduations and dedications, senior proms and charity balls, the World Series, the Superbowl, the U. S. Open, the Kentucky Derby. Much of what passes for ancient tradition, like the cap and gown worn at graduations, is of rather recent invention, but venerable anyway.

At that earlier stage of modernization in which sociology became an academic discipline, most of the population spent most of their waking hours at work and the energetic pursuit of leisure was limited to a small elite. Our categories for the description of social trends still bear the imprint of those vanished times by treating unemployment, welfare, and poverty as more descriptive of social structure than the life-style of retired persons, the development of commercial sport, or the growth of mass media audiences. As we discuss social trends, the division of labor and its effects on individual lives will continue to be emphasized, but the division of leisure and its multiple consequences will not be neglected.

Some trends will be omitted, of course. There is no way to paint a comprehensive picture of social change in a modern society. The subject is vast, its boundaries vague, and its facets innumerable. Even though our inquiry focuses on the 30-year period from 1960 to 1990, which is relatively well documented, there are huge gaps in the data on such basic topics as health, crime, and productivity. And some trends must be excluded because 30 years is too short an interval. There are no chapters on social class or occupational inheritance in this book because they require a longer time frame.

Our reliance on numerical data for the description of contemporary American trends has drawbacks as well as advantages. The official statistics of the United States are inferior in quality and coverage to those of most other advanced industrial nations and in some respects they are deteriorating. We depend upon the decennial enumerations conducted by the Bureau of the Census to count the population and to provide sampling frames for surveys. But the census information, which was collected by door-to-door interviewing from 1790 to 1960, is now extracted from mail questionnaires that have higher rates of error and omission.* The situation is no better with respect to statistics of business activity, working conditions, housing, religion, health, and crime. The *Statistical Abstract of the United States*, issued annually, is the source most frequently cited in the following pages.[2] Although it contains an inexhaustible wealth of information, it is in some respects a statistician's nightmare. In many tables, the latest data are years out of date. When the same entry appears in several tables, the numbers are likely to disagree. Topics and categories shift capriciously from year to year. Many of the terms used in captions and legends are undefined. Many entries are implausible. Errors are particularly noticeable in national tables constructed by collating reports from state and local agencies, like the Uniform Crime Reports assembled by the Federal Bureau of Investigation. When the people who report events have clear motives for inflating or deflating the numbers and the people who receive the reports have no authority to demand verification, inaccuracy is guaranteed. The net effect of the poor quality of official statistics in the United States is that it is quite impossible to ascertain such elementary facts as the number of resident aliens, the rate of criminal recidivism, the volume of imported oil entering the country, or the frequency of malpractice claims against physicians. With the exception of voting patterns in national elections, there is no social issue before the American public for which the statistical information is as detailed and reliable as the statistics of major league baseball.

---

*The 1990 Census was probably the most defective decennial enumeration since the series began in 1790.

This situation requires us to be constantly vigilant when examining trends. The possibility that the numbers are wrong can seldom be completely excluded when working with U. S. time series. The best protection against being misled by defective data is to cross-check continually, one time series against another, one source against another, official data against private studies, enumerations against sample surveys, national series against local series. I have sometimes used trend information from Middletown,[3] which is more detailed and more easily verified than national data, to cross-check national trends. Although Middletown is not a microcosm of the nation, most of its trends run parallel to national trends. Similarly, the sample surveys conducted by polling organizations like Gallup and Roper provide abundant information to cross-check with official statistics. The *General Social Survey*, an omnibus survey of a sample of the national population repeated every year since 1972 by the National Opinion Research Center, has been particularly helpful in the preparation of this volume.[4]

I have drawn trend data from many sources, where they were presented in tables and charts of various styles, interspersed with other information. For the sake of clarity, the statistical tables in this book are presented in a very simple format that includes only the most essential information. Full citations are given so that the reader can track every number back to its source.

Our discussion of social trends will continue, in Chapter 2, with an examinination of the connection between scientific-technological progress and social change. That turns out to be the thread on which the dominant paradigms of social science have been strung since the mid-nineteenth century. But contemporary research shows the connection to be more complex than was previously suspected, because of the sheer diversity of social trends, which may be long-term or short-term; continuous or episodic; universal or local; linear, curvilinear, oscillating, cyclical, or random. Mingling with this intellectual menagerie are imaginary trends based on misperceptions and astonishing continuities that go completely unnoticed. Chapter 2 emphasizes the distinction between an important set of social trends that are directly linked to scientific-technological progress and other social trends that are not.

Chapter 3 describes the big trends that *are* closely linked to technology and that have been running for two centuries or more without interruption. The big trends are long-term increases in population, wealth, mechanical energy, and knowledge; in industrial and agricultural productivity; in the volume and velocity of commerce and communication; the improvement of health; the availability of human services; the number and size of great cities; the expansion of governmental authority; the intensification of war; the erosion of local cultures; the increasing interference with nature; and hundreds of parallel trends that reflect the steady expansion of human capabilities made possible by the advancement of science and the discovery of new technologies. Collectively, they constitute the unique historical event we call modernization, which began in northwestern Europe around the middle of the seventeenth century, eventually expanded to cover the entire world, and as yet shows no loss of momentum.[5]

Chapter 4 compares the recent paths of the big trends for the U. S. and for the rest of the world; some of the comparisons are alarming. In the 30 years from 1960 to 1990, the United States lost its enormous lead over the other advanced nations in the modernization procession and transformed itself from the world's largest creditor to the world's largest debtor. That this abrupt decline was largely attributable to inept public policies is one of the central themes of this book.

Chapter 5 describes some of the imaginary trends that color contemporary views of social change, with special attention to the decline of religion, diminishing literacy, increasing mobility, the growing burden of mental illness, and the acceleration of social change— nonproblems for which new solutions are proposed every day. Though imaginary, these trends are widely believed and therefore have real consequences.

In Chapters 6 to 11, the American social structure is divided into six institutional sectors for the more convenient analysis of trends in family, work, education, leisure, religion, and government. This simple classification, originally devised by a British anthropologist, W. H. R. Rivers, was used by the Lynds as the framework for their Middletown studies and proved durable enough to be used in the Middletown III study half a century later. Although the classification is unpretentious, it has surprising analytical power, as will appear in Chapter 12, where the six institutional sectors are treated as a causal matrix and we examine the influence of trends in each sector on each of the other sectors.

In each of the institutional chapters, we try to identify the most significant trends of the past three decades, those that involve large changes and important consequences. That judgment is partly subjective, of course, but in most instances, the significant trends seem to jump out of a mass of inconclusive trends and command our attention. In the chapter on the family, such conspicuous trends as the decline of fertility, the deregulation of premarital sex, the increasing employment of married women, the spectacular rise in the number of illegitimate births and of single-parent families, and the increasing differentiation of white and black family patterns, would be hard to ignore. In religion, the growth of the evangelical denominations at the expense of the mainstream Protestant churches, and their increasingly divergent political tendencies, are equally conspicuous. In the chapter on work, the spotlight necessarily falls on the increasing ratios of white-collar workers to blue-collar workers and of women to men in the labor force, the gradual disappearance of dangerous and disagreeable jobs, and the lagging growth of productivity. In discussing leisure, we dwell perforce on the leisure explosion and the simultaneous expansion of active and passive pastimes, the increasingly minute division of leisure, and the lessening differentiation of leisure activities by gender, social class, race, and age. Considering trends in government, our attention is inevitably drawn to the expansion of federal authority into areas formerly reserved for state, local, and private authorities, the dramatic increase in government expenditures at all levels, the dizzying escalation of health and educational costs under the spur of third-party payments, the commercialization of politics, and the civilianization of the armed forces. In each of these institutional sectors, the identification of significant trends seems to be a straightforward task, driven by the available data. Another analyst might see the picture in a different light, but it ought to be recognizably the same picture.

The next four chapters, 13 to 16, describe recent trends in American attitudes and practices about money, sex, health, and intoxication. The chapter on money considers such matters as the distribution of income and expenditure, the long-term movement of prices, and the varieties of pecuniary emulation. The chapter on sex summarizes the dramatic changes that have occurred in erotic attitudes and practices within a generation together with some overlooked continuities. The chapter on health describes trends in general health, the popular mythology of health, the development of new medical and surgical capabilities, the overgrowth of the health care system, and the recent appearance of new plagues in place of old ones. The chapter on intoxication describes the rapidly changing attitudes and practices associated with the consumption of alcohol, tobacco, prescribed mood-changing drugs, and illegal mood-changing drugs, together with the extraordinary consequences of attempting to suppress the illegal ones.

Chapter 17 on ethnicity traces the recent evolution of social divisions based on race, religion, national origin, and various combinations of these. The two most important trends of the past three decades were the achievement of full legal equality by ethnic minorities and the disappointing outcome of efforts to achieve social and economic equality. Chapter 18 considers recent social movements and describes their successes and failures, with special attention to civil rights, women's liberation, and the environmental movement.

Chapter 19 on future trends presents a summary list of the 90 leading trends described in previous chapters, followed by an inventory of the social problems that became intractable between 1960 and 1990: the debt burden, the condition of the underclass, the deteriorating infrastructure, single-parent poverty, diminished industrial competitiveness, the excessive costs of health care and education, the unwinnable "war on drugs," environmental pollution, excessive litigation, political corruption, and the apparent decline of bureaucratic competence. The question of how this packet of problems can be resolved is considered in several different lights as we speculate in a moderately hopeful way about America's future.

NOTES

1. Robert S. Lynd and Helen Merrell Lynd, *Middletown: A Study in American Culture* (New York: Harcourt and Brace, 1929).
2. Published annually in midsummer by the U. S. Department of Commerce, Bureau of the Census. The 1989 edition was the 108th. It contains nearly 1,000 pages and nearly 1,500 tables, and is cited in the notes to subsequent chapters as *SAUS89*, followed by a table or page number. Because no consistent practice is followed with respect to the number of years included in tables showing trends, the construction of time series of reasonable length requires frequent use of other than current editions (denoted for example as *SAUS79* or *SAUS66*) and of another indispensable reference work from the same source, *Historical Statistics of the United States: Colonial Times to 1970*, published in two volumes in 1975.

3. In addition to the Lynd book referenced in footnote 1, there is also the follow-up work: Robert S. Lynd and Helen Merrell Lynd, *Middletown in Transition* (New York: Harcourt and Brace, 1937). Recent studies include Theodore Caplow, Howard M. Bahr, Bruce A. Chadwick et al., *Middletown Families: Fifty Years of Change and Continuity* (Minneapolis: University of Minnesota Press, 1982) and *All Faithful People: Change and Continuity in Middletown's Religion* (Minneapolis: University of Minnesota Press, 1983). A list of other publications is available from the Center for Middletown Studies at Ball State University in Muncie, Indiana.

4. Published annually in the form of a cumulative codebook reporting the results of the omnibus annual surveys of national samples of about 1,500 respondents conducted every year since 1972, and also circulated on diskettes for direct consumer entry. In notes to subsequent chapters, the *General Social Survey, 1972–1989*, published in 1989 by the National Opinion Research Center, will be cited as *GSS89*, followed by an item number.

5. The best concise account of this historical sequence is Daniel Chirot, *Social Change in the Modern World* (San Diego: Harcourt Brace Jovanovich, 1986).

2

HOW SOCIAL CHANGE DIFFERS FROM TECHNOLOGICAL PROGRESS

During the nineteenth century, thoughtful observers in Europe and America were fascinated by the unprecedented growth of population and production that was occurring around them, accompanied by new machines, new forms of organization, and new modes of sensibility. Their efforts to interpret these spectacular developments created the social sciences of anthropology and sociology, which still bear the marks of their origin. The founders of these disciplines looked at first for a single formula—a sort of magic key—to explain the phenomenon that we now call modernization. Once discovered, it would be able to unlock the future as easily as the past.

The quest for the magic key eventually produced three influential models of social change: the linear progress model, the transformation model, and the apocalyptic model.

The linear progress model visualized social development as mankind's steady ascent up a ladder of predictable stages, each stage marked by parallel improvements in technology, social organization, and moral excellence. It was unquenchably optimistic about the future and expected social problems to solve themselves, as you may read in the works of Herbert Spencer:

> The advance from the simple to the complex, through a process of successive differentiation ... is seen in the evolution of humanity, whether contemplated in the civilized individual or in the aggregate of races; it is seen in the evolution of society in respect alike of its political, its religious and its economical organizations.[1]

The transformation model identified the transition from traditional to modern forms of social organization as the central event of recent history. It predicted the eventual modernization of all societies and all institutions but was a little vague about what would happen after that. The several versions of this model are easily recognized by their paired labels for the conditions before and after the transformation: status–contract, Gemeinschaft–Gesellschaft, mechanical solidarity–organic solidarity, traditional–modern, folk–urban. Emile Durkheim supplied the most sophisticated account of the transformation in his famous book, *The Division of Labor in Society.*[2]

The apocalyptic model described modern societies as moving towards a culminant struggle which would change them beyond recognition. In the Marxist version of the apocalyptic model, which is the most familiar, history is the record of class struggles but the final victory of the proletariat will abolish social classes and put an end to history. This theory was elaborated in a long series of nineteenth-century writings from *The Communist Manifesto* in 1848 to *The Class Struggle* in 1893.[3] Another apocalyptic model, Gobineau's theory of racial inequality,[4] eventually flowered into the racial policies of the Third Reich.

As crystal balls, these nineteenth-century theories of social change were remarkably flawed. The events of the early twentieth century bore no resemblance to what had been predicted by the best minds of Europe and America a few years earlier. The continued progress towards individual freedom anticipated by Spencer was rudely interrupted by the rise of the authoritarian state. The decline of national solidarity perceived by Durkheim in the 1890s was illusory; nationalism would be one of the dominant themes of the twentieth century. The proletarian revolutions that were to cause the state to wither away caused it instead to become larger and more tyrannical.

The failure of the classical theories of social change to deliver accurate predictions did not diminish their influence very much. The idea that society might be perfected in one way or another—by social evolution or by modernization or by revolution—was too deeply embedded in the foundations of the social sciences to be easily dislodged. But after 1900, as it became apparent that events were not conforming to the dominant models of social change, two new models were proposed: the cyclical model and the linear regress model.

The cyclical model describes social change as an oscillation between opposing possibilities. The most elaborate version is found in Pareto's gigantic 1916 *Treatise on General Sociology,*[5] which describes many cyclical sequences such as this one: the decentralization of power in a society increases the reliance of the rulers on

voluntary compliance, which leads to a breakdown of their authority, which is remedied by the reconcentration of power, which involves an increase of coercion, which provokes resistance, which
leads eventually to the decentralization of power, whereupon the
sequence begins again. Another cyclical theory, which sees societies
as perpetually fluctuating between sensual and spiritual values, was
the work of the Russian-American sociologist Pitirim Sorokin, set
forth at length in his *Social and Cultural Dynamics* in 1937.[6] The im-
plicit argument of cyclical theories is that social improvement is
impossible.

The linear regress model, of which innumerable versions have
been presented since Oswald Spengler launched the genre with *The
Decline of the West* in 1918,[7] turns the linear progress model upside
down, asserting that the ultimate consequence of technological
progress is not the perfecting of society but the destruction of social
order. Some versions anticipate universal calamity; others hold out
the hope that modern societies can be saved by abandoning high
technology and large-scale organization.

So far as the record goes, the cyclical models seem to yield
somewhat better predictions than the others, although when it
comes to specificity, none of them has much of an edge over Chinese
fortune cookies.

To understand why these grand models of social change predict
the future so badly we must recall the question to which they are
responses: What is the connection between scientific-technological
progress and social change in modern industrial societies?

Since about 1650, scientific-technological progress has been
continuous, cumulative, consistent, and irreversible. The effort to
discover the principles governing natural phenomena has not met a
serious check. Although scientific theories are even less durable
than theories of social change, the technology derived from physics,
chemistry, and biology grows steadily more competent year by year.
The leading edge of any technology based on the natural sciences
moves inexorably forward. The lowest temperatures that can be produced in the laboratory this year will be surpassed by lower temperatures next year. The velocities obtained in the newest particle
accelerator will be exceeded in the next generation of accelerators.

Although it now appears that technology, population, and productivity began their unprecedented upward movement in northwestern Europe before the end of the seventeenth century, it was not
until the middle of the nineteenth century—the era of railroad
building—that the direct effects of technology on social organization

became too obvious to ignore[8] and scholars set to work to clarify the connection.

The easiest solution was to equate social progress with technological progress. Social progress too would be continuous, cumulative, consistent, and irreversible. But difficulties appeared very soon. Even the most ardent apostles of linear social progress noticed that social progress often faltered and sometimes went into reverse. The more closely the differences between technological and social progress were exan.ined the larger they loomed. The transformation models allowed social change to be discontinuous but still required it to be consistent and irreversible. The apocalyptic models abandoned the requirement that social change be cumulative but insisted that it be consistent and irreversible. The cyclical theorists were forced to ignore the unique features of modernization in order to make their point that social change is perpetually reversible. And the linear regress models, like the linear progress models they challenge, ascribe more continuity and consistency to social change than can be found in trend data.

Each of these theories attributed some of the features of technological progress to social change; the element common to all of them was the expectation that social change would be consistent, in other words, that all the parts of a social system would develop in the same direction in response to the same social forces. Because the classical models took social change to be consistent, they encouraged the misinterpretation of empirical data, and the habit has persisted to this day. We hear, for example, that in contemporary American society, accelerating mobility has loosened the attachments of individuals to communities; that the bonds of kinship no longer offer support to the isolated nuclear family; that religion has become irrelevant to practical concerns; and that permissiveness has undermined traditional standards of conduct.

The most cursory review of empirical data is sufficient to show that these generalizations are inaccurate. Some types of mobility have been increasing in recent decades while others—like residential and occupational mobility—have declined or remained unchanged. Kin networks have become more active and important as other aspects of family structure have weakened. The influence of religion has been growing in national politics and declining in local politics. As to permissiveness, the trend data show us just how inconsistent social change can be. We are much more permissive than our grandparents about premarital sex, illegitimacy, and bankruptcy; much less permissive about drug addiction, domestic violence, professional errors, and defective goods; and neither more nor less permissive about adolescent crime, extramarital sex, and political corruption. Each of these separate trends makes sense when we descend to the examination of details, but nothing useful can be said about the trend of permissiveness in general.

Permissiveness is part of the invisible subject matter of sociology, which is at least as important as the visible part. The visible part consists of people and things. The people can be counted and many of their attributes like gender, age, skin color, height, and location can be objectively described. The things, including both human artifacts and features of the natural environment, can also be counted and objectively described.

Changes in the visible parts of a social system—people and things—are relatively easy to measure. If sociology restricted itself to the study of these, it would be as straightforward a subject as botany. The prospect is so attractive that it has been repeatedly attempted, under such headings as behaviorism, social physics, and sociobiology.[9] It always produces interesting results without, however, coming to grips with the invisible subject matter of sociology, which consists of the social roles, relationships, attitudes, values, sentiments, symbols, and myths that define the meaning of human experience.

What we find when we look closely at social change in modernizing societies is that trends in the visible subject matter of sociology are directly linked to technological progress and for the past two or three centuries they have been continuous, cumulative, consistent, and irreversible. Technological progress has made possible the uninterrupted increase of people and things, reflected in the growth of population, the increase of goods, occupational specialization, decreasing work effort, the increasing number and size of cities, rising living standards, the increasing velocity of transportation and communication, and hundreds of parallel trends that reflect the steady enlargement of human capabilities by science-based technology. Many of these big trends of modernization conform in a general way to the linear progress model; they have so far been as continuous and irreversible as the technological progress on which they depend. They are very long-term trends. There has not been a single decade since 1650 during which the size of the world's population, the production of coal, the number of printed books, or the efficiency of ships failed to increase.

Along with the big trends that conform to the linear progress model are those that represent linear regress, like the intensification of war, the destruction of plant and animal species, the pollution of the natural environment, and the exhaustion of resources. These too have been continuous, cumulative, consistent, and irreversible, although less beneficent.

The big trends of modernization are the background for, but not the direct causes of, the innumerable trends that can be observed in the invisible parts of modern society: in family relationships, educational goals, worker motivation, religious beliefs, leisure preferences, government policies, attitudes towards money, sexual morality, health care practices, drinking customs, ethnic stratification, modes of conflict resolution, and so forth. These latter trends involve shifts of meaning, changes in patterns of relationships, innovations in the social construction of reality. They are seldom continuous, cumulative, consistent, or irreversible.

Social meaning may be derived from a closed action system, like a game, a ritual, or a market. In a closed action system like baseball, each participant occupies a named position (pitcher, batter) with motives and relationships specified by the rules of the game. There are other kinds of action systems that may be described as open—families, communities, and publics, for example—in which the specification of motives and relationships is less precise but no less important. The behavior that occurs in open systems is extensively coded, but the coding is not highly reliable. The meanings ascribed to acts command general agreement only occasionally and by chance. The Rashomon principle is constantly operative; the participants in an event give quite different accounts of what happened. Social scientists observing this disorderly scene must choose between imposing their own interpretation of motives and relationships—in which case their account of events will not match the accounts of participants—or accepting the local frame-of-reference—in which case their findings will not be generalizable.[10]

When we trace the connection between the big trends of modernization, based directly on technological progress, and the shorter and less reliable trends that reflect changes in motives and relationships, we discover many connections, direct and indirect, but nothing that resembles simple causality. The effects of modernization on motives and relationships are always intricate and partly unpredictable.

For practical purposes, we are going to divide the social trends discussed in this book into several categories:

- First, the "big trends" that show the enlargement of human capabilities by technological progress during the past three centuries.

These trends are directly driven by technology but their rates are not constant and their patterns vary.

- Second, trends in the major action systems that are called social institutions: family, work, education, religion, leisure, government. These huge slow-moving clusters of motives and relationships exhibit a great variety of trends—long-term and short-term, linear and cyclical, local and general, cumulative and episodic, along with many surprising continuities.

- Third, trends in the areas of high-intensity motivation in which individual choices are concentrated: money, sex, health, intoxication. The attitudes and practices of Americans with respect to money, sex, health, and intoxication underwent extraordinary changes during the period with which we are concerned.

- Fourth, changes in the way Americans divide themselves into potentially hostile groups by ethnicity and ideology, and in the conflicts produced by those divisions, and in how they are resolved.

NOTES

1. Herbert Spencer, *Progress: Its Law and Cause* (1857; New York: Appleton, 1915), 35. Spencer's *The Study of Sociology*, published in 1873, was the textbook of the earliest sociology courses taught in American colleges.

2. Emile Durkheim, *The Division of Labor in Society* [*De la Division du Travail Social*] (1893; Glencoe, IL: Free Press, 1960).

3. Karl Marx and Friedrich Engels, *The Communist Manifesto* (1848; New York: Washington Square Press, 1965); and Karl Kautsky, *The Class Struggle* (1893; New York: Norton, 1971).

4. Joseph Arthur de Gobineau, *L'Inégalité des Races Humains* (1853–55; Paris: Firmin-Didot, 1933), 2 vols.

5. Vilfredo Pareto, *The Mind and Society: A Treatise on General Sociology* (1916; New York: Dover Publications, 1963), 2 vols.

6. Pitirim A. Sorokin, *Social and Cultural Dynamics: Fluctuation of Social Relationships, War, and Revolution* (New York: Bedminster Press, 1962), 3 vols.

7. Oswald Spengler, *The Decline of the West* [*Der Untergang des Abendlandes*] (New York: Knopf, 1926–28), 2 vols. For a discussion of the current versions of linear regression, see Charles Tilly, *Big Structures, Large Processes, Huge Comparisons* (New York: Russell Sage Foundation, 1984).

8. Even so perspicacious an observer as Alexis de Tocqueville had only a hazy image of modernization when he wrote his great book on American democracy in the 1830s.

9. Among the most notable attempts: John B. Watson, *Behaviorism* (1925; Chicago: University of Chicago Press, 1962); George Kingsley Zipf, *Human Behavior and the Principle of Least Effort* (Cambridge, MA: Addison-Wesley, 1949); and Howard L. Keys, *The Social Meaning of Modern Biology* (New Haven, CT: Yale University Press, 1986).

10. This is the famous "emic-etic" issue in ethnography. See Marvin Harris, *The Nature of Cultural Things* (New York: Random House, 1964); and Derek Freeman, *Margaret Mead and Samoa: The Making and Unmaking of a Sociological Myth* (Cambridge, MA: Harvard University Press, 1983).

3

THE BIG TRENDS OF MODERNIZATION

The big trends that have been running in the United States since its first settlement by Europeans, and in the rest of the world for varying lengths of time, go under the general name of modernization. They include a continuous increase of population, and more than proportionate increases in mechanical energy, goods and services, information and images, together with urbanization, militarization, the erosion of local cultures, and the disturbance of ecological balances. These major trends, in turn, include thousands of smaller trends. The increase of services, for example, includes the spectacular growth of education, health care, government, transportation, marketing, communication, and entertainment services and of the organizations that provide them.

Modernization appears to be a single, unprecedented historical event, which began in northwestern Europe around 1650 and gradually spread to the rest of the world, reaching the remotest countries—those that had the least contact with Europe—towards the middle of the twentieth century. The choice of 1650 as the starting point is somewhat arbitrary, but there does seem to have been a significant quickening of science, technology, and energy production at just about that time. Robert Merton counted 45 important discoveries and inventions in Britain between 1601 and 1650 but no fewer than 135 between 1651 and 1700. The annual production of British coal was around 200,000 tons at the beginning of the seventeenth century and around 3 million tons at its end.[1] The population surged at the same time.

With a few exceptions, the nations of today's world are arrayed in a rank order of development that reflects the diffusion of modernization from its original core. The most developed nations are those where modernization originated: Britain, France, Germany, the Netherlands, Scandinavia, and the overseas territories originally settled by emigrants from those countries: the United States, Canada, Australia, and New Zealand. The least developed nations are those few which, like Ethiopia, Afghanistan, Yemen, and Nepal, were insulated from the influence of the European core until recently. Japan is an exception. It managed to modernize in the nineteenth century without submitting to European dominance, and then leaped ahead of the procession under the American occupation, carrying its neighbors—South Korea, Thailand, Taiwan, Singapore—along. Saudi Arabia and the small Persian Gulf states are exceptional also, having been modernized under forced draft in the past two decades with the aid of huge profits from the sale of oil.

Modernization is often attributed to the invention of the steam engine and other machinery, but the original causes of the phenomenon are not self-evident. Technology was more advanced in China than in Europe before 1600 but modernization did not occur there. Karl Marx attributed the development of machines to the efforts of bourgeois capitalists to reduce labor costs. Max Weber located the main source of the same capitalism in the religious precepts of Calvinism. Sociologists of the "world system" school credit the transfer of overseas wealth to Europe that began with the Spanish conquest of Mexico and Peru. William Cottrell suggested that modernization started with the European development of high-energy convertors, especially the sailing ship. For Emile Durkheim, the engine of modernization was the division of labor. Jean Fourastié pointed to improvements in markets and roads that released Europe from the periodic scourge of famine. There is no good way to decide among these conflicting interpretations, since modernization is a unique historical event and the cause of such an event is always a matter for speculation rather than proof.

The increase of population was the first sign that something unusual was afoot. The world's population grew as shown in Table 3–1.

TABLE 3–1   TOTAL WORLD POPULATION

1650	510 million
1700	625 million
1800	944 million
1900	1,673 million
1950	2,417 million
1980	4,333 million
1990	5,320 million

SOURCE: Based on World Bank, *World Development Report 1984*, Figure 1.3, p. 6; *World Almanac 1989*, p. 487; and *Statistical Abstract of the United States 1989*, Table 1402.

This trend ran for a long time before it became visible, because nobody was counting. The first careful estimate of a national popula-

tion was made in England in 1688. The first national system for re-
cording births and deaths was established by Sweden in 1750. But by
the end of the eighteenth century, the rapid growth of population
could no longer be ignored. One reaction was alarm. In his famous
Essay on Population, first published in 1798, Thomas Malthus proposed that population was increasing geometrically while food supplies could only increase arithmetically, so that misery and starvation must eventually result. The theory was so plausible that it still
has adherents today. But, in fact, the production of food and other
commodities has increased geometrically in the past two centuries,
and at a much higher rate than population. Table 3–2 illustrates this
growth in world production:

TABLE 3–2   TOTAL WORLD PRODUCTION (in 1980 dollars)

1800	$ 230 billion
1900	970 billion
1950	2,630 billion
1980	11,720 billion

SOURCE: Based on World Bank, *World Development Report 1984*, Figure 1.3, p. 6.

Instead of misery and starvation, the world's expanding population
has enjoyed a sharply rising level of living, and the rate of improvement has been accelerating, as shown in Table 3-3:

TABLE 3–3   PER CAPITA WORLD PRODUCTION (in 1980 dollars)

1800	$ 244
1900	580
1950	1,088
1980	2,705

SOURCE: Based on World Bank, *World Development Report 1984*, Figure 1.3, p. 6.

It seems unlikely that this pace can be maintained indefinitely,
given the depletion of natural resources that accompanies these
high rates of production but, for the time being, the counter-Malthu-
sian trend continues unabated. Between 1970 and 1985 alone, the
world production of wheat increased 69 percent, of corn and rice 51
percent, of electricity 91 percent, of iron ore 74 percent, while world
population increased by 29 percent.[2] The growth of services was
equally dramatic. In approximately one generation, from 1960 to
1984, the number of teachers in the world rose from 15 to 34 million
and the number of physicians from 1.8 to 4.7 million.[3]

Although the big trends now cover the entire world, their effects vary greatly from one region to another. Modernization has created a kind of procession, with the advanced industrial countries at the head, and the least developed countries of the Third World at the tail. For example, if we take telephones per thousand people as an index of modernization (it is one of the best), the nations at the head of the procession—Sweden, Switzerland, the United States, France, West Germany, Japan, Australia, and the United Kingdom—all have more than 50 telephones per 100 people while the countries at the tail of the procession—Burma, Nigeria, Uganda, Afghanistan, Ethiopia, Yemen, and Nepal—all have fewer than 3.[4] On the other hand, while the natural increase of the population is negligible or negative in the countries at the head of the procession, it is very high at the tail.

In premodern societies, the size of the population was roughly constant over long periods of time, with very high birth rates offset by very high death rates. Most of the deaths were concentrated in the first year of life. In many times and places, most of the babies died in infancy. When the infant mortality rate started to fall, as it did in Europe after 1650, the birth rate remained for a while at its customary level and the population grew very fast. But over several generations, the birth rate slowly fell, the size of the average family declined, and infant mortality attained so low a level that further reductions had no significant influence on population. Eventually, birth rates caught up with death rates and the population approached or passed the point of zero growth.* At the same time, the average age of the population rose, decreasing the proportion of women of childbearing age to such an extent that even a sharp rise in the birth rate could not restore earlier rates of population growth.

This sequence of events is known as the demographic transition. It took about 300 years to run its course in western Europe, because the reduction of infant mortality was slow and gradual. In the developing countries of Latin America, Asia, and Africa, the reduction of infant mortality in recent decades occurred about ten times faster, thanks to health measures imported from the most modernized societies, and the gap between customary high birth rates, which decline slowly, and the suddenly reduced death rates, generated explosive population growth. The populations of some

---

*The fertility ratio of West Germany and the Netherlands currently stands at 1.8, that of Quebec at 1.4 and most of eastern Europe falls into the same range. A ratio of 2.1 is necessary to maintain zero population growth. The lower rates presage the decline of these populations.

Third World countries, like the Dominican Republic, now double in less than 15 years. Growth at this rate reduces the average age of the population, increases the proportion of women of child-bearing age, and assures that these populations will continue to grow rapidly even when their birth rates decline.

The United States has more or less completed the demographic transition. The fertility of the native-born white population is too low for zero population growth, but the national population continues to grow at about one percent annually because of immigration and the somewhat higher fertility of blacks and hispanics. This modest rate of increase forecasts an aging population for the foreseeable future.

The increase of goods and services at various places in the modernization procession varies in another way. In general, nations at the head of the procession show relatively low rates of growth but large absolute amounts of growth, as they add automobiles or physicians to their already huge numbers of automobiles and physicians. The contrary is true for those at the tail of the procession. Most of them show high percentage increases from year to year in such things as automobiles and physicians, but the absolute numbers remain small.

Some trends top out at advanced stages of modernization. Elementary education and indoor plumbing, for example, have ceased to show significant growth in the United States and other advanced countries because almost everybody is already provided with these amenities. A more interesting case is the per capita consumption of energy, which increases rapidly in the early stages of modernization but ceases to increase at a later stage when more sophisticated technology permits energy to be used more efficiently. This is illustrated by Table 3–4, which shows the consumption of energy in the U. S. since 1850.

TABLE 3–4   **CONSUMPTION OF ENERGY IN THE U. S.**
(trillions of BTUs)

	Energy	Annual Increase
1850	219	
1880	2,150	29.4%
1910	14,261	18.8
1940	22,991	2.0
1970	66,400	6.3
1985	73,900	0.7

SOURCE: Based on *Historical Statistics of the United States: Colonial Times to 1970*, Table M76–92; and *Statistical Abstract of the United States 1989*, Table 904.

In addition to quantitative growth trends, modernization is associated with important changes in modes of life, organizational patterns, culture traits, and psychological attitudes. All premodern societies are predominantly rural; they cannot produce enough surplus food to feed a large number of nonproducers. Even in partly modernized societies like the United States in 1850 or China in 1980, the great majority of workers were directly engaged in the cultivation of food crops. (Fewer than 2 percent of U. S. workers are so engaged today.) As food supplies become steadily more abundant, farmers leave the land and go into factories, and as manufactured goods become more abundant, workers leave the factories and go into offices. Factory work is more diversified than farm work, and office work is more diversified than factory work, so that the number of distinct occupations grows from a few dozen to many thousands in the course of modernization. These occupational shifts are accompanied by a great drift of population from farms and villages to towns and cities, and the combined effect of this migration and of steady population growth is a spectacular increase in the size and number of metropolitan cities as shown in Table 3–5.

TABLE 3–5   **CITIES OF MORE THAN A MILLION PEOPLE IN THE WORLD**

1800	0
1850	2
1900	10
1950	29
1970	142
1984	225

SOURCE: Based on *United Nations Demographic Yearbooks* 1967, Table 6; 1971, Table 9; 1986, Table 8; and on A. F. Weber, *The Growth of Cities in the Nineteenth Century* (1899; Ithaca, NY: Cornell University Press, 1963).

New metropolitan cities enter the list every year while most of the older ones continue to grow. The three largest, Mexico City, Sao Paulo, and Tokyo-Yokohama, are each approaching 20 million. The ten largest, taken together, increased by 62 percent between 1970 and 1985. New York was the only American metropolis and London the only European metropolis among the ten largest, and both of them declined slightly during that period.

Urbanization is followed in due course by suburbanization, which distributes metropolitan residents and facilities far out into the countryside, and makes them dependent on motor vehicles. Metropolitan cities all over the world resemble each other much more than their hinterlands do. Nearly all of them have such characteristic metropolitan features as high-rise office buildings, luxury hotels, traffic jams, daily newspapers, museums, television stations, specialized hospitals, a criminal underworld, juvenile gangs, ethnic slums, organized gambling and prostitution, branches of multinational enterprises, and easy access to other metropolitan centers, as well perhaps, as certain habits of mind like wariness, worldliness, and responsiveness to new fashions.

Although a great deal of manufacturing takes place in metropolitan cities[5] their principal products are services, such as trade, transportation, administration, litigation, education, health care, and entertainment. In the course of modernization, the increase of food and other raw materials is outpaced by the faster increase of manufactured goods, by the still faster increase of services and by the virtually unlimited increase of information. Innovations in information technology—telephones, computers, copiers, audio and video recorders, radio, and television—have affected every type of human activity. To an extent never approached before, modernized societies are awash in remotely transmitted symbols and images. The growth rates in this sector are too high to be extrapolated. It appears, for example, that the number of scientific papers published (2,880 per *day* in more than 40,000 journals in 1987) has been doubling about every six years.[6] Much of information technology, like television and personal computers, is more easily transmitted to societies at the tail of the modernization procession than innovations in agriculture and manufacturing that require a more elaborate infrastructure. Afghan guerrillas use personal computers to plan ambushes. Transistor radios bring rock music to New Guinea tribes that have not yet adopted the wheel.

The benefits of modernization are incontrovertible. The great majority of people throughout the world today are healthier, better fed, longer-lived, and better protected against pain and suffering than their grandparents. They are better educated, better housed, and more frequently entertained than any preceding generation. Whether these benefits are offset by certain spiritual losses is an interesting question. That is often asserted but difficult to prove. As Jean Fourastié remarked:

> A man who, two centuries ago, would not even have learned to read, if he had survived to maturity, profits by his windows, the central heating of his apartment, and the 300,000 copies of the newspaper for which he writes, to announce that humanity has arrived at the last stage of barbarism.[7]

But although it is difficult to deny that modernization contributes to the comfort and happiness of individuals, the long-term cost-benefit ratio may yet turn out to be unfavorable. One pessimistic conservationist refers to

> ... the shock of recognizing that the vaunted progress of modern civilization is only a thin cloak for global catastrophe.[8]

The principal negative effects of modernization are the intensification of war, ecological damage, the erosion of local cultures, and the exhaustion of energy resources. They may not portend a global catastrophe but the possibility cannot be denied.

The intensification of war is inextricably connected with modernization, both as cause and effect. The surpluses of food and other materials that sustain modernization also make it possible to raise larger armies and to keep them in the field for longer campaigns. The technological progress that improves the efficiency of production machines does as much or more for the efficiency of lethal machines.

The Napoleonic wars were the first wars of the modern type and the destruction of life and property was correspondingly great, but the remaining European wars of the nineteenth century were relatively quick and cheap. The most modernized nineteenth-century war was the American Civil War, which introduced automatic rifles, explosive shells, the military use of railroads and the telegraph, and even aerial observation, in a conflict that involved mass armies, year-round campaigning, heavy casualties, and extensive property damage. But the real potential of industrialized warfare was not realized until the twentieth century as the numbers in Table 3–6 suggest:

TABLE 3–6   DEATHS IN WARS (millions)

18th century	4.4
19th century	8.3
20th century to 1980	98.8

SOURCE: Based on Ruth Leger Sivard, *World Military and Social Expenditures*, 1986, Chart 17, p. 26.

Although the total of twentieth-century casualties thus far is enormous compared to any previous era, it might easily be exceeded by a single day's fighting with nuclear weapons, whose destructive potential is almost unimaginable. One nuclear bomber or submarine carries more explosive power today than has been used since the invention of gunpowder. About 50,000 nuclear warheads are presently deployed. Some reputable climatologists maintain that the detonation of any large part of the existing nuclear arsenals would make the earth uninhabitable for mammals, including ourselves.

In addition to nuclear weapons, the advanced technology of war offers the prospect of efficient mass killing by chemical and biological weapons, and by the lasers and particle beams that are currently being developed. This set of trends may eventually raise the aggregate costs of modernization above the benefits.

There are other ominous trends in the effects of human activities on the natural environment. These effects are now much greater than ever before because the human population has increased by a factor of 3 in the twentieth century, and our ability to interfere with nature by a factor of 50 or more. Ecological balances that evolved over millions of years are now upset in a decade or two, and the rate of disturbance seems to be accelerating. The specific problems include the extinction of plant and animal species, the increasing dependence of food production on fossil fuels, the release of immense quantities of carbon dioxide and other pollutants into the atmosphere, the destruction of a large part of the world's forest cover by mechanized logging operations during the past 20 years, acid rain in Europe and North America, overcutting for firewood in Africa and India, the potential warming of the earth's climate by the combined action of chemical pollutants and deforestation, the destruction of aquatic life by acid rain and the dumping of sludge, the attrition of the ozone layer by the release of fluorocarbons and nitrates into the atmosphere, the escape of toxic radiation from nuclear waste, and widespread ecological damage by other inorganic products. Many of these effects interact in ways not clearly understood, and the problems develop with awesome rapidity. In the single decade from 1970 to 1980, the per capita use of chemical fertilizers worldwide increased by 53 percent, the aggregate emission of carbon from fossil fuel combustion increased by about 30 percent, and the world's forests diminished by about 25 percent.[9] The order of nature, which used to be self-adjusting, now requires extensive human management to restore the equilibria that have been disturbed by population pressure and by new technologies that are introduced without much attention to their long-term consequences. Some of these new technologies are ecologically perverse, like the substitution of detergents for soap and of plastic bottles for glass, but others, like the increasing use of chemical fertilizers in grain production, are driven by short-term imperatives that can only be evaded by new technology.

One type of ecological damage that probably cannot be halted by improved technology is the extinction of plant and animal species by reckless exploitation and the destruction of habitats. This diminution in variety is an important aesthetic loss; when the last wild elephant dies, the world will be much less beautiful. And the loss of irreplaceable genetic resources may ultimately be very costly for the human species.

A similar loss of variety has been occurring on the cultural level as richly varied local cultures are destroyed by the homogenized metropolitan culture. The destruction is well advanced everywhere in today's world:

> Now the people who inhabit the Kentucky mountains came into the region nearly two centuries ago, bringing with them what many students affirm to be survivals of Elizabethan culture, and even Chaucerian speech. These they modified somewhat, of course, in the new situation . . . and naturally they added something of their own until they had one of the most distinctive or individually flavored cultures in the United States. The whole culture complex—their special way of looking at life and doing things—was kept intact right down to the most recent times: their speech, their balladry, their music, their social codes, and their religiosity. . . . Then came the radio and the television, and the Kentucky mountaineer was no more.[10]

The phenomenon is almost too common to be noticed. As recently as 1910, every coastal area in North America and Europe had locally built boats of distinctive design, splendidly adapted to local conditions. They survive only in museums. As recently as 1940, phonetic experts were able to locate the birthplace of any American by listening to his accent. As recently as 1970, Russians and Chinese dressed quite differently than Americans and Germans. The basic trend of modernization is towards cultural uniformity, although family roles, religious practices, work habits, and ideologies are less amenable to homogenization than styles of clothing, architecture, scholarship, and entertainment.

The loss of autonomy and variety in the cultural environment is analogous to the loss of autonomy and variety in the natural environment. Both situations invite an expansion of centralized management, which takes the form of continuous growth in the scale and functions of national governments and of transnational organizations as well. As official bureaucracies and their regulatory functions expand, all other large organizations—manufacturing enterprises, voluntary associations, political parties, churches, universities—must become increasingly bureaucratized also in order to comply with the regulatory and record-keeping requirements of government agencies.

The most disputed issue on the negative side of the modernization balance sheet is the rate of depletion of the fossil fuels—oil, coal, natural gas—which provide most of the electric power, furnace heat, chemical fertilizer, and motor fuel that make it possible for the earth to support more than 5 billion people and all those metropolitan cities. There is no question that the fossil fuels are being used up, but experts differ vehemently about how long it will take to exhaust them, and whether they can be replaced by alternative energy sources. From 1900 to 1970, the world's production of petroleum grew at approximately 7 percent per year and doubled every ten years—an exponential series. Such a series has the arithmetic property that the amount consumed between one doubling and the next exceeds the total of all previous consumption.[11] This property tells us that the amount of petroleum consumed in the decade 1960–1970 was greater than the total of all previous consumption. By 1970, about 16 percent of the world's estimated total reserves of 2,000 billion barrels had been extracted and if the rate of production had continued to double every decade, the supply would have run completely out around 1999. In fact, as Table 3–7 illustrates, the rate slowed down after 1970.

TABLE 3–7	ANNUAL WORLD PRODUCTION OF PETROLEUM (billions of barrels)
	1990 0.2
	1920 0.8
	1940 4.0
	1960 14.9
	1970 20.4
	1980 18.2
	1986 18.4

SOURCE: Figures for 1900 to 1940 are taken from Albert A. Bartlett, "Forgotten Fundamentals of the Energy Crisis," *American Journal of Physics* (September 1978), 876–88, Figure 2; figures for 1960 to 1986 are derived from *Statistical Abstract of the United States 1988*, Table 905.

The world's annual production of petroleum (and also of natural gas) has not been increasing since 1970, and if it continued at present levels, the point of exhaustion would not arrive for about 100 years. The welcome stability in oil consumption has been achieved in part by a shift to coal, and while total coal reserves are much larger than total oil reserves, they too are exhaustible. World coal production doubled between 1960 and 1980 and is expected to double again by the end of the century. If this rate were continued, the world's enormous supply of coal would also be exhausted in 100 years or so.

Whether alternative sources of energy can take the place of the disappearing fossil fuels remains uncertain. As of 1986, about 4.5 percent of the world's energy was produced by nuclear reactors, but the early enthusiasm for nuclear power cooled in the United States after the accident at Three Mile Island, and in Europe after the Chernobyl accident. Moreover, reserves of recoverable uranium are not unlimited. Hydropower accounts for about 3 percent of the world's total energy but most of the best sites have already been utilized, and further development will be limited. All other power sources, including solar, geothermal, tidal, and wind systems taken together, contribute much less than 1 percent of total energy and their future potential is uncertain. One way or another, additional energy sources must be found if modernization is to continue.

NOTES

1. Robert K. Merton, *Science, Technology and Society in Seventeenth Century England* (New York: Harper and Row, 1970), Tables 3 and 10.
2. Based on *SAUS88*, Table 1373.
3. Based on Ruth Leger Sivard, *World Military and Social Expenditures 1986*, 32, Table II.
4. Based on *Telephones of the World 1987* (Whippany, NJ: American Telephone and Telegraph Company, 1989).
5. According to one theory, practically all economic development is attributable to import-substitution by cities, as they begin to produce for themselves items formerly brought from abroad. See Jane Jacobs, *Cities and the Wealth of Nations* (New York: Random House, 1984).
6. Michael J. Mahoney, "Scientific Publication and Knowledge Politics," *Journal of Social Behavior and Personality*, 2 (1987): 165–76.

7. Jean Fourastié, *The Causes of Wealth* (Glencoe, IL: Free Press, 1960), 229.

8. Barry Commoner, "The Closing Circle," *New Yorker* (October 2, 1971), 90.

9. Data from Lester R. Brown et al., *State of the World 1987* (New York: Norton, 1987).

10. Richard M. Weaver, *Life without Prejudice and Other Essays* (Chicago: Henry Regnery, 1966), 109.

11. Albert A. Bartlett, "Forgotten Fundamentals of the Energy Crisis," *American Journal of Physics* (September 1978), 876–88.

4

AMERICA AND THE WORLD

From 1900 to about 1980, the United States was the unchallenged leader of the modernization procession, leading the other industrialized countries by wide margins in telephones, automobiles and highways, industrial and agricultural productivity, the electronic media, higher education, real wages, home ownership, and almost every other measure of technological progress and affluence. American preeminence was reinforced by the two world wars, which inflicted severe damage on most of the other advanced countries but not on this country, and stimulated our industrial and financial expansion. By the end of World War II, the United States produced and consumed about as much as the rest of the world combined, and its products were universally admired. In the 1950s there was much talk of the American Century and whether it would last forever.

The decade of the 1960s administered severe shocks to this complacency: Sputnik, the assassinations of the Kennedy brothers and of Martin Luther King, defeat in Vietnam, rioting on campuses and in black ghettos, and widespread denial of America's traditional claim to moral superiority. But it was also a decade of notable progress in civil rights and social services, and it is difficult to trace the connection between the social and political turmoil of the 1960s and the loss of America's competitive advantages in the 1970s and 1980s.[1]

Table 4–1 that follows is more complicated than the others in this book, but it contains a great deal of information and is worth study. A nation's telephone index (the number of telephones per capita) is one of the best measures of modernization and is especially suitable for international comparisons. It shows very high rank-order correlations, generally above .95, with such other indicators of modernization as per capita income, energy, and food consumption; the proportion of physicians and teachers in the labor force; life expectancy and infant mortality; agricultural productivity per acre and industrial productivity per worker; but it is more accurate than these other indicators because telephone systems require directories and are therefore self-enumerating and because a count of telephones does not require currency conversions or demographic adjustments as measures of income or productivity do. Moreover, the telephone index gives us an unusually long international series, essentially complete since 1896.

TABLE 4–1   THE MODERNIZATION PROCESS, 1950–1985
(based on telephones per capita)

A 1950 Rank	Country	B 1950	C 1965	D 1985	E 1950	F 1965	G 1985	H '50–'65	I '65–'85
		U.S. Equivalent Date			Time Lag in Years			Change in Time Lag	
1	United States	1950	1965	1985	0	0	0	—	—
2	Sweden	1947	1964	—	3	1	—	− 2	—
3	Canada	1946	1958	1973	4	7	12	+ 3	+ 5
4	Switzerland	1943	1958	—	7	7	—	0	—
5	Australia	1936	1947	1969	14	18	16	+ 4	− 2
6	Great Britain	1916	1944	1967	34	21	18	− 13	− 3
7	Belgium	1910	1940	1963	40	25	22	− 15	− 3
8	Netherlands	1909	1944	1971	41	21	14	− 20	− 7
9	Austria	1906	1924	1966	44	41	19	− 3	− 22
10	France	1906	1920	1971	44	45	14	+ 1	− 31
11	West Germany	1905	1937	1972	45	28	13	− 17	− 15
12	Argentina	1905	1907	1915	45	58	70	+ 13	+ 12
13	South Africa	1903	1907	1925	47	58	60	+ 11	+ 2
14	Czechoslovakia	1902	1915	1947	48	50	38	+ 2	− 12
15	Italy	1902	1918	1963	48	47	22	− 1	− 25
16	Spain	1901	1911	1957	49	54	28	+ 5	− 26
17	Chile	1901	1902	1906	49	63	79	+ 14	+ 16
18	Cuba	1901	1902	1905	49	63	80	+ 14	+ 17
19	Japan	1901	1936	1969	49	29	16	− 20	− 13
20	East Germany	1900	1913	1946	50	52	39	+ 2	− 13
21	Portugal	1900	1906	1942	50	59	43	+ 9	− 16
22	Venezuela	1899	1902	1910	63	63	75	+ 12	+ 12
23	Hungary	1899	1906	1936	51	59	49	+ 8	− 10
24	Mexico	1898	1900	1912	52	65	73	+ 13	+ 8
25	Algeria	1898	1899	1903	52	66	82	+ 14	+ 16
26	Greece	1898	1906	1956	52	59	29	+ 7	− 30
27	Brazil	1898	1900	1910	52	65	75	+ 13	+ 10
28	Poland	1898	1904	1917	52	61	68	+ 9	+ 7
29	Colombia	1898	1901	1907	52	64	78	+ 12	+ 14
30	Rumania	1898	1901	(na)	52	64	(na)	+ 12	(na)
31	Bulgaria	1897	1903	1945	53	62	40	+ 9	− 22
32	USSR	1897	1903	1917	53	62	68	+ 9	+ 6
33	Morocco	1897	1898	1899	53	67	86	+ 14	+ 19
34	Egypt	1896	1898	1901	54	67	84	+ 13	+ 17

SOURCE: Based on *Telephones of the World*, published intermittently by American Telephone and Telegraph Company, 1912 to 1989.

Because the United States led the rest of the world in telephones per capita in 1950, 1965, and, with two exceptions, in 1985, it is possible to show for each of the 34 countries in the table how far it lagged behind the United States in each of those years. Column A of the table arrays the 34 major countries by their telephones per capita as of 1950. Column B gives the year the United States was at the other country's 1950 level with respect to telephones per capita. For example, the entry for France in Column B is 1906, meaning that France's 1950 telephone index (.0576 per capita or 6 telephones for every 100 people) was approximately the same as the U. S. figure for 1906. Column C gives the year the United States was at the other country's 1965 level. The entry for France in Column C is 1920, because France in 1965 had 12 telephones for every hundred people, like the United States in 1920. Note that France did not gain on the United States between 1950 and 1965. Column D gives the year the United States was at the other country's 1985 level. The entry for France in Column D is 1971, because France in 1985 had 61 telephones for every 100 people, like the United States in 1971. Columns E, F, and G express the same facts in a different way by showing how far each country lagged behind the United States in 1950, 1965, and 1985. (Sweden and Switzerland fall out of the table in 1985, having moved *ahead* of the United States.) Columns H and I show for each country whether its lag behind the United States increased or decreased from 1950 to 1965, and from 1965 to 1985. Following France again, we see that its lag increased slightly from 1950 to 1965 but decreased dramatically— by 31 years—between 1965 and 1985, as France began to gain on the United States in the modernization procession.

Table 4–1 incidentally helps us to see just how large the American lead was. In 1950, only five countries had surpassed the level reached by the United States in 1910 and more than half of the world's independent nations had to be excluded from the table because they had not yet reached the American level of 1896!

From 1950 to 1965, the United States lost ground to 8 countries and gained on 24. From 1965 to 1985 it gained on 14 countries, and lost ground to 17. Japan and every west European country gained on the United States, while the Latin American and African countries fell further behind. Austria, Italy, Spain, Greece, and Bulgaria reduced their respective lags by more than 20 years; West Germany, Japan, East Germany, and Portugal by more than 10 years.

The declining American advantage shows itself in more painful ways than the count of telephones. The merchandise trade balance of the U. S. with the rest of the world was modestly positive until 1980, when it turned sharply negative, as shown in Table 4–2.

TABLE 4–2   **U. S. MERCHANDISE TRADE BALANCE (billions of dollars)**

1960	$ 4.6
1970	2.7
1980	− 24.2
1987	− 152.1

SOURCE: Based on *Statistical Abstract of the United States 1989*, Table 1369.

One after another, American manufacturing industries lost their competitive edge in the face of vigorous price and quality challenges from Japan, the newly industrializing countries of the Pacific Rim, and the countries of the European Economic Community. Between 1980 and 1987, the share of imported products in the domestic American markets for aluminum, machine tools, construction machinery, food machinery, transformers, computers, furniture, telecommunications equipment, textiles, and apparel, more than doubled, and there were major increases in imports of steel, farm machinery, aerospace, industrial and scientific instruments, motor vehicles, and household appliances.[2] In several product lines—phonographs and videorecorders, for example—the American share of the domestic American market has fallen to zero. The United States, with a gross national product three times as large as West Germany's, had a slightly smaller total of exports in 1988.[3]

In 1989, a research team at MIT reported the results of their attempt to discover why American manufacturers had been losing ground to overseas producers in automobiles, electronics, machine tools, textiles, and other key industries, and to find remedies for the creeping loss of competitive edge.[4] They attributed the problem to a number of interlocking defects in American industrial organization, including a parochial approach to technological innovation, outdated strategies of product development, the neglect of human resources, a lack of intra-industry cooperation, an adversarial relationship between industry and government, and excessive devotion to short-term profits. They blamed the primary and secondary schools for not turning out better-qualified workers and the engineering schools for insufficient attention to process engineering.

What most of these conditions have in common is that they are deeply rooted in national institutions and not amenable to improvement by individual managers. There is no way the president of the XYZ Company can reform the high school curriculum or change the mental habits of bankers. But towards the end of the MIT report, the authors begin to talk about "flattening organization hierarchies" and "dismantling functional barriers"—steps that can sometimes be taken by strong managers and that might be more effective than anything else. The typical American enterprise has a much more elaborate managerial hierarchy, and many more functional barriers, than it had a generation ago when American industry was the envy of the world. Everywhere, there are too many specialists ruling petty fiefdoms, too many forms, too many procedures, too much administration, too many vice presidents. When the head of the personnel department becomes a human resources administrator or the president's secretary becomes an executive associate and gets a secretary of her own, a little life goes out of the organization. Bureaucratic overgrowth in the private sector is less visible than in government, but it has become equally pervasive. Virtually all American enterprises have more managers and larger administrative components than their foreign competitors.

There are intricate connections between the loss of competitiveness reflected by the merchandise trade deficit and the federal debt, whose growth after 1965 acquired momentum, doubling from 1965 to 1975, doubling again from 1975 to 1980, and again from 1980 to 1985. It is expected to complete another doubling by 1992.

TABLE 4–3   U. S. FEDERAL DEBT (billions of dollars)

1950	$ 256
1965	272
1975	533
1980	907
1985	1,823
1990	3,150

SOURCE: Based on *Statistical Abstract of the United States 1988*, Table 477; and *Economic Indicators: November 1989*, Prepared for the Joint Economic Committee of Congress by the Council of Economic Advisers. The 1990 figure is an estimate based on press reports.

The annual increase in the federal debt, which averaged $260 billion in the five years preceding 1989, is a much better measure than the more familiar federal deficit, which ran about $100 billion lower because of the accounting devices commonly described as "blue smoke and mirrors." The aggregate amount added to the debt from December 1985 to February 1989, a period of only 38 months, exceeded the total debt of 1980.

The federal government, staggering under the burdens of the most costly military establishment in history; runaway inflation in its badly designed health care system; a set of huge, inflexible entitlement programs; and the rising cost of servicing the debt itself; has so far made only token efforts to extricate itself. The growth in the federal debt has been largely financed by an inflow of foreign capital which, together with the trade deficit, transformed the United States from the world's largest creditor to its largest debtor. The turning point occurred in 1985. Thereafter, the imbalance grew so fast that by 1988, it exceeded all other international debts combined. By the end of 1988, foreign claims on U. S. assets amounted to $1.79 trillion, and exceeded U. S. claims on foreign assets by $533 billion.[5] The magnitude of these figures can be grasped by recalling that the total value of all the companies listed on the New York Stock Exchange at that time was about $2 trillion.

Almost unnoticed besides the federal debt was the growing debt of state and local governments, which reached $659 billion in 1986, the most recent year for which the total has been published, and like the federal debt, has a doubling time of about six years.[6]

The extraordinary borrowing of government was matched by the profligacy of consumers. Between 1975 and 1985, the total of mortgage debt and outstanding consumer debt tripled, to approximately $3 trillion,[7] half again as much as the federal debt, while the debt-to equity ratio of U.S. corporations rose to around .90,[8] and the savings and loan sector of the banking industry collapsed under a mountain of bad loans. It was, by any standard, the largest spending spree in history, and it bought a decade of apparent prosperity, with nearly full employment, only moderate inflation, virtual stability in the real income of the median family[9] and a proliferation of new millionaires. Meanwhile, financial dominance shifted from New York to Tokyo, which now has the world's largest stock exchange and most of its largest banks. Foreign investors, British, French, German, and Japanese, acquired American companies and established American subsidiaries. Foreign owners bought heavily into residential and commercial real estate, in New York, Hawaii, Virginia, and California. The share of imported products in U. S. markets continued to grow, as American industry continued to labor under the disadvantage of relatively aged machinery and plant, relatively inflexible labor costs, lagging automation, and excessive debt. Despite the general air of prosperity, some regions and economic sectors suffered severely during the 1980s: iron and steel in Pennsylvania, grain farming in the Midwest, oil and real estate in Texas. Parts of the national infrastructure—roads, bridges, railroads, water systems—were wearing out much faster than they were being replaced. Problems like the alleviation of poverty and the disposal of toxic waste became more intractable in the United States than in other industrialized countries because of the government's lack of discretionary funds. The heartland of industrial capitalism was running out of capital.

The trouble seems to have begun with the oil crisis of 1973, during which the price of oil rose by several hundred percent and the United States, largely dependent on imported oil, began to contribute to foreign oil producers $50 to $75 billion a year that might otherwise have gone into domestic investment.* The growth of the economy faltered but the growth of consumer expectations and the expansion of government did not. As a result, net national saving and investment by Americans dropped from around 9 percent of the gross national product in the 1960s to less than 3 percent from 1982 to 1988,[10] by far the lowest rate of any industrialized nation. The missing capital was supplied by foreign investors, out of savings in their own economies, but that solution compounded the problem. The payment of interest and profits to foreign investors further diminished the capital available for the renewal of machinery and highways in this country, while the necessity of attracting and holding foreign capital required interest rates in the United States to be kept at higher levels than German and Japanese rates, lest the flow of capital reverse. This placed the American economy at a double disadvantage, making investment in productive facilities relatively more expensive here than abroad and diverting resources from productive investment to debt service. The consequences of operating under these disadvantages were reflected in the loss of competitiveness by American industry and the deteriorating performance of the American welfare state. By 1990, the United States was unique among the advanced industrial nations in failing to guarantee adequate housing, health care, education, transportation, or public safety, and

---

*The problem did not disappear after the 1973 crisis. Although conservation efforts checked the growth of petroleum consumption in the U. S. and even reduced it slightly (*Statistical Abstract of United States 1989*, Table 926), the U. S. imported much more oil in 1989 than in 1973 (*SAUS89*, Table 946) and the prospects for lessening that dependence are dim.

there was some doubt that its existing level of effort in these areas could be maintained. It is arithmetically impossible for public debts to continue indefinitely to double every few years, and it will be difficult to recover the capital already squandered or to check the growing influence of foreign investors. Most of the imaginable resolutions of the problem—massive inflation, a planned reduction of living standards, dismantling the military establishment, the curtailment of entitlements, debt repudiation—would involve rude shocks to the American way of life, and given the close-knit web of economic and political relationships between the United States and the rest of the world, those shocks would be felt in other countries, with consequences that are difficult to predict.

Nevertheless, the United States still had the world's largest national economy; a disproportionate share of coal, iron, and agricultural land; the world's largest and most productive system of higher education, undisputed leadership in popular culture, and an awesome military establishment. It was plain by 1990 that America had won the cold war. The communist bloc was in economic and political disarray. Marxism was no longer a persuasive creed, and the goal of world revolution had been nearly forgotten. Communist governments were experimenting with private entrepreneurship, free markets, family farms, multiparty elections, and other capitalist institutions in efforts to overcome the stagnation created by over-centralized and corrupt state management. The Soviet Union was in effect suing for peace. Looking back at Table 4–1, we see that by 1985, Czechoslovakia, the most advanced nation with a state socialist regime, had barely attained the level of modernization of the United States in 1947, while the Soviet Union was only at the level reached by the United States *in 1917*.

The average American's view of the world was strained by these two sets of facts. On the one hand, the evil empire was beaten and asking for help to reform itself. "America," in Ronald Reagan's phrase, "was standing tall." On the other hand, more and more of the goods in American stores were "made in Japan" or in West Germany, China, Thailand, Italy, France, Taiwan, or South Korea; more and more newspapers and television stations were owned by foreigners; more and more Americans worked for foreign employers. When the average American family traveled, they found it difficult to afford hotel rooms or restaurant meals in Tokyo or Paris, while Japanese and French tourists thronged to American cities and found them delightfully cheap.

Since the founding of the Republic, Americans had felt comfortably superior to the inhabitants of less favored countries, and that superiority was confirmed by the eagerness of foreigners to settle here. In this regard, too, the signals of the 1980s were confusing. Immigrants, legal and illegal, continued to pour in—mostly from Mexico, Central America, and the Caribbean, but also from the Soviet Union, Ireland, China, Vietnam, and Iran. America was still the land of opportunity. But at the same time, there were disquieting signs of European and Asian superiority. By 1989, real wages in most of the leading industrial countries were higher than in the United States; international comparisons of student achievement in various fields consistently put American high school students close to the bottom of the list; most of the leading industrialized countries had higher life expectancy, lower infant mortality, much less poverty, much less crime, and much less political corruption than the United States, and all of these gaps seemed to be widening. Every international comparison was likely to turn up unpleasant surprises. Italy, for example, has a higher rate of home ownership than the United States, France has a more versatile telephone system, Japan has ten times as many industrial robots, West Germany, with a quarter of the U. S. population, has a greater volume of exports. Standing tall may not be enough to overcome the consequences of America's self-imposed insolvency.

Many different explanations have been suggested for the loss of America's lead in the modernization race: excessive military expenditures, excessive welfare expenditures, excessive wage rates, shortsighted business management, profligate energy use, overregulation of the private sector, underregulation of financial institutions, unfair foreign competition, the low savings rate of American families, the excessive borrowing of American corporations, inadequate support of basic research, a decline of labor discipline, affirmative action, drug abuse, illegal immigration, the growth of the legal profession, and the declining effectiveness of public education. The choice among these explanations is guided, more often than not, by the politics of the observer. Those who attribute the decline of competitiveness to the poor education and low commitment of rank-and-file workers have an understandable quarrel with those who blame corporate managers for ignoring long-term objectives in favor of short-term profits. But almost everyone agrees that the federal government is ultimately responsible for the problem and obligated to resolve it.

NOTES

1. For two interesting attempts to do so, see Michel Crozier, *The Trouble with America: Why the System Is Breaking Down* (Berkeley: University of California Press, 1984), and John Lukacs, *Outgrowing Democracy: A History of the United States in the Twentieth Century* (Garden City, NY: Doubleday, 1984).
2. Based on Joint Economic Committee, *The Education Deficit*, 100th Cong., 2nd Sess. (Washington, D.C.: Government Printing Office, 1988); and data from International Trade Administration, Department of Commerce, 1989.
3. Based on data from GATT, quoted in *News from France*, March 23, 1989.
4. Suzanne Berger et al., "Towards a New Industrial America," *Scientific American*, June 1989.
5. Felix Rohaytn, "America's Economic Dependence," *Foreign Affairs*, 68, no. 1 (1989): 53–65.
6. Based on *SAUS89*, Table 453.
7. Based on *SAUS88*, Tables 793 and 795; and current news releases, March 1989.
8. Federal Reserve Board, quoted in Goldman, Sachs, *Portfolio Strategy*, December 1988: 6.
9. Based on Office of Educational Research and Improvement, U.S. Department of Education, *Youth Indicators*, Table 10.
10. Francis M. Bator, "President Bush Needs a Team B on the Economy," *Washington Post*, 28 January 1990, C7.

5

IMAGINARY TRENDS

The invention of imaginary social trends is one of the most thriving branches of American popular culture. The decline of religion is widely lamented along with the abandonment of reading, increasing mobility, the growing burden of emotional disorder, and the general acceleration of social change, but each of these trends—along with many others that are commonly taken for granted—is imaginary, part of a rich mythology. Imaginary trends are too numerous to count but fairly easy to catalog. Most of them pretend to report the imminent collapse of social institutions, the erosion of personal relationships, or a weakening of social control. The trends briefly mentioned above are so widely believed that it seems almost impious to challenge them. Everybody knows about our increasing mobility, but what everybody knows is not necessarily so.

Imaginary trends, like other myths, serve real social purposes, but before we consider what those are, it may be useful to review the empirical evidence that makes some well-known trends imaginary.

The Decline of Religion   Religion, we hear, no longer has any important influence on people's lives. Church membership and church attendance continue to decline. The clergy are no longer taken seriously. The shared religious faith that once held society together has shattered under the impact of technology and popular culture. American society is increasingly secular.

The Abandonment of Reading   Television has nearly done away with the reading of books and serious literature has been displaced by mindless fiction. The debasement of language is reflected in the mass media and in everyday life. "Until recently," a prominent book editor tells us, "this was a country of readers; people of all trades and professions and habits of mind read books. Now only students read, and that rarely."[1]

Increasing Mobility   This powerful trend, as everyone knows, has broken the strong bonds that used to attach Americans to their neighborhoods, communities, and regions, as well as to occupations, firms, and old friends. Restless and rootless, we move with accelerating velocity from house to house, from place to place, from job to job, and from one style of life to another.

The Growing Burden of Mental Illness   The pressure imposed on individuals by a dynamically changing society is reflected by a dramatic rise of all forms of psychic disorder and of neurotic, psychotic, and self-destructive behavior. "Given few clues as to what kind of behavior is rational under the radically new circumstances, the victim may well become a hazard to himself."[2]

The Acceleration of Social Change   This familiar concept implies that with each passing year, we are compelled to make more and more changes in our habits and attitudes in order to meet the increasing velocity of change in the social environment. The further implication is that, sooner or later, we will be unable to match the pace and some sort of breakdown will occur. "While the shift from an agricultural to an industrial society took 100 years, the present restructuring from an industrial to an information society took only two decades. Change is occurring so rapidly that there is no time to react . . ."[3]

With Fontenelle's rule firmly in mind, let us not hasten to explain these disturbing trends until we are sure that they exist.

The decline of religion is called secularization and has been continuously deplored in this country since the middle of the seventeenth century. The data are sparse for the seventeenth century but, in our own era, religious practices and beliefs have been extensively studied, and the data are abundant and reliable. Religion is an intricate phenomenon and secularization—if it occurred—would have multiple indicators, including: a decline in the number of churches, declining attendance at religious services, a decline in the frequency and variety of private devotions, the waning of religious beliefs, the secularization of rites of passage like weddings and funerals, a decline in religious endogamy, a declining proportion of religious workers in the labor force, a decline in the financial support of religious activities, a decline in the number and circulation of religious books and periodicals, a decline in the attention given to religion in the mass media, a decline in new sects and in new movements in existing churches, increased attention to secular issues in sermons and liturgy, a decline of political activity by organized religious groups, and a decline in the political influence of the clergy.[4]

In the United States in the past half century, the number of churches increased significantly while church attendance kept pace with the growth of population. About 40 percent of the adult respondents in recent national surveys report attending religious services within the past week—the same proportion as in the 1940s, although the stability of the figure masks a decrease of attendance among Catholics and an increase among Protestants and Jews. Private devotions are difficult to measure but seem to continue at a high level. The proportion of the population who *never* attend religious services and the proportion who have no religious preference vary from survey to survey but remain small. The proportion of U. S. survey respondents who say they believe in God was 94 percent in 1947 and 95 percent in 1986. The proportion believing in life after death was 76 percent in 1944 and 74 percent in 1988.[5] Rites of passage under religious auspices—baptisms, confirmations, weddings, funerals—are not counted nationally, but local studies show them to be increasing. The proportion of religious workers in the labor force has been approximately stable since 1950; the proportion of income devoted to religious purposes shows a slight increase. The volume of religious literature shows a significant and continuing increase, as does the attention given to religion in the mass media, the appearance of new sects and religious movements, the intervention of religious groups in politics, and the political role of the clergy.*

In sum, the empirical evidence contradicts the imaginary trend of religious decline, and more detailed analyses of religious practices and belief by age, sex, family composition, occupation, ethnicity, and other attributes confirm the growing strength and salience of the religious elements in American society. (We will examine religion in much more depth in Chapter 7.)

The abandonment of reading by the American population, and by young people in particular, is another trend more frequently deplored than demonstrated. It rests upon a number of false perceptions—that American schools do not educate their pupils, that the educational level of high school and college graduates is much lower than it used to be, that television has displaced the printed page, and that the quality of popular literature has declined.

There are grains of truth in each of these misperceptions but they are rather small grains. American elementary school pupils show remarkable ignorance of subjects like geography, in which they

---

*In the 1988 campaign for the presidential nomination, two of the major contenders were Protestant ministers—an unprecedented situation.

get no serious instruction. American high school students compare unfavorably in science and mathematics with secondary school students in other industrialized countries. The average scores of high school seniors on scholastic aptitude tests have declined over the past 20 years. The median American adult spends more than 20 hours a week in front of a television screen.

On the other hand, elementary school pupils in most of the nation's schools score reasonably well in most of the subjects they have been taught. The inner-city schools that perform custodial rather than educational functions are the exceptions not the rule. Although American high school graduates do not know quite as much as the graduates of French lycees and German gymnasia, the American graduates represent a much broader segment of the population and they have more years of schooling still ahead of them. The decline of SAT scores over the past three decades, while statistically significant, is quite small and is adequately explained by the expansion of the college-bound cohort taking the tests.

The median Americans who spend so much time watching television somehow manage to read many more serious books and magazines than their parents or grandparents. The Lynds found not a single bookstore in Middletown in 1935; we counted 13 in 1978, together with hundreds of paperback outlets in supermarkets and other retail establishments.[6] The number of new books and editions published in the United States increased from 15,000 titles in 1960 to 53,000 in 1986.[7] In the ten years between 1975 and 1985, the number of book copies sold in the United States increased by 31 percent, the ratio of fiction to nonfiction fell sharply, and the number of bookstores nearly doubled.[8] The number and circulation of magazines increased as well. A 1983 survey by the Census Bureau classified more than 50 percent of every age group from 16 to 50 as book readers.[9]

The principal factor that accounts for the trend of *rising* literacy in the United States is the steady rise in the average level of educational achievement, shown in Table 5–1:

TABLE 5–1   **MEDIAN SCHOOL YEARS COMPLETED**
(U. S. residents over age 25)

1940	8.6
1960	10.6
1980	12.5

SOURCE: Based on *Statistical Abstract of the United States 1988*, Table 201.

The proportion of the adult population with fewer than five years of formal schooling, among whom illiteracy is most common, dropped from 14 percent in 1940 to 2 percent in 1987, while the proportion with 12 or more years of formal schooling rose from 25 percent in 1940 to 76 percent in 1987. Among blacks, this rate has risen much faster, from 7 percent in 1940 to 63 percent in 1987.[10] The enormous improvement in the educational level of the population explains why, despite television and other distractions, the readership of books and magazines has increased so dramatically in recent decades and why the intellectual level of best-selling books and popular magazines is now so much higher than it used to be.

Mobility is a sociological term that covers several different kinds of behavior. *Residential mobility* is the movement of an individual or family from one dwelling to another within the same community. *Geographic mobility*, also called migration, is the displacement of individuals and families to new communities, states and regions. *Occupational mobility* is the movement of workers among occupations. *Vertical mobility* refers to a gain or loss of status, either within a single lifetime, or from one generation to the next.

When people refer to "our increasingly mobile and rootless society" they are usually thinking about geographic mobility, although the supposed increase of geographic mobility may be assumed to imply a parallel increase in other kinds of mobility also.

Geographic mobility in many parts of the United States is much lower today than it was in the nineteenth century. The original settlers of every successive frontier area moved astonishingly often as they searched for economic and social niches. In his study of nineteenth-century Boston, Stephen Thernstrom discovered that about a million new arrivals were needed to increase the permanent population of Boston by 100,000.[11] The remaining 900,000 moved on to other places, from which most of them moved on again. In a somewhat similar study of Muncie, Indiana, based on the original records of the censuses of 1850 to 1880, Alexander Bracken found that barely a tenth of the population remained there from one census to the next, not to mention the people who were never counted because they arrived and departed between censuses.[12]

Today's U. S. population is not conspicuously mobile either by historic or international standards. The overall rates of residential and geographic mobility have been remarkably stable since 1950. About a fifth of the population change their addresses in any given year and about a third of these go to another county. There is no trace of a trend towards increasing mobility.

TABLE 5–2   **GEOGRAPHIC AND RESIDENTIAL MOBILITY IN THE U. S. (percent of population remaining after one year)**

	In Same House	In Same County
1949–50	81%	94%
1959–60	80	93
1969–70	81	93
1985–86	81	93

SOURCE: Based on *Statistical Abstract of the United States 1959*, Tables 136 and 1170; and *Statistical Abstract of the United States 1988*, Tables 204 and 1350.

Several different kinds of occupational mobility are commonly recognized: intergenerational mobility is the movement of workers to occupations of higher or lower status than those of their parents; career mobility is the shifting of individuals from one occupation to another in the course of their working careers. There are no official statistics on either topic, but there have been numerous studies. In studies of intergenerational mobility, the hypothesis of diminishing opportunity, which translates into decreasing mobility, has been advanced more often than the hypothesis of increasing opportunity, but the most careful studies do not show a clear-cut trend either way. Summarizing the many studies that have attempted to measure intergenerational mobility in the United States in the past century, Bahr concludes that:

> . . . when structural changes were taken into account, there was virtually no change in the association between fathers' occupational origins and sons' occupational destinations.[13]

As to mobility within individual careers, there seems to have been a *decline* in the rate of movement between jobs and between occupations over the past half century,* because of the barriers interposed by the expansion of credential requirements, the vesting of seniority and pension rights, and the emptying of the rural reservoir from which urban workers were formerly recruited.

It is customary and commonplace to attribute the growing burden of emotional disorders in contemporary American society to the stresses and strains imposed by rapid social change, but it is not commonplace to inquire whether that burden has really been growing. The problems of enumeration are formidable. The diagnostic

---

*Although national data on this point are apparently unavailable.

categories of modern psychiatry are fluid and unreliable. The number of patients hospitalized for emotional disorders in any given period is too heavily affected by changing institutional policies and therapeutic theories to provide much information about the true incidence of these conditions. Subjective conditions like anxiety and depression cannot be counted accurately. Disordered behaviors like child abuse and alcoholism have been redefined too often to permit the construction of satisfactory time series. To get an idea of the general trend, we have only a few reliable indicators, of which the most important are the suicide rate and the diagnoses of emotional disorders in a few institutional settings where relatively constant criteria have been used. The U. S. suicide rate, shown in Table 5–3, is particularly interesting:

TABLE 5–3	U. S. SUICIDE RATES (suicides per 100,000 of the population)	
	1940	14.4
	1950	11.4
	1960	10.6
	1970	11.8
	1985	11.5

SOURCE: Based on *Historical Statistics of the United States: Colonial Times to 1970*, Tables B149–166; and *Statistical Abstract of the United States*, Table 118. The figures for 1970 and 1985 are age-adjusted, which makes a difference of no more than 0.3 points.

The figure in Table 5–3 for 1940 reflects the unusually high level of suicide that prevailed from 1930 through 1940 and is plausibly attributed to the Great Depression. Otherwise, there has been no discernible trend.

It is not necessary to insist that every suicide is a sign of emotional disorder. Some suicides are undoubtedly based on cool and rational decisions. But enough is known from the study of attempted suicides and of the surviving spouses of successful suicides to identify most suicides with severe emotional disorders arising from stressful situations.[14]

Similar conclusions about the absence of any upward trend in the incidence of emotional disorders must be drawn from the few diagnostic series that are usable for this purpose.[15]

The acceleration of social change is a metaphor without a precise meaning. Since there is no way to measure the speed of social change, there is no sure way of detecting an acceleration or deceleration, but the metaphor might stand for several different conditions. It might signify that the life experience of successive generations was increasingly different from each preceding generation. Or that the average number of significant decisions taken by members of a population increased in successive intervals of time. Or that rates of social and technical innovation increased. Or that attitudes and relationships were increasingly volatile. Or simply that more people had feelings of estrangement from their surroundings as they grew older.

The last experience being nearly universal, the metaphor of accelerating social change is automatically plausible to anyone over 30. But the other conditions are theoretically amenable to proof or disproof.

If we compare the collective experience of the cohort of Americans born in 1950, and now approaching middle age, with the cohorts born in 1920 and 1890, it is immediately apparent that the 1950 cohort is closer to the 1920 cohort in educational experience, occupational distribution, family size, marriage and divorce, housing, possessions, leisure patterns, and physical appearance, than was the 1920 cohort to the 1890 cohort. The great transitions from rural to urban, from Europe to America, and from the horse to the automobile, separated the 1920 cohort from their parents. Very few of the 1890 cohort grew up in houses with central heating and electricity, played football, graduated from high school, drank wine, or practiced contraception, as did the majority of both the 1920 and the 1950 cohorts. The 1920 cohort enjoyed an enormous advantage in lifetime real income over the 1890 cohort, but most of the 1950 cohort entered the labor force in the early 1970s, when the growth of real income slowed to a crawl, and their real incomes remain close to those of their parents. On this dimension, social change seems to have decelerated.

Can we detect acceleration in the number of significant decisions required of individuals? Significant decisions include educational choices, friendship choices, vocational choices, the choice of sexual partners and spouses, choices of location, the decision to have or not to have children, decisions to save or spend, religious and political commitments, and so forth. As an action, like having children, becomes elective rather than obligatory, the occasions for decision increase. As another action, like finishing high school, becomes obligatory rather than elective, occasions for decision decrease. And the number of housing decisions should remain approximately unchanged if residential mobility is stable. All in all, there is no evidence of a consistent increase in the number of decisions required of individuals.

Have rates of social and technical innovation been increasing, then? Before reaching the age of 30, the cohort born in 1890 witnessed the general diffusion of the automobile, the airplane, motorcycles, outboard motors, amateur photography, motion pictures, the phonograph, radio, electric light, vacuum cleaners, central heating, washing machines, toasters, typewriters, skyscrapers, jazz, musical comedy, night clubs, comic strips, synthetic fabrics, mutual funds, income taxes, newsmagazines, relativity, trench warfare, communist governments, and high school basketball. Before reaching 30, the cohort born in 1920 saw the arrival of air travel, limited access highways, television, radar, jet engines, social security, unemployment insurance, guaranteed bank deposits, voting machines, electric typewriters, audio recorders, microwave ovens, air conditioning, antibiotics and steroids, multinational corporations, motels, credit cards, supersonic planes, nuclear weapons, fascist governments, and mainframe computers. Before the age of 30, the cohort born in 1960 saw the introduction of personal computers and computer networks, video recorders, space travel, civil rights legislation, women's liberation, legal abortion, condominia, child pornography, AIDS, retirement communities, organ transplants, aerobic exercise, industrial robots, lasers, shopping malls, and nuclear arms agreements. If anything, the rate of innovation seems to be slowing down, although the recent innovations in computer technology may eventually outweigh all the rest.

The ultimate claim of the accelerating change metaphor is that habits and attitudes have become unstable because of the difficulty of adjusting to an unstable environment. For this assertion there is no evidence at all. Since the *General Social Survey* of the National Opinion Research Center began its annual surveys of the U. S. population in 1972, putting some of the same questions to national samples year after year, they have accumulated a body of evidence that shows the prevailing stability of American attitudes and habits.[16]

There are dozens of other imaginary trends that are as widely believed today in the United States and as unsupported by facts, as the ones just described. The common feature is that all of them purport to trace the passage from a former state of social order to a present disorder that is likely to get worse. The current mythology conforms to the linear regress model. It compares the real present with a fictional past and finds that every day in every way motives and relationships are getting worse. In that fictional past, families were happy and united, everybody read the Bible and went to church, sex was mostly confined to marriage, cities were clean and safe, crime was rare and quickly punished, employers were considerate, teachers were stern but conscientious, officials were honest, prices were reasonable, and a man could repair his own automobile. This view of 1950 or 1890 is strangely comforting. It matches the nearly universal sentiment of nostalgia for one's past and it provides a natural platform from which to inveigh against the objectionable features of the world around us. But most of it is false.

NOTES

1. Elizabeth Sefton, editor-in-chief of the Viking Press, quoted in *Washington Post*, 23 May 1962, A3.
2. Alvin Toffler, *Future Shock* (New York: Bantam Books, 1971), 12.
3. John Naisbitt, *Megatrends: Ten New Directions Transforming Our Lives* (New York: Warner Books, 1982), 18.
4. For a fuller description of the indicators of secularization, see Theodore Caplow, Howard M. Bahr, Bruce A. Chadwick, et al., *All Faithful People: Change and Continuity in Middletown's Religion* (Minneapolis: University of Minnesota Press, 1983), Chapter 14.
5. Based on Richard G. Niemi, John Mueller, and Tom W. Smith, *Trends in Public Opinion: A Compendium of Survey Data* (New York: Greenwood Press, 1989), Tables 13.1 and 13.6.
6. Theodore Caplow, Howard M. Bahr, Bruce A. Chadwick, et al., *Middletown Families: Fifty Years of Change and Continuity* (Minneapolis: University of Minnesota Press, 1982), 24–25.
7. *SAUS79*, Table 997; and *SAUS89*, Table 382.
8. *SAUS89*, Table 380.
9. *Ibid*, Table 381.
10. Based on *SAUS89*, Table 211.
11. Stephen Thernstrom. *The Other Bostonians: Progress and Poverty in the American Metropolis, 1880–1970* (Cambridge, MA: Harvard University Press, 1973).
12. Alexander E. Bracken, "Middletown as a Pioneer Community" (Ph.D. diss., Ball State University, 1973).
13. Howard M. Bahr, *Social Mobility*, a trend report prepared for the International Research Group on the Comparative Charting of Social Change,

March 1989. The most authoritative of these studies was Otis Dudley Duncan, David L. Featherman, and Beverly Duncan, *Socioeconomic Background and Achievement* (New York: Academic Press, 1972).

14. Two particularly illuminating studies are Samuel E. Wallace, *After Suicide* (New York: John Wiley, 1973), and Jack P. Gibbs and Walter T. Martin, *Status Integration and Suicide: A Sociological Study* (Eugene, OR: University of Oregon Press, 1964).

15. S. Kirson Weinberg, ed., *The Sociology of Mental Disorders* (Chicago: Aldine, 1970).

16. See National Opinion Research Center, *General Social Survey: Cumulative Codebook*, published annually.

6

TRENDS IN THE FAMILY

The family is an institution that ordinarily resists short-term change. The attitudes and practices of existing families are not very flexible, and new families are founded by people whose expectations were shaped in existing families. Many features of the American family— the division of labor between husband and wife, the way children are disciplined, sibling rivalry, the free choice of marital partners— were already present in the eighteenth century. When new patterns appear, they spread slowly and the old patterns persist in many families. Nevertheless, there were some extraordinary changes in American family patterns between 1960 and 1990.

Family relationships in the present generation are stronger in many respects than in previous generations. Communication between husbands and wives and between parents and children has improved, if the studies can be trusted.[1] Although divorce is more frequent, most divorced persons remarry quickly. White Americans continue to be the most married population in the world. Fewer than one in twenty have not been married by the time they reach the age of 55. The number of men and women who reach their early thirties without ever having married was slightly lower in 1985 than in 1890, although higher than in 1960.[2] Moreover, Reuben Hill calculated in 1982 that the average duration of marriage was still rising in the U. S.; the effect of increased life-expectancy outweighed the effect of increased divorce.[3]

The four percent of white Americans who now pass middle age without ever marrying is probably close to the irreducible minimum. Some of them have physical or mental handicaps that exclude marriage; others are confirmed homosexuals. But middle-aged bachelors and spinsters of heterosexual inclination are astonishingly rare. Two recent trends may presage their reappearance, however. The average age of first marriage rose by more than three years for both sexes between 1960 and 1990, to 26 for men and 24 for women—a very steep rise in a measure that usually changes very slowly.[4] And the proportion of each year's marriages that were first marriages fell from more than three-quarters to less than half. Taken together, these two trends raise the possibility that people born after 1960 will have a lower lifetime propensity for marriage than their parents and grandparents.

There are signs of strain in the increasing number of illegitimate births and single-parent families in the majority population, but these signs occur at the margin, so to speak: 84 percent of the white infants of 1986 were born to married mothers, 87 percent of the white families were headed by a married couple.[5]

The case is otherwise for black and hispanic families; they have developed dual family patterns since 1960, one following the majority pattern, and the other evolving in a new direction. We will consider trends among white families first, and then return to black and hispanic families.

The most basic family indicator is the birth rate. Among white women in the United States, the birth rate declined steadily from 1800 to 1940, was interrupted by the postwar baby boom, and resumed its long-term decline around 1960, as Table 6–1 shows.

TABLE 6–1   **THE U. S. WHITE BIRTH RATE (live births per 1,000 white women aged 15–44)**

1800	278
1840	222
1880	155
1920	115
1940	77
1950	102
1960	113
1970	84
1980	65
1988	64

SOURCE: Based on *Historical Statistics of the United States: Colonial Times to 1970*, Series B-5, 10; *Statistical Abstract of the United States 1988*, Table 83; and National Center for Health Statistics, *Monthly Vital Statistics Report*, February 1989, Table 4.

A falling birth rate routinely accompanies modernization and is adequately explained by the declining value of children's labor, the increasing cost of child-raising, the decrease of infant mortality, and the increasingly voluntary control of conception. The gross reproduction rate for U. S. white women now stands at 850, signifying that, if present rates continue, each 1,000 women now of childbearing age will bear 850 daughters and that the next native-born generation will be smaller than the current one. The long-term decline in the birth rate is associated with a long-term, very gradual decline in the size of the median family, from 5.8 persons in 1790 to 2.7 in 1985. Most of the decline is attributable to the declining proportion of families with many children.

Four major developments transformed the life-situation of American families after 1960—childbearing became elective, the legal prohibition of unmarried cohabitation was abandoned, no-fault divorce became available, and large numbers of mothers with young children entered the labor force. Given the speed and magnitude of these changes, it is surprising that so much of the institutional pattern has remained intact.

Although contraception was widely used before 1960, all of the available methods then had high rates of failure, so that coitus usually involved a serious risk of pregnancy. Voluntary abortion was illegal everywhere in the United States; illegal abortions were expensive, dangerous, and disreputable. Sterilization was rare. The pregnancy of an unmarried woman or the unwanted pregnancy of a married woman was a major crisis that might end tragically. All this changed with the introduction, around 1962, of reliable oral contraceptives. Surgical sterilization became generally available soon afterwards and in 1973, in the famous case of *Roe* v. *Wade*, the U. S. Supreme Court unexpectedly legalized abortion throughout the 50 states. A woman's decisions about whether and when to have children were suddenly separated from her decisions about whether and with whom to go to bed. So fundamental a change in the relation between the sexes was bound to have far-reaching consequences.

The most obvious consequence was an extraordinary drop in fertility; as Table 6–1 shows, the birth rate fell by nearly half between 1960 and 1988. As soon as women could freely choose how many children to have, they chose to have fewer.

The methods of contraception available before 1962 had failure rates of five to ten percent *per month*; the failure rate of oral contraceptives, properly used, was near zero. But sterilization and abortion probably accounted for more of the fertility decline. By 1988, nearly two out of five married women of childbearing age (and/or their husbands) were surgically sterile—more than the combined number of those who used condoms or the pill.[6]

No one knows how many illegal abortions were performed in the U. S. before the *Roe* v. *Wade* decision and data on legal abortion are still fragmentary; but in the 13 states reporting abortions in 1986, there were 286 abortions per 1,000 live births for white women and

634 for black women.[7] If abortions had been effectively prohibited in 1986, the birth rate for married white women would have risen by only five percent, but births to unmarried white women would have more than doubled, and births to white girls under age 15 would have more than tripled. Legal abortion reduces illegitimacy even more than it reduces fertility. The overwhelming majority of abortions took place in the first trimester of pregnancy, the period excluded from state regulation by *Roe* v. *Wade*. Complications were very rare. Despite the strength of the antiabortion movement that developed in the 1980s, it is most unlikely that abortion will be delegalized. It is difficult to argue that society would benefit from the birth each year of more than 1 million babies to unmarried mothers, many of whom are 12 or 13 years old and otherwise unqualified for child-raising, and few opponents of abortion take that position. Some of them rely on the dogma that the ovum becomes a person at the moment of conception, contrary to the traditional Christian beliefs, which dated personhood either from birth or from the "quickening" of the fetus in the second trimester. Those who take the new position cannot condone abortion even in cases of rape and incest or when the mother's life is endangered by a pregnancy, because these circumstances cannot excuse a premeditated murder. They are, however, a small minority compared to the much larger body of citizens who are uneasy about abortion because it seems self-indulgent and antifamilial, or because they visualize it as the destruction of a fetus almost ready to be born. The regulation of second-trimester abortions and the prohibition of third-trimester abortions—a prospect opened by the Supreme Court's 1989 *Webster* opinion—would not have any appreciable effect on existing practices. Moreover, RU-486, a pharmaceutical product that accomplishes the same purpose without surgical intervention, is already marketed in Europe and will inevitably spread to the United States. However the political issue of abortion is ultimately resolved, it is almost certain that large numbers of women, mostly unmarried, will continue to obtain prompt and safe abortions when they discover themselves to be pregnant.

The availability of effective contraception before coitus and of safe abortion afterwards had a depressing effect on the marriage rate as well as on the birth rate. Before 1960, "shotgun weddings," in which a reluctant groom took a pregnant bride under some degree of social pressure, were fairly common. Since then, they have virtually disappeared. By the same token, it became less risky for unmarried couples to set up housekeeping together, with or without the prospect of eventual marriage.

Until about 1960, American law, following and elaborating on the common law of England, attempted to enforce monogamy by a variety of ingenious provisions. The cohabitation of unmarried couples was repressed by local laws against false registration in lodging houses, a Federal statute that prohibited the interstate transportation of females for immoral purposes, and regulations that made it impossible for unmarried couples to buy a house or rent an apartment. Hotel keepers and landlords often went beyond the law in refusing to accommodate them. In colleges and other institutional settings, men and women were kept out of each other's rooms by locked gates and armed guards. Sexually active adolescents were defined as juvenile delinquents and sometimes imprisoned. Adolescent girls who became pregnant were automatically expelled from school and were likely to be placed in institutions that kept them out of public sight and gave their babies out for adoption. Adolescent boys were often convicted of statutory rape for consorting with girls of their own age. Adultery was a criminal offense in theory and sometimes in practice but was more effectively punished in civil actions for separation, support, divorce, or custody where the husband or wife accused of adultery was treated very harshly. Illegitimate children had few inheritance rights. Custom required the exclusion of an identified homosexual from any position of responsibility.

This entire structure was swept away, mostly by judicial rulings, between 1965 and 1975. The U. S. Supreme Court led the way in the 1965 case of *Griswold* v. *Connecticut* when it struck down a state law proscribing the use of contraceptives by discovering in the Constitution a hitherto unknown right of marital privacy. That right was soon extended to other intimate relations between consenting adults.

As the structure of official regulation was dismantled, the private regulators had no choice but to follow suit. College deans abandoned the *in loco parentis* role that made them responsible for student chastity. Dormitories became co-ed and moderately tolerant of student cohabitation. Hotel keepers lost interest in the marital status of their guests. Banks encouraged homosexual couples to take out mortgage loans. One of the most important changes was a shift in the policies of social agencies so that unmarried mothers became fully entitled to welfare payments and other kinds of family assistance.

Contrary to a widespread impression, the divorce rate does not show a constant upward trend. Prior to 1940, the national data are

unreliable. From 1940 to 1965, the rate fluctuated in the neighborhood of 10 divorces per 1,000 married women per year, except for a
spike in the immediate aftermath of World War II when it reached 18.
Between 1965 and 1975, it doubled to 20, and has remained in that
vicinity ever since.[8] The sharp increase from 1965 to 1975 is no
mystery:

> Twenty-five years ago a couple could only get a divorce by prov-
> ing that one party was at fault, and thus the other was justified
> in suing for divorce. Different states had different rules about
> the kinds and degrees of fault that were necessary, but in all
> cases the laws were intended to be obstructive . . . In 1966, New
> York state started the move for reform, when it rewrote its di-
> vorce law. This was one of the oldest in the nation, having been
> written by Alexander Hamilton. It was also one of the most rigid,
> allowing divorce only upon proof of adultery. The new law al-
> lowed divorce . . . for an agreed-upon separation of two or more
> years. Though no one recognized it at the time, this was the first
> no-fault divorce law. California produced a new and explicit no-
> fault divorce law in 1969, and by 1985 all fifty states had some
> form of no-fault divorce.[9]

All of this did not happen in a vacuum. It was closely linked to other
social movements of the Vietnam era: the counterculture, women's
liberation, gay rights, participatory democracy, and the extension of
Federal authority over education and health care.

The increasing employment of married women is a long-term
trend that has greatly accelerated in recent years, as the employment of women has gained on the employment of men, the employment of married women has gained on the employment of single
women, and the employment of married women with children has
gained on the employment of married women without children. The
figures are fairly spectacular. In 1940, 45 percent of single women
were in the labor force but only 15 percent of married women (with
husbands present.) By 1987, the proportion of single women who
were in the labor force had risen by almost half, to 65 percent, but the
proportion of married women had almost quadrupled, to 56 percent, and the employment of married women with children under
age six, which had been negligible in 1940, reached 57 percent in
1987, slightly *above* the rate for married women in general. Most of
this increase has taken place since 1960. The figures in Table 6–2
refer to married women living with their husbands who have one or
more children under the age of six:[10]

TABLE 6–2	EMPLOYMENT OF MARRIED WOMEN WITH YOUNG CHILDREN (percent in labor force)

1960	19%
1970	30
1980	45
1987	57

SOURCE: Based on *Statistical Abstract of the United States 1988*, Tables 607, 622, 624.

Divorced and separated mothers had even higher rates. Divorced women with children between ages 6 and 17 achieved a labor force participation rate of 85 percent in 1987, considerably higher than that of married men.[11]

In earlier times, the employment of married women was confined to underprivileged families. In their 1924–25 study of Middletown, the Lynds found that more than half of the wives of factory workers participated intermittently in the labor force when their husbands were out of work or incapacitated. The wives of office workers almost never took paid employment.[12] But the recent surge of women's employment involved all occupational levels and all sections of the country.

The primary reason seems to have been economic necessity. The growth of real wages virtually ceased in the U. S. after 1970 while living standards continued to rise and the cost of housing, health care, automobiles, and college educations, rose faster than the general rate of inflation. The earnings of one middle-income breadwinner were no longer sufficient to provide a family with a middle-class standard of living. But other factors played an important part. The simplification of housework, which began half a century earlier with the electric washing machine and the vacuum cleaner, continued with such innovations as wash-and-wear clothing, precooked frozen meals, and microwave ovens. The doctrines of feminism called upon women to shake off their dependence on men and compete with them on equal terms. The domestic role was denigrated and married women came to see employment more as an opportunity for self-fulfillment than as a burden. The new viewpoint was widely accepted by married men too; it decreased their obligations without much affecting their comfort, since working wives continued, for the most part, to be responsible for housekeeping and child care. Studies of the division of family labor showed that it changed only slightly when wives entered the labor force, except, of course, for an enormous increase in external child care, both in the homes of relatives and friends and in group care centers.[13]

As previously noted, the great majority of the white population continue to live in households headed by a married couple and the great majority of white infants are born to married couples. Consensual unions—what the Census Bureau quaintly calls concubinage—often lead to marriage. Illegitimacy presently accounts for about one in every seven white births, but about half of these are eventually legitimated by marriage. Most of the unmarried mothers are very young; contrary to a general impression, unmarried white women over 30 have few babies.

That is one side of the coin. The other is more startling. From 1960 to 1985, the number of infants born to unmarried white women increased from 82,000 to 433,000, or 428 percent! The number doubled from 1960 to 1970, and doubled again from 1970 to 1982. Between 1970 and 1985, the number of white families headed by a woman increased from 4 million to almost 7 million, more than half of them with children living at home.[14]

These trends, if they continue, will have drastic consequences on the life-experience of future generations. For the time being, it is uncertain whether they will continue. The pace of female entry into the labor force must necessarily slacken, since most women are already at work. The rise in adolescent sexual activity has run most of its course also, since most unmarried women in the high childbearing ages of 18 to 24 are already sexually active. Meanwhile, the new venereal epidemics seem to be discouraging promiscuity and encouraging the use of contraceptives. On balance, traditional family patterns have been shaken but not destroyed.

Despite the demographic stresses, attachment to family values has not decreased in any measurable way in recent decades, and the research evidence does not indicate any decrease in family solidarity or kinship interaction. The great majority of American adults with living parents maintain close and affectionate relationships with them. The great majority of American households interact frequently and extensively with households of kin.[15]

The networks composed of related households living in the same vicinity and continually exchanging visits, telephone calls, and personal services, were long overlooked by sociological observers, who were gripped by the myth of the isolated nuclear family. The numerous, careful descriptions of American family life in many different settings that appeared between 1920 and 1970 took no particular notice of these networks so that it is now impossible to determine whether the ties of kinship among urban and suburban households have recently become more important than they used to be. Some analysts think they have but the evidence is scanty. The same question is raised but not answered by recent studies of kin networks—French sociologists call them *parenteles*—in urban communities in western Europe.[16] Whatever the irrecoverable trend may have been, the present importance of these networks is beyond dispute.[17] Most American families live within easy reach of the households of close relatives, with whom they are constantly in touch. Most adults see their parents several times a month, although the number of parents who live in the same household as their married children has been declining for many years. Nearly all parents, children, siblings, and grandchildren, including those who live far apart, exchange gifts at Christmas and celebrate each other's birthdays. Most Americans live where they do to be "near their families" which in this context signifies a kin network. Since American kinship is fully bilateral, paternal and maternal relatives are equally close. Married people are absorbed into the kin networks of their spouses; even unmarried people who live together participate in each other's networks. It is not uncommon for Americans to attend half a dozen family gatherings at Christmas and to buy Christmas gifts for 50 or 60 relatives.[18] These networks cut across social class and occupational lines, include all living generations, and provide emotional and material support to their members in innumerable ways. They are particularly important for elderly widows and widowers, and for single-parent families, substituting in many ways for the missing spouse or parent. Kin networks are particularly important for wealthy families of high status, for whom they conserve and transmit social influence, and for poor families at the bottom of the class system, for whom they provide more effective protection than the remote, impersonal welfare agencies.

The support offered by kin networks is especially important for the single-parent families who make up most of the "underclass" living in misery and poverty in the black ghettos of every large American city. Their numbers have greatly increased since 1960 and will continue to increase for the foreseeable future—an unwelcome and paradoxical outcome of the social reforms of the 1960s.

The family patterns that developed among blacks in the slave-holding regions of North America, the Caribbean, and Brazil were strongly matricentric, as the constraints of slavery dictated.[19] The mother-child relationship was very strong; the father-child relationship was relatively weak. Consensual unions were more prevalent than formal marriages and were easily dissolved. Grandmothers often presided over three- and four-generation households with no adult males. Vestiges of the system persisted long after emancipation. The earnings of black men were often too low and insecure to support a family, lower and less secure than the earnings of their wives. When Franklin Frazier studied black families in the United States[20] two generations ago, he described a dual system in which middle-class families were characterized by marital solidarity and working-class families by its absence. This situation remained more or less unchanged until the 1960s, when the factors impinging on the white family—discretionary childbearing, the deregulation of sexual relations, the increased employment of married women—had much more sweeping effects on the black family.

A few numbers tell the story. By 1986, 43 percent of never married black women aged 18 to 29 had borne one or more children, compared to only 6 percent of single white women. Sixty percent of all black births in 1985 were to unmarried women; the ratio has been climbing from year to year. Of the 4.8 million black families with children under 16 in 1986, 54 percent were headed by a woman without a husband and only 42 percent by a married couple. The majority of black children were being raised without fathers or stepfathers, and a majority of these in poverty.[21] Among more affluent blacks, the trend was towards later marriage and fewer children. It is a curious fact that the black illegitimacy *rate*, the number of illegitimate births per 1,000 black women aged 15 to 44, declined slightly from 1963 to 1983, while the illegitimacy *ratio*, the number of illegitimate births per 1,000 births, skyrocketed. The explanation of this apparent paradox lies in the steep decline of marital fertility and the changing age structure of the black female population during this period.[22]

The situation of the hispanic family is more difficult to summarize, because the hispanic minority in the United States is not culturally homogeneous. Its three main components—Puerto Ricans, Mexicans, Cubans—have very different family patterns although all of them stem from a Latin American model characterized by male dominance, elaborate codes of sexual morality, durable marriages, and large families. The current profile of Puerto Rican families in the U. S. closely resembles that of black families. Most births are illegitimate, most children are raised by unmarried mothers, many are poor. Cuban-Americans, by contrast, have relatively stable families and an illegitimacy ratio close to the national average. Mexican-Americans fall between.[23]

The black and Puerto Rican children who grow up without paternal authority, without economic security, and sometimes without much care of any kind, do not all turn out badly, by any means. But in later life, they make a disproportionate contribution to the numbers of functional illiterates, high school dropouts, youth gang members, robbers and rapists, teen-age prostitutes, drug dealers and addicts, welfare recipients, family service clients, the unemployed and the unemployable, AIDS patients, death row inmates, and lost souls. The dramatic and continuing increase in the size of this underclass does not bode well.

The great recent changes in family structure that we have just reviewed suggest that we ought to look for correspondingly important changes in family attitudes and values, but they turn out to be rather elusive.[24] One reason is that the traditional attitudes and values are both persistent and flexible. Contemporary Americans continue to disapprove of divorce in general while accepting and even welcoming the divorces of their relatives and friends. Parents favor adolescent chastity but discover as little as they possibly can about the sex lives of their adolescent children. Unmarried welfare mothers, whose own mothers were unmarried, express as much attachment to the ideal of a happy marriage as suburban housewives.

In survey after survey, about 70 percent of married Americans rate their own marriages as very happy; only about 2 percent admit to being unhappily married. Presumably, most of the marriages that turn unhappy are promptly dissolved by divorce. Respondents in national samples invariably report more satisfaction with their family lives than with their work, their hobbies, or their friendships. There was no discernible change in these responses between 1972 and 1987.[25] The respondents may be exaggerating to some extent but that would hardly account for such lopsided distributions or for the parallel findings of in-depth biographical studies. A very large proportion of American adults regard their families as a safe haven where they can escape from the impersonal cruelty of mass society.

Everyone in the United States who reads newspapers or watches television knows about the "crisis of the contemporary family." Since most Americans have been told that the family as an institution is at the point of collapse, but regard their own families as happy and successful, they derive great psychic satisfaction from the contrast—at very low social cost.

Despite the general and surprising stability in family attitudes and values, there are two important trends that began long before 1960 and will probably continue long after 1990. One is a shift in the qualities that parents value in their children, away from obedience and conformity towards autonomy and self-direction.[26] The other is the equalization of power between husbands and wives, which has now been under way for several generations, although it is obscured by the great diversity of power configurations that can be observed in any set of contemporary families.

NOTES

1. See, among many other studies, Bruce A. Chadwick, "The Quality of Marriage," and Howard M. Bahr, "Parents and Children," Chapters 6 and 7, respectively, in Theodore Caplow, Howard M. Bahr, and Bruce A. Chadwick et al., *Middletown Families* (Minneapolis: University of Minnesota Press, 1962).
2. Based on Bureau of the Census, *Marital Status and Living Arrangements, March 1985*, CPS, Series 20, no. 4, 1986.
3. Reuben Hill, "American Families during the Twentieth Century," Chapter 12 in Caplow, *Middletown Families*.
4. Based on Bureau of the Census, *Marital Status*.
5. Based on *SAUS89*, Tables 93 and 60.
6. National Center for Health Statistics, *Contraceptive Use in the United States, 1973–88*, Advance Data Release, no. 182, 20 March 1990.
7. National Center for Health Statistics, "Induced Terminations of Pregnancy: Reporting States, 1985 and 1986," *Monthly Vital Statistics Report*, 37, no. 12 supp. (April 18, 1989); and *SAUS89*, Table 127.
8. National Center for Health Statistics, *Vital Statistics of the United States III*, 1975, Table 2.1; and *Monthly Vital Statistics Report*, 38, no. 1 (1989). Contrary to a widespread belief, there has been no recent reduction in the duration of marriages broken by divorce (See *SAUS89*, Table 132).
9. Achsah Carrier, "A Sexual Revolution? Changing Sex Law in the Twentieth Century," unpublished manuscript, 1989.
10. Based on *SAUS88*, Tables 607, 622, 624.
11. *Ibid.*
12. Robert S. Lynd and Helen M. Lynd, *Middletown: A Study in American Culture* (New York: Harcourt and Brace, 1929).
13. See Judith W. Weaver and Carol A. Cartwright, *Child Care Administration* (Belmont, CA: Wadsworth, 1987); and Select Committee on Children, Youth and Families, *U. S. Children and Their Families: Current Conditions and Recent Trends* (Washington; Government Printing Office, 1986).

14. Based on *SAUS88*, Tables 87, 58, 70.
15. According to data from Howard M. Bahr, *Trend Report on Parenthood* (Quebec, Canada: International Research Group on the Comparative Charting of Social Change, 1990).
16. The best recent discussion of parenteles is found in Henri Mendras, *La Seconde Revolution Française* (Paris: Presses Universitaires de France, 1988).
17. Among the most informative studies of kin networks in the U. S. are Bert N. Adams, *Kinship in an Urban Setting* (Chicago: Markham, 1968); George Rosenberg and Donald F. Anspach, *Working Class Kinship* (Lexington, MA: Lexington Books, 1973); Louis Harris and Associates, *The Myth and Reality of Aging in the United States* (Washington, D.C.: National Council on the Aging, 1975); Gary R. Lee, "Kinship in the Seventies: A Decade Review of Research and Theory," *Journal of Marriage and the Family*, 38 (1980): 749–56; and Robert Joseph Taylor, "The Extended Family as a Source of Support to Elderly Blacks," *The Gerontologist*, 25, no. 5 (1985): 488–95.
18. Theodore Caplow, "Christmas Gifts and Kin Networks," *American Sociological Review*, 47, no. 3 (1982): 383–92; and "Norm-Enforcement without Visible Means," *American Journal of Sociology*, 89, no. 6 (1984): 1306–23.
19. See, for example, M. G. Smith, *The Plural Society in the British West Indies* (Berkeley, CA: University of California Press, 1965) 92–115; and Gilberto Freyre, *Casa-grande & Senzala*, 4th ed. (Rio de Janeiro: J. Olympio, 1943).
20. E. Franklin Frazier, *The Negro Family in Chicago* (Chicago: University of Chicago Press, 1932), and *The Negro Family in the United States* (Chicago: University of Chicago Press, 1939).
21. Based on *SAUS88*, Tables 43, 66, 87.
22. Herbert L. Smith and Phillips Cutright. "Thinking about Change in Illegitimacy Ratios: United States, 1963–1983," *Demography*, vol 25, no. 2, 235–47.
23. Based on *SAUS88*, Tables 43, 66, 87.
24. For an interesting demonstration of this point, see Nicholas Leman, "Stressed Out in Suburbia," *Atlantic Monthly*, November 1989, 34–48.
25. *GSS80*, items 161 and 116; and *GSS87*, items 155 and 161.
26. Duaine P. Alwin, "From Obedience to Autonomy: Changes in Traits Desired in Children, 1924–1978," *Public Opinion Quarterly*, 52 (1988): 33–52.

7

TRENDS IN RELIGION

Americans have been exceptionally pious for a very long time. More than 150 years ago, Alexis de Tocqueville wrote that,

> America is still the place where the Christian religion has kept the greatest real power over men's souls . . . . The religious atmosphere of the country was the first thing that struck me on arrival in the United States. The longer I stayed in the country, the more conscious I became of the important political consequences resulting from this novel situation.[1]

That novel situation persists to this day. About 40 percent of American adults attend religious services every week, in contrast to fewer than 10 percent of the Germans, the French, or the British. Three out of four Americans, but only one in four Europeans, assert the divinity of Jesus. Americans spend more money on religious activities and more time in private devotions than the inhabitants of any other advanced industrial country.[2] Tocqueville attributed the strength of religion in the United States to its division into "innumerable sects." This fragmentation prevented American denominations from exercising any political authority, like the Catholic church in France, or any alliance with the state, like the Protestant churches of Germany. Religion was inevitably weakened, he thought, by involvement in the shifting currents of political and social issues. American religion was protected by the separation of church and state. At a deeper level, he argued that an egalitarian society encourages the pursuit of self-interest to the point of social breakdown unless selfishness is checked by norms of duty imposed from outside. Since democratic governments lack the moral authority to impose such norms, people turn to religion to provide the restraints on their own behavior which they sense to be necessary.

Whether or not this reasoning is valid, the pattern that Tocqueville sought to explain is still visible today. The church is more fragmented in America than anywhere else, and has fewer connections with the state. Everywhere in Europe, from Spain to the Soviet Union, the state is directly involved in the management of churches and religious organizations in ways that would be inconceivable in the United States. Religious education is supported by the state in countries as unlike as Switzerland and Bulgaria. Sweden, with practically no church attendance, taxes all of its citizens for the support of the national church. Everywhere in Europe, as Jean Stoetzel showed in his monumental study of European values,[3] religious and political affiliations are so closely linked that the political opinions of a survey respondent can be inferred from his or her response to questions about religion.

The nearly perfect separation that Tocqueville observed between state and church in early nineteenth-century America has given way to a web of intricate transactions whereby absolute separation is proclaimed in principle and breached in a thousand small ways in practice. For example, government aid to religious schools must conform to a series of judicial decisions that can only be described as whimsical. At various times in the 1970s, the Supreme Court decided that transporting parochial students to and from school at public expense is constitutional but transporting them on field trips is unconstitutional, that the loan of a public school textbook to a parochial school is constitutional but the loan of audiovisual equipment is not, that a state may provide guidance counseling for parochial schools in a mobile unit but not on their school grounds.[4] As of this writing, a large number of lawsuits about Christmas decorations in and around public buildings are wending their way through the courts. Nevertheless, the principle of separation between church and state endures.

The other side of the system is that the principle of separation permits government to assume a nondenominational religious identity. The peculiarly American faith in the joint working of democracy and divine Providence goes back to the seventeenth century when the Mayflower Compact was dedicated to the "Glory of God and the Advancement of the Christian Faith," and John Donne exhorted the Virginia colonists to "be a light to the Gentiles that sit in darkness." William Penn wrote in 1682, "Government seems to me a part of religion itself, a thing sacred in its institution and end."[5] A century later, the Declaration of Independence closed with an appeal to the "Supreme Judge of the world and to the Protection of Divine Providence." Nearly a century after that, Abraham Lincoln wrote, in his Emancipation Proclamation, "I invoke the considerate judgment of mankind and the gracious favor of Almighty God." In our own century, Dwight Eisenhower said that "Our government makes no sense unless it is founded on a deeply-felt religious faith," adding "And I don't care what it is."[6] Every recent U. S. president has echoed that theme in his public statements. The religious freedom sought by so many Catholic and Jewish—and lately Orthodox and Buddhist—immigrants to the United States is not an indifference to religion but a benevolent neutrality towards denominational differences.

While the fundamental pattern of religious organization in the United States is very stable, there have been frequent changes in the details. These are easy to track through recent decades with the help of abundant survey data, but longer-term trends are more elusive. There was a fairly steady increase in church membership from about 10 percent of the population in 1800 to about 65 percent in 1950, declining slightly, to 60 percent, by 1985.[7] Long-term trends in church attendance seem to have been much more irregular than trends in church membership, being strongly affected by revival movements and by complex intergenerational shifts. Table 7–1, for example, illustrates the long-term trend of church attendance by married women in one midwestern community:

TABLE 7–1   **CHURCH ATTENDANCE BY MARRIED WOMEN IN MIDDLETOWN**

Frequency	1890	1924	1978
Regular	59%	23%	48%
Occasional	11	24	34
None	30	53	17

SOURCE: Based on T. Caplow, H. M. Bahr, B. A. Chadwick et. al., *All Faithful People: Change and Continuity in Middletown's Religion* (Minneapolis: University of Minnesota Press, 1982), Table 3–2, 306.

As these figures suggest, the long-term trend in regular church attendance must be distinguished from the trend in nonattendance. The proportion of married Middletown women who went to church regularly (weekly or more often) was lower in 1978 than in 1890 but so was the proportion who stayed away altogether.

Church attendance is a convenient measure of religiosity but hardly a sufficient one. It is conceivable that church attendance might remain approximately level while religious faith declined. The general conclusion that religion has not weakened in the United States in recent decades rests on a broad range of evidence.[8] In Gallup surveys extending from the 1940s to the 1980s, the proportion of U. S. respondents expressing belief in God as a universal spirit has hovered around 95 percent, the proportion asserting the divinity of

Jesus around 70 percent. The proportion who could name all four gospels increased from 35 percent in 1954 to 46 percent in 1982. Most strikingly perhaps, the proportion of Americans who say they read the Bible at least daily increased gradually from 10 percent in the 1940s to 15 percent in 1984.[9] When the Middletown women whose 1978 church attendance is recorded in the table above were interviewed, they were asked three questions that had been put to a similar sample of women in the same community in exactly the same words in 1924, 54 years earlier:

- What are the thoughts and plans that give you courage to go on when thoroughly discouraged?
- How often have you thought of Heaven during the past month in this connection?
- What difference would it make in your daily life if you became convinced that there was no loving God caring for you?

The most interesting result of this replication was that the responses of 1978 were indistinguishable in tone and content from those of 1924; when cards bearing the verbatim answers to these questions were shuffled into a single pile, readers were unable to separate them. The distributions were similar too. In response to the third question, about half the women at both points in time said that life would be intolerable or utterly changed without their belief in God; a smaller number rejected the suggestion as unthinkable. In response to the first and second questions, large proportions of both the 1924 and the 1978 respondents drew their courage from religion and thought of Heaven almost constantly. In 1924, working-class women were more fervent about their beliefs than business-class women; in 1978, the responses were not much affected by social class or education.[10]

By contrast, there was a striking increase in religious tolerance over the same interval. When the Lynds surveyed the entire high school population of Middletown in 1924, 94 percent agreed with the statement that "Christianity is the one true religion and all people should be converted to it." When the same statement was presented to the comparable population of 1977, only 38 percent agreed.[11] Throughout the United States, the people immersed in religion, who used to hate heretics and infidels with a clear conscience, are now inclined to ecumenical harmony.

The relative stability of church attendance and membership between 1960 and 1990 masks a number of significant trends within and among denominations. Between 1960 and 1975, the percentage of Catholics attending mass every week fell sharply, from about 75 percent to about 55 percent, at which level it has since remained. The decline is commonly ascribed to the Vatican II reforms, which did away with the traditional Latin mass and weakened customary practices like confession and fasting; but Greeley shows, by means of survey evidence, that it is properly attributable to Pope Paul VI's 1968 encyclical, *Humanae Vitae*, which attempted to prohibit contraception and was strongly resisted by American Catholics.[12] But even after that decline, the church attendance of American Catholics remains higher than the church attendance of American Protestants and very much higher than the church attendance of European Catholics. Protestant church attendance has not changed appreciably since 1960, oscillating around a weekly rate of 41 percent. Jewish synagogue attendance was much lower—under 30 percent—in 1960 and showed a slight upward trend in recent years.[13]

The statistics of church attendance take no account of the rapid growth of the "electronic church" audience, the viewers of syndicated religious programs supported by voluntary contributions. That audience grew from a handful of viewers in 1955 to more than 21 million in 1981,[14] and continued to grow until checked by the scandals that overtook some of the leading televangelists in 1987 and 1988.

The growth of the electronic church reflected a shift of Protestants out of mainline denominations (especially Methodism and Presbyterianism) towards the more evangelical churches that emphasize personal commitment to Jesus Christ (being "born again") and a literal interpretation of the Bible. About one out of three Protestants now claims the born-again experience, urges others to make the same commitment, and accepts the Bible as the literal word of God. Evangelicals figure largely in right-wing political groups that are both antiliberal and antilibertarian. They favor the use of state power to enforce sexual morality, family solidarity, and the work ethic; they are pronuclear, antiabortion, and somewhat inclined to racial intolerance.[15]

Numerous and influential though they are, the Evangelicals represent a reaction against the movement of American mainline churches in the other directions—towards more liberal positions on religious and social issues. This movement has dominated the history of the mainline denominations since 1960. The clergy have led the way while the laity have, in many instances, been dragged unwillingly along. The movement has been reinforced by recent American theology, which challenges the traditional alignment of the church with the powers that be.[16]

The principal signs of the liberal drift have been:

- Liturgical reform, aimed at modernizing and democratizing traditional forms of worship.

- The ordination of women in the Protestant denominations and the "empowerment" of Catholic nuns.

- The abandonment of exclusionary practices that prohibited, for example, the remarriage of divorced persons, the marriage of church members to the unchurched, the religious burial of suicides, and the acceptance of homosexuals as clergy.

- An extraordinary decline in long-standing hostilities between Christians and non-Christians, between Protestants and Catholics, and among Protestants of different convictions.

- A strong commitment to racial equality, the abolition of compulsory segregation in church organizations (although the voluntary segregation of blacks and hispanics in local congregations is accepted as innocuous) and preferential treatment of minority clergy.

- Increasing disregard of the doctrinal differences which nominally distinguish Catholics from Protestants and the mainline Protestant denominations from each other.

The joint effect of the liberal drift in the mainline churches and the conservative countercurrent among Evangelicals and Fundamentalists has been a great increase in political participation by churches and church-related organizations. Beginning around 1965, with the protest movement against the Vietnam war, the traditional abstention of American clergy from overt political activity began to weaken. In 1988, for the first time in U. S. history, two clergymen were candidates in the presidential primaries. Religious organizations currently engage in lobbying on a wide range of public questions, from foreign policy to genetic engineering. As the churches become more politicized, their politics become increasingly complex. The Catholic hierarchy looms large on the liberal side of the nuclear issue and on the conservative side of the abortion issue. Most Episcopalians are politically conservative but the Episcopal hierarchy is predominantly liberal. Evangelicals lobby for school prayer and nuclear modernization.

An admirable summary of recent and ongoing trends in denominational composition and orientation is provided by Roof and

McKinney.[17] They identify four categories of Protestants: Liberal Protestants (Episcopalians, United Church of Christ, Presbyterians) Moderate Protestants (Methodists, Lutherans, Disciples, Northern Baptists, Reformed) Black Protestants (Methodists, Northern Baptists, Southern Baptists) and Conservative Protestants (Southern Baptists, Evangelicals/Fundamentalists, Nazarenes etc.) as well as Catholics, Jews, and Others (Mormons, Jehovah's Witnesses, Christian Scientists, Unitarian-Universalists). Combining the annual replications of the *General Social Survey* from 1972 to 1982 to obtain a larger sample, they arrived at the following estimates of the distribution of religious preferences in the United States around 1980:

TABLE 7–2   SELF-REPORTED RELIGIOUS PREFERENCES OF U. S. ADULTS

Preference	Percent of Population
Moderate Protestants	24%
Conservative Protestants	15
Liberal Protestants	9
Black Protestants	9
Catholics	25
Jews	2
All others	8
No religious preference	7
Total	100

SOURCE: Wade Clark Roof and William McKinney, *American Mainline Religion: Its Changing Shape and Future* (Rutgers, NJ: State University Press, 1987), 82. Since the survey responses were obtained over an 11-year period, no exact date can be assigned to this table. It is not feasible to chart year-to-year trends in religious preference for the U. S. population because the annual numbers in survey samples are too small and the annual data on membership published by the major denominations are not strictly comparable. However, membership figures for any given denomination are usually comparable from year to year and the trends cited in the text can be confirmed by examining the annual membership figures reported by Catholic, Methodist, Episcopal, Southern Baptist, and other, national offices.

Recent growth trends have favored Catholics, Conservative Protestants, Black Protestants, and Others, at the expense of Moderate Protestants, Liberal Protestants, and Jews. Since Catholics are closer to Moderate and Liberal Protestants than to Conservative and Black Protestants in their social characteristics and in their religious and political views, the growth of the Catholic population has offset the growing strength of the Conservative Protestants.

The major religious groups differ among themselves in a number of interesting ways:

- Liberal and Moderate Protestants have lower rates of church attendance than Conservative and Black Protestants and Catholics. Jews have the lowest rate.

- Catholics and Jews are much more committed to their denominations than Liberal and Moderate Protestants, but Conservative and Black Protestants are even more committed.

- White Protestants believe more firmly in life after death than Catholics or Black Protestants and much more than Jews.

- With respect to socioeconomic status, as reflected by education, income, and occupation, Liberal Protestants and Jews are in the top group. The middle group is composed of Catholics, Moderate Protestants, and some Conservative Protestants; the bottom group includes Black Protestants and most of the Conservative Protestants.

- Liberal and Moderate Protestants and Jews are older on the average than Conservative and Black Protestants who, in turn, are older than Catholics.

- There are no significant differences in marital status among these religious groups except for Black Protestants who are much more likely than the others to be single or divorced. Conservative and Black Protestants have significantly higher birth rates than Moderate Protestants and Catholics; these in turn are significantly more fertile than Liberal Protestants. Jews are the least fertile of all.

- Black Protestants and Jews are more enthusiastic about civil liberties and racial justice than Liberal Protestants, who exceed Moderate Protestants and Catholics in this regard. Conservative Protestants cling to older racial attitudes.

- Liberal Protestants and Catholics are about equally feminist, Black, Moderate, and Conservative Protestants somewhat less so, but the differences are rather small.

- The abortion issue aligns them differently. Jews and Liberal Protestants favor discretionary abortion far more than Moderate Protestants, who are more favorable than Black Protestants, and Catholics, who are more favorable than Conservative Protestants.

- On issues of sexual morality, Jews are the most permissive, followed by Black Protestants, Liberal Protestants, Catholics, Moderate Protestants, and least permissive, the Conservative Protestants.

The four marginally Protestant denominations in the "Other" group—Mormons, Jehovah's Witnesses, Christian Scientists, and

Universalist-Unitarians—divide sharply on most of these matters. In general, Mormons and Jehovah's Witnesses are more conservative than the Conservative Protestants while Christian Scientists and Universalist-Unitarians are distinctly more liberal than the Liberal Protestants.

On balance, it would appear that at both extremes of the liberal-conservative spectrum in religion, the United States is beginning to develop the linkage between religious and political attitudes whose absence has been celebrated for so long. Jews and Unitarian-Universalists are likely to vote for Democrats. Southern Baptists are drawn to Republicans. But it remains true for the great majority of Protestants and Catholics that there is not much connection between their religious beliefs and their political opinions. Although some observers predict a continued increase at the conservative end of the denominational spectrum and a concomitant decline at the liberal end, the data do not support that prediction. American religion continues, as before, to be more resistant to change than other institutional sectors.

NOTES

1. Alexis de Tocqueville, *Democracy in America* (1835–40; New York: Alfred A. Knopf, 1945).
2. For a fuller discussion of these differences, see Theodore Caplow, "Contrasting Trends in European and American Religion," *Sociological Analysis*, 46, no. 2 (1985):101–108.
3. Jean Stoetzel, *Les Valeurs du Temps Présent: Une Enquête Européene* (Paris: Presses Universitaires de France, 1983).
4. Robert T. Miller, *Towards Benevolent Neutrality: Church, State and the Supreme Court* (Waco, TX: Baylor University Press, 1977); and Arthur Selwyn Miller, *The Supreme Court: Myth and Reality*, (Westport, CT: Greenwood Press, 1978).
5. This quotation and those in the following paragraph are taken from an unpublished paper by Paul Johnson, "The Almost Chosen People: Why America Is Different," 1984.

6. The postscript, although it may sound cynical, is pure Tocqueville, "Society has nothing to fear or hope from another life; what is most important for it is not that all citizens should profess the true religion, but that they should profess religion." Johnson, 290.

7. Robert T. Handy, *A History of the Churches in the United States and Canada* (Oxford: Clarendon Press, 1976), 162; and *SAUS89*, Tables 78, 79.

8. Best summarized in Andrew Greeley, *Religious Change in America* (Cambridge, MA: Harvard University Press, 1989).

9. Gallup Report, *Religion in America: 50 Years: 1935–1985*, Report no. 236, May 1985.

10. Theodore Caplow, Howard M. Bahr, and Bruce A. Chadwick, "Piety in Middletown," *Society*. January–February 1981: 34–37.

11. *Ibid.*

12. Andrew M. Greeley, *The Catholic Myth: The Behavior and Beliefs of American Catholics* (New York: Charles Scribner's Sons, 1990), Chap. 5.

13. Gallup, *Religion in America*.

14. See George H. Hill, *Airwaves to the Soul: The Influence and Growth of Religious Broadcasting in America* (Saratoga, CA: R & E Publishers, 1983); Jeffrey K. Hadden and Anson Shupe, *Televangelism: The Marketing of Popular Religion* (Carbondale, IL: Southern Illinois University Press, 1987); and Steward M. Hoover, *Mass Media Religion: The Social Sources of the Electronic Church* (Newbury Park, CA: Sage Publications, 1988).

15. See James Davison Hunter, *Evangelicalism: The Coming Generation* (Chicago: University of Chicago Press, 1987).

16. See David Nicholls, *Deity and Domination* (London and New York: Routledge, 1989), especially Chap. 5.

17. Wade Clark Roof and William McKinney, *American Mainline Religion: Its Changing Shape and Future* (Rutgers, NJ; State University Press, 1987). Another perspective on the same trends may be found in Robert Wuthnow, *The Restructuring of American Religion* (Princeton, NJ: Princeton University Press, 1988).

8

TRENDS IN EDUCATION

In education, as in manufacturing, the United States registered spectacular progress during the 100 years that followed the end of the Civil War. The ratio of high school graduates to the total number of 17-year-olds rose year after year, from 2 percent in 1870 to 9 percent in 1910 to 29 percent in 1930 to 76 percent in 1965, which turned out to be the peak year. Thereafter it ceased to rise; it stood at 73 percent in 1985.[1] Enrollment in colleges and universities rose in parallel—from less than 1 percent of the 18- to 24-year-old population in 1870 to 3 percent in 1910, 8 percent in 1930, and 32 percent in 1970, near which level it has remained ever since.[2]

The interruption of educational progress around 1970 is reflected in the average educational achievement of American adults, which began to level off at that time after decades of dramatic growth. Blacks, however, continued to catch up to whites in educational achievement until 1980, when they too leveled off, with only a slight remaining disadvantage.

TABLE 8–1   **MEDIAN YEARS OF SCHOOL COMPLETED FOR U. S. POPULATION OVER 25**

	White	Black
1940	8.6	5.7
1950	9.3	6.8
1960	10.6	8.0
1970	12.1	9.8
1980	12.5	12.0
1986	12.6	12.3

SOURCE: Based on *Statistical Abstract of the United States 1988*, Table 201.

There were close parallels between the interruption of educational progress after 1970 and the slowing of economic progress at the same time. Just as people accustomed to steadily rising real incomes found it difficult to adjust to level incomes, the abrupt halt in educational progress upset many expectations. And just as the country was forced in the 1980s to acknowledge the competitive superiority of foreign manufacturers in many lines of production once dominated by American firms, we discovered at the same time that the American system of primary and secondary education was no longer fully competitive with the educational systems of other developed countries. In a 1981–82 study of the mathematics level of eighth graders in many countries, conducted by the International Association for the Evaluation of Educational Achievement, the American scores were lower than those of Belgium, Canada, Great Britain, Finland, France, Hong Kong, Hungary, Japan, and the Netherlands. In a slightly later study of science achievement, involving high school students in 14 countries, the U. S. was outscored by every country except Thailand. And according to the National Center for Education Statistics, the U. S. has a shorter school year than any other industrial country except Sweden.[3]

It became the accepted wisdom in the 1980s that the public schools were to blame for the declining competitiveness of U. S. firms in the world market. A subcommittee of the Congress held hearings in the fall of 1988 on "Competitiveness and the Quality of the American Work Force" and published a report on "The Education Deficit."[4] The report acknowledged that the educational system was performing about as well as it had 20 or 30 years before but insisted that the earlier standards had become irrelevant because of more demanding work force requirements. A parade of witnesses accused the schools of following an outmoded factory model, described teachers as ill-prepared, expressed misgivings about the quality of future teachers, announced that a large proportion of high school graduates were functionally illiterate, and deplored the school performance of the black and hispanic students who are a large and growing proportion of the school population. The final witness said that "most Americans . . . see radical change in education as the biggest key to making the country competitive again."

Much stronger complaints against the public schools are commonly heard, like this 1979 diatribe:

> The quality of public-school education in the United States has been declining for the last decade and a half. The almost universal decline has been marked by plummeting Scholastic Aptitude Test scores, functionally illiterate high school graduates and the general alienation of many students. It has been paralleled by an explosive growth in the nonteaching

school bureaucracy, overall cost increases vastly exceeding inflation, declining enrollments and a radical redefinition of school objectives.[5]

Such tirades go beyond the facts. The national average of verbal SAT scores, for example, declined between 1965 and 1975 from 471 to 431 while the average of quantitative scores went from 496 to 472, 10 percent in the one case and 5 percent in the other. Thereafter they remained approximately level: the 1986 average scores were 430 and 476 respectively.[6] The decline from 1965 to 1975 was probably attributable to the enlargement of the test cohort by affirmative action during that decade. In any case, there was no plummeting. The assertions about functional illiteracy and about alienation are too vague to assess. That school costs have outraced inflation is undeniable, but not inexplicable. Salaries are the largest component of every school budget and the real incomes of teachers, like those of other American workers, outraced inflation by about 3 to 1 from 1950 to 1970, although lagging behind the gains of other professionals. Between 1970 and 1985, the income gains of school personnel were minimal, but the rapid decline of school enrollments as the baby boom cohorts gave way to the thin cohorts of the following years, left most schools overstaffed and increased their per pupil costs, as did the federally mandated inclusion in school budgets of special education for handicapped, disadvantaged, and bilingual pupils. As to bureaucratic proliferation, it has been relatively modest in most school systems, despite the increasing burden of federal and state regulation. High school dropout rates have been falling, not rising, since 1970.

Yet if much criticism of the schools is unfounded, the loss of public confidence is real and has important consequences. Since about 1975, teachers and their professional organizations have been obsessed with their low prestige and the unfavorable ratings the public gives to their work.

When people criticize the schools, they mean the 84,000 public elementary and high schools administered by local school boards and supported by taxes. There is virtually no public criticism of the private schools that enroll 17 percent of elementary pupils and 9 percent of high school students and are supported by tuition fees and private contributions. These church schools, day schools, alternative schools, and boarding schools are highly regarded by their constituencies; most of them claim success in teaching, discipline, and character formation. But contrary to appearances, there has been no increase in the relative size of the private school sector since

1955.[7] The growth of private day schools has been offset by a decline of Catholic parochial schools.

Nor does the customary denigration of the schools apply to the American system of higher education. That enormously complex structure—more than 2,000 colleges and universities offer bachelor's degrees, several hundred award advanced degrees, and more than 1,000 community and junior colleges provide abridged versions of the undergraduate curriculum—is generally viewed with complacency.[8] The leading research universities and liberal arts colleges are universally respected and draw financial support from all levels of government and a wide range of private contributors. The less pretentious institutions attract strong local support. Higher education is one field in which American preeminence is still taken for granted. The number of foreign students studying in the United States has approximately tripled since 1970, to about 350,000, and greatly exceeds the number of American students studying abroad.

Over and beyond these major divisions—public schools, private schools, colleges, and universities—there are thousands of small, mostly proprietorial, schools that teach every imaginable art and skill, from karate to filmmaking, as well as a vast and growing network of preschools, nursery schools, tutoring schools, day camps, and summer camps, which extend schooling to earlier ages and beyond the school day, and another growing network of adult education facilities that extend schooling to later ages.

Although educational theories are constantly changing, educational curricula are highly resistant to change. In the midwestern industrial city we call Middletown, the first grade pupils of 1890 were taught reading, writing, arithmetic, language, spelling, drawing, music, and science. The same subjects were taught in 1984, together with health, physical education, and social studies, but these subjects, under slightly different names, had entered the curriculum by 1924. The seventh grade curriculum of 1984 was essentially the same as that of 1890, except for the disappearance of geography, the addition of social studies, and a greater emphasis on physical education and health. The subjects taught in the twelfth grade, the senior year of high school, expanded significantly between 1890 and 1924, but thereafter the main categories—English, mathematics, science, social science, foreign language, commercial, vocational, home economics—remained unchanged through 1984, except for the addition of elective courses within these categories: Computer math and calculus under mathematics, aerospace, genetics, and physiology under science, principles of management among the commercial subjects. There is no reason to think that the curriculum was trivialized by these new electives or that the Middletown high schools demanded less effort of their college-bound students in 1984 than in 1930, although for various reasons, they were somewhat more tolerant of poor academic performance.

But as Howard Bahr points out in the paper from which the above information was drawn, the community's demands upon the school have expanded dramatically since 1924 when according to an official brochure, pupils were expected to acquire "the various uses of language, the accurate manipulation of numerical symbols, training in patriotic citizenship, familiarity with the physical surroundings of peoples, the leisure-time skills of singing and drawing, and some useful manual skills." By 1986, the long list of objectives in the school system's annual report included, among other things, the opportunity to develop self-direction, individuality, personal achievement, integrity, moral responsibility, creativity, positive self-concepts, appreciation for the dignity of work, and "an understanding of others including appreciation for differences."[9]

In an acid commentary on such inflated goals, Richard Mitchell writes:

> Our educators have said that they would teach love and the brotherhood of mankind as well as the importance of brushing after meals. They have promised to teach social consciousness and environmental awareness, creativity, ethnic pride, tolerance.... They have said they will straighten everybody out about sex and venereal disease and the related complications of family life and about how to operate voting machines and balance checkbooks.... Very few Americans will recall asking the educators to pursue such goals.... it was the educators who decided not only that such an enterprise was mandated by the people but that it belonged properly to the public schools....[10]

Regardless of how it arose, the proposition that the public schools are responsible for forming the characters and shaping the future behavior of their students is by now taken for granted and partly explains the widespread dissatisfaction with the schools. Schools are blamed not only for the declining competitiveness of U. S. industry in world markets but also for poverty, illegitimacy, drug abuse, and violent crime. These perceptions are linked to developments in some large metropolitan school systems after 1965, where the vigorous efforts of federal courts and regulatory agencies to achieve school-by-school desegregation was countered by the flight of white families to the suburbs and to private schools, with the paradoxical effect that entire school systems became segregated by race and social class.* Since affluent minority families were also moving to the suburbs and to private schools, these metropolitan school systems became the exclusive preserve of children from the urban underclass, afflicted by all the problems associated with poverty, unstable homes, and cultural deprivation. During the same period, by an unhappy coincidence, the authority of teachers and school principals was drastically curtailed by regulatory and judicial actions that were intended to protect the civil rights of students but had the unintended effect of undermining discipline in some metropolitan schools until they could no longer ensure the physical safety of teachers or students.

That is still the situation today in scores of metropolitan schools, commonly described as jungles. "Back in the '40s when most of us were in school" wrote a prominent industrialist in 1989, "the top problems were talking, chewing gum, making noise in the classrooms and running in the halls. That what the really bad guys did. Now let's look at top problems of the '80s: drug abuse, alcohol abuse, pregnancy, suicide, rape, robbery and assault. You cannot have learning in that environment."[11] Although there are no easy solutions, many problem schools have been successfully reformed by forceful principals, as was done in Atlanta's George Washington Carver High School.[12]

Other sources of instability in public education were the school closings, redistrictings, and mass transfers that became routine in the 1970s and 1980s, partly to conform with desegregation plans and partly because of large shifts in school-age populations caused by the fluctuations of the birth rate, residential movement within communities, interregional migration, and immigration from abroad. For the country as a whole, high school enrollment rose from 8.5 million in 1960 to 14.3 million in 1975. The 68 percent increase in student population in 15 years required new schools to be built at a frantic pace. From 1975 to 1985, high school enrollment declined by 13 percent to 12.3 million, and many of the new schools completed in the previous decade had to be closed.[13]

The population shifts were of course more extreme in particular localities than in the nation as a whole. Some cities, like Minneapolis,

---

*Minority enrollment in the public schools of the District of Columbia reached 99 percent in 1989; the figures for New York, Detroit, Chicago, and Los Angeles were not much lower.

closed more than half of their schools between 1975 and 1985, while the schools of other cities, like Miami, were running double shifts. Rapid declines in enrollment raised per pupil costs because of underutilized facilities and shrinking class size. But rapid increases in enrollment had the same effect, because they required large capital outlays and increased payroll costs disproportionately. As population shifts strained available resources, little attention was given to the possibilities of improving the technology of instruction. A study published in 1989 by the Office of Technology Assessment found that:

> Education is tied (with social work) as the most labor-intensive business in the economy with labor costs equal to 93 percent of output value—compared with 54 percent for all private business ... education has by far the lowest level of capital investment of any major industry: only about $1,000 per employee. The average for the U.S. economy as a whole is about $50,000 of capital investment per job; in some high-tech industries it is $300,000 or more.[14]

The federal intervention into the management of local schools has introduced some additional uncertainties into school planning. Federal involvement in local public education was negligible until about 1965, but by 1975, almost every activity of local schools, from the planning of cafeteria menus to the content of classroom teaching, had come under federal supervision. The speed of this movement and the imposition of a third control structure on top of the existing dual structure of state and local control, hampered school administration in many ways.[15] The federal contribution to public school expenditures, which was negligible in 1965, rose to 6 percent in 1975 and 9 percent in 1985, but both the amounts and their designated purposes fluctuated unpredictably from year to year[16] creating periodic crises for local school systems.

During this time of troubles for the public schools, U. S. colleges and universities followed a different trajectory. From 1960 to 1975, the number of colleges and universities nearly doubled, with junior colleges showing especially rapid growth, and total enrollment more than tripled, from 2.2 million to 7.5 million. This growth stopped abruptly around 1975. Total enrollment in 1986 was only 7.6 million, and the proportion of high school students entering college was essentially the same as in 1975. The enrollment of black students followed a similar trend except that their numbers quintupled between 1960 and 1975, and continued to increase, although at a much slower rate through 1986. However, the proportion of black high school graduates going on to college declined from 1975, when it was approximately the same as for white high school graduates, to 1986, when it was significantly lower.[17]

Except for the sharp increase in black enrollment from 1960 to 1975, these trends were driven mostly by the demographics of successive youth cohorts. The historic trend towards more extensive involvement in higher education virtually stopped during this period.[18] As Table 8–2 shows, there was no increase after 1975 in the propensity of high school graduates to go to college or of college graduates to go on for advanced degrees:

TABLE 8–2   DEGREES EARNED IN U. S. HIGHER EDUCATION

	Bachelor Degrees	Percent of High School Graduates 4 Years Earlier	Advanced Degrees	Percent of College Graduates 5 Years Earlier
1960	392,000	28%	84,000	41%
1975	923,000	31	382,000	48
1986	979,000	32	394,000	40

SOURCE: Based on *Statistical Abstract of the United States 1988*, Table 232.

Still driven by demographics, total enrollment in institutions of higher education is expected to decline slowly until the year 2000 and then recover rather quickly.

The apparent stability in the number of advanced degrees awarded annually after 1975 masks a great deal of volatility in student's choices of professional and scholarly fields. For example, while the number of Ph.D.'s (and equivalent scholarly degrees) awarded by American universities in 1986 was about the same as in 1971, the number of doctorates in mathematics, the physical sciences, and the social sciences declined sharply during that period, while the number of doctorates in psychology, theology, and the health sciences increased. Among professional degrees, the number of medical and engineering degrees doubled from 1970 to 1985, the number of law degrees more than doubled, while professional degrees in education dropped by half.[19]

The demographic fluctuations that made it difficult to match facilities and students during this era were compounded in the colleges and universities by (1) unpredictable fluctuations in the distribution of student choices among fields of study, (2) a dramatic increase in the regulatory and reporting requirements imposed by federal agencies, (3) the continuing exponential expansion of scholarly knowledge, and (4) the successive additions of mainframe computers, minicomputers, and personal computers to the equipment needs of colleges and universities. As a consequence, costs continued to escalate at a time of very moderate enrollment growth. Between 1975 and 1985, the total enrollment of American institutions of higher education increased hardly at all, while their annual dollar expenditures rose by 157 percent.[20]

These costs were met by drawing more heavily on public and private resources and by dramatic increases in tuition and fees. By 1990, the basic charges for tuition, fees, room, board, and books for an undergraduate student at an Ivy League college exceeded $20,000. A complex system of scholarships, part-time employment, guaranteed and unguaranteed student loans, and parental loans filled the gap between what parents could afford to pay and what the colleges charged. Unlike all other industrialized countries, where higher education had become free or nearly free for qualified students, the United States had developed a system that imposed crushing burdens on middle-income families and mountainous debts on graduates beginning their careers. But although cost escalation has become the principal problem of higher education, no serious interest in cost containment had developed as of 1990.

With minor exceptions, the technology of instruction, like the structure of academic organization, was regarded as immutable and not subject to improvement. Most colleges and universities responded to the growing financial pressure by further raises in tuition, more ambitious fund-raising campaigns, and intensified lobbying for state and federal support. The crisis on the horizon was not allowed to threaten the status quo.

NOTES

1. Based on *Historical Statistics of the United States: Colonial Times to 1970*, Series II, 598–661; and *SAUS88*, Table 232. These two official sources give slightly different figures; the latter shows a peak at 1970 instead of 1965, but both show a slight decline after 1970.

2. Based on *Historical Statistics of the United States*, 1970, Series II, 700–715; and *SAUS88*, Table 233. Again the two sources show different figures but the same trend.

3. National Center for Education Statistics, *Youth Indicators*, 1988, 64.

4. Joint Economic Committee, 100th Cong., 2nd Sess., S. Prt. 100–139, December 14, 1988. (Washington, D.C.: Government Printing Office, 1989).

5. Charles M. Frye, quoted in Richard M. Brandt, *Public Education under Scrutiny* (Washington: University Press of America, 1981), 5.

6. National Center for Education Statistics, 68.

7. Based on *SAUS88*, Table 189.

8. Although that complacency may be coming to an end. See, for example, the recent denunciations of American higher education in Charles J. Sykes, *Profscam: Professors and the Demise of Higher Education* (New York: St. Martin's Press, 1988); Allan Bloom, *The Closing of the American Mind* (New York: Simon & Schuster, 1987); and the more thoughtful critique of graduate education in Theodore Ziolkowski, "The Ph.D. Squid," *American Scholar*, Spring 1990, 177–95.

9. Howard M. Bahr, "Training the Young in Middletown and Other Topics Relevant to the Study of Education in Muncie, Indiana," unpublished paper, 1986.

10. *Ibid.*

11. Lee Iacocca, quoted by the Associated Press.

12. Described in Sarah Lawrence Lightfoot, *The Good High School* (New York: Basic Books, 1983), 29–55.

13. Based on *SAUS89*, Table 205.

14. Lewis J. Perelman, "Schools: America's $500-Billion Flop," *Washington Post*, 3 December 1989, C3.

15. An account of conflicting regulations in the public schools may be found in Theodore Caplow, "Conflicting Regulations: Six Small Studies and an Interpretation," in Roger C. Noll, *Studies of the Regulatory Process* (Berkeley: University of California Press, 1985), 37–48.

16. Based on *SAUS88*, Table 191.

17. Based on *SAUS89*, Tables 242–246.

18. Based on *SAUS88*, Tables 233–236.

19. Based on *SAUS88*, Tables 254–256.

20. Based on *SAUS89*, Table 247.

9

TRENDS IN WORK

The evolution of the American labor force since 1960 has been dominated by two trends that are still running strongly: an increasing proportion of women and an increasing proportion of white-collar workers. The ratio of employed women to men rose from .50 in 1960 to .62 in 1970 and to .80 in 1986. The ratio of white-collar to blue-collar jobs went from .49 in 1960 to .61 in 1970 and to 1.24 in 1986.[1]

The increase in women's employment was described from the standpoint of the family in Chapter 6. It was perhaps the most important social change to occur in the United States between 1960 and 1990. Women moved into hundreds of occupations that had been the exclusive preserve of men and increased their representation in nearly every occupation where they had been in the minority. In large organizations, increasing numbers of women occupied supervisory and executive positions, and the reluctance of men to accept female supervision, which was taken for granted in 1960, virtually disappeared by 1990. By then, women were legally entitled to equal opportunity in employment and in some large organizations they were hired and promoted on the same basis as men, but they were still very far from achieving real equality. The persistent disadvantage of women workers is reflected in the ratio of women's incomes to men's incomes among full-time year-round workers. The ratio rose from .59 in 1970 to .66 in 1988; the average female worker still earns a third less than the average male worker.[2] The ratio of women's *weekly* wages to men's is even less favorable and according to one careful study: it declined from 1950 to 1980.[3] The difference is not primarily attributable to men and women being paid unequally for the same work (although such cases are not uncommon and have given rise to litigation and "equivalent work" statutes) but to differences in the career patterns of men and women. Women continue to be heavily underrepresented in the skilled crafts, the construction trades, and the unionized factory jobs that pay high hourly wages. They are similarly underrepresented among middle- and upper-level corporate managers, senior elected and appointed officials, airline pilots, commission salespeople, and in the more lucrative professional specialties.

This is partly the effect of the former exclusion of women at the entry levels of long careers so that, for example, relatively few women have had time to reach the rank of full professor in academic fields that were formerly reserved for men but are now entirely open to women at the entry level. But in larger measure, the persistent difference of earnings reflects the weaker continuity of women's careers, the subordination of married women's careers to their husbands', the interruption of careers by childbearing and child care, women's more frequent job entries and exits, and the large numbers of women, even in skilled and professional occupations, who hold part-time or temporary jobs. O'Leary's careful study of a national sample of dual-earner families revealed the surprising fact that when paid work and housework were lumped together, wives and husbands worked approximately the same number of hours; the wives put in more hours of work at home and fewer hours at their outside jobs.[4] Initial career choice is also an important factor; women still direct themselves and are directed towards lower-paying careers, family medicine rather than surgery, office work rather than the construction trades.

The shift from blue-collar to white-collar jobs that took place between 1970 and 1986 was an historic turning point. Workers who handled tools and materials had outnumbered workers who dealt with symbols and relationships from the beginning of time. The recent increase in white-collar jobs was concentrated in two large occupational categories. Between 1970 and 1986, an interval of only 16 years, the number of people in managerial, supervisory, and administrative occupations rose by 57 percent and the number in clerical and technical occupations by 76 percent. Contrary to a widespread belief, the proportion of service workers remained unchanged, as did the proportions of craftsmen, professionals, and farmers. But the number of "operatives" and "laborers"—the core of the factory work force—dropped precipitously.[5]

There are many anomalies in the conventional distinction between white-collar and blue-collar workers so that, for example, a dentist is white-collar although he works mostly with tools and materials, and a policeman is blue-collar although he deals mostly with relationships. But taking the system as a whole, there can be no doubt about the massive shift from such activities as digging and hammering to such activities as filling out forms and negotiating agreements. The advent of small computers around 1970 gave new impetus to an old trend—the replacement of human operations by machines. Computers were able to perform complex mental tasks and to operate many kinds of power-driven machinery more effectively than human workers. But the increase of speed and complexity in computer-controlled operations enhanced the need for surveillance, scheduling, planning, accounting, and other administrative functions; the number of work hours devoted to the manipulation of tools and materials continued to decline while the hours spent with papers, telephones, and keyboards continued to increase. This trend involved not only the migration of workers from blue-collar to white-collar occupations but notable growth in the clerical component of blue-collar occupations and the gradual elimination of physically punishing work. There are still millions of dirty and dangerous jobs in heavy industry, mining, and transportation, but there are fewer of them each year as forklifts take over the lifting of heavy packages and robots take over the cleaning of contaminated vats. The slow but steady elimination of dangerous work is reflected by the trend in job fatalities, which declined from 21 per 100,000 workers in 1960 to 15 in 1975, to 10 in 1987. In coal mining, an especially dangerous occupation, the fatality rate fell from 171 in 1960 to 71 in 1975 to 37 in 1987.[6]

The intangible factor of comfort on the job showed parallel improvement, due in part to the modernization of production facilities, in part to increased government oversight of occupational health and safety, and in large part to the enlargement of employers' liability by the courts. Adequate light, heat, ventilation, and washrooms, can now almost be taken for granted at industrial worksites.

Rather surprisingly, there has been no change at all in the length of the average workweek, which has hovered around 38 hours since 1935. But the work *year* has been slowly declining, because of longer vacations; more generous leaves for sickness, emergencies, and military service; and longer breaks during paid working time.[7]

The improvement in physical working conditions since 1960 has not been matched by any perceptible improvement in job security or promotional opportunities for the average worker. The United States is unique among industrialized countries in not giving wageworkers any general right to job security or to advance notice and severance pay in case of unavoidable layoff. The common law doctrine of "employment-at-will," which allows employers to discharge employees without notice or cause, still applies in the United States except for certain categories of employees who have acquired job security by statute, contract, or custom.

Most public employees—federal, state, and local—enjoy permanent tenure after a probationary period and are virtually immune from dismissal or layoff. Workers covered by collective bargaining agreements are usually protected against individual dismissal, except for serious cause and with due process, and partially protected against group layoff by seniority arrangements. Many nonunionized employees in the private sector, especially salaried personnel in large corporations, have a kind of customary tenure which is seldom breached unless the employer goes out of business or is reorganized. Many specialists and technicians work under contracts that guarantee employment for a fixed term and specify conditions for renewal. In the unionized construction trades and a few similarly organized occupations, the employer-employee relationship is temporary but access to employment is regulated by seniority. Finally, the anti-discrimination measures adopted by the federal government after 1964 to protect racial minorities and later extended to women, homosexuals, handicapped persons, and the elderly, protect people in these categories against arbitrary dismissal although not against layoff. A 1988 federal statute requires large employers to give workers 60-days notice of a plant closing. It was the first attempt to limit the industrial employer's privilege of laying off workers without notice or compensation, and although the limitation was not severe, it was vigorously opposed by industry.

The risk of abrupt layoff is the greatest disadvantage of blue-collar jobs relative to white-collar jobs in the American economy. The salaried employees of large corporations are seldom laid off during seasonal or cyclical lulls and when their jobs are terminated by reorganization, they receive much more generous treatment than wageworkers in the same enterprise. The higher an employee's rank in the corporate hierarchy, the more ample his or her severance benefits are likely to be. At the very top of the pyramid, dismissed executives may be consoled with golden parachutes that make them financially independent. But the wageworker, however well paid, is never safe from sudden unemployment.

Unemployment rates vary cyclically—there are no consistent long-term trends. The general unemployment rate fluctuated in the range between 1.3 and 6.0 from 1948 to 1975. From 1976 to 1990, it fluctuated within a higher range, reaching 9.7 in 1982, but dipping below 6.0 from 1988 to 1990.[8]

Unemployment rates for women were consistently higher than those for men until 1981, since when they have been consistently lower. The relative advantage of education has been increasing slightly: the unemployment rate of workers who have not graduated from high school runs about six times as high as the unemployment rate of college graduates. Youth unemployment (or more accurately, joblessness) runs about twice as high as the general unemployment rate, as does the unemployment of black workers of all ages. Where these two disadvantages are combined—among young black workers—unemployment is chronically very high. There has been no recent change in these differentials.

The precariousness of blue-collar employment has been aggravated during the past 20 years by severe, localized recessions in such key industries as steel, oil, and textiles; by numerous plant closings in the face of foreign competition; by the reorganization of long-established companies as a result of leveraged buyouts; and by the steep decline of union membership and bargaining power.

The proportion of union members in the nonagricultural labor force has been declining for many years, from 33 percent in 1955 to 28 percent in 1965, 25 percent in 1975, and 17 percent in 1987. Between 1975 and 1986, while the number of wage and salary workers increased from 77 million to 100 million, the total membership of the unions associated with the AFL-CIO decreased from 14 million to 12 million.[9]

The highest proportions of unionized workers are found today in three fields where employment is unusually secure and seniority is exceptionally important: government, transportation, and utilities. In the traditional strongholds of organized labor, manufacturing and construction, less than a quarter of the work force is unionized.

The decline in membership was accompanied by a sharp decline in the effectiveness of collective bargaining. The average first-year wage increase secured by collective bargaining agreements declined from 11.4 percent in 1975 to 1.1 percent in 1986, when a considerable number of agreements called for wage *cuts*. The use of union labor's primary weapon—the strike—declined correspondingly. From 1960 to 1980, an average of 306 strikes were begun each year; the annual average from 1983 to 1986 was only 67.[10] The declining effectiveness of collective bargaining after 1980 was partly attributable to an unsympathetic federal administration but more particularly to the economic weakness of industries, such as steel, railroads, and women's clothing, that were traditional union strongholds; the shift from blue-collar to white-collar occupations; increas-

ing numbers of female and part-time workers; the weakening of the
adversarial relationship between management and labor; the erosion of union influence in local and national elections; the deterioration of organized labor's public image; and widespread distrust of
union leadership.[11] To some extent, collective bargaining is being
replaced by alternative devices like participatory management, employee ownership, and profit sharing. But the overall position of labor vis-à-vis management has deteriorated since 1970.

Whether the decline of American competitiveness in world markets has been accompanied by changes in the motivation and commitment of American workers is a much debated question. During
the 1970s there was much talk about worker alienation, but Hamilton
and Wright, reviewing the empirical evidence, concluded that the
great majority of American workers continued to be satisfied with
their jobs and proud of their work.[12] Although the lagging productivity of some industries is commonly blamed on inadequate motivation, it is almost impossible to isolate worker attitudes from such
other elements of productivity as invested capital, the age of machinery, hiring restrictions, plant design, regulatory burdens, accounting
procedures, and managerial competence.

Nevertheless, some knowledgeable observers see a fairly direct
link between worker attitudes and productivity. Yankelovich and
Harman[13] argue that American industrial dominance after the turn
of the century was based on a low-discretion workplace where
workers had little control over product quality or the amount of effort they put into their jobs. Under that system, with a largely uned-
ucated and unskilled work force, management controlled the content and pace of work and did not call upon workers for
commitment, creativity, or innovation. The employer paid as low a
wage as the market permitted, and the employee did only as much
work as was necessary to avoid dismissal. Today, say these authors,
an educated work force has expanded the sphere of discretionary
effort and discretionary effort has become crucial to product quality
and overall competitiveness. They attribute the change to high technology on the one hand and to the shift from blue-collar to white-
collar work on the other. High technology replaces simple assembly-
line work by complex control functions that involve discretion, and
even at the lowest levels, white-collar work always involves some degree of individual judgment. They go on to suggest that most workplaces are still managed on low-discretion principles so that
workers are encouraged to withhold effort, and they cite recent survey data to show that most jobholders consciously work below their

maximum capacities and do not expect their earnings to be much affected by how hard they work. The implications are that management must become more flexible to make the most of high-discretion workers and that pay should be tied more closely to performance to enlist their discretionary support. Similar views were expressed by a distinguished group of experts who published a comprehensive report on U. S. industrial performance in 1989.[14] But such modest and sensible proposals are not easy to insert into bureaucratic employment systems.

According to Elliot Jaques,[15] more than 90 percent of American workers held jobs in bureaucratic employment systems in 1985—a vast increase over 1960. Bureaucratic employment systems have tables of organization that specify the titles, locations, and reporting relationships of positions; they have job classifications that specify qualifications, duties, and pay ranges; they have formal procedures for hiring, promotion, dismissal, retirement, transfer, and payroll calculations; and they have written policies about seniority, discipline, vacations, sick leave, bonuses, profit sharing, insurance, accident reporting, discrimination, grievances, and many other matters. This structure was formerly confined to government agencies and a few very large corporations, but since about 1960 it has been adopted by many other types of organizations, from religious denominations to professional associations, as well as by enterprises of every size down to the smallest. The driving force behind this trend has been the extensive new regulation of the workplace by federal agencies, so that even the smallest employer must install a miniature bureaucracy in order to comply with the numerous regulations by which employers are now governed.

The MIT Commission on Industrial Productivity remarked that,

> The issue is not simply whether there is too much government or too little. What is clear to the commission, however, is that a lower level of cooperation between government and business exists in the U. S. than it does in the countries of American firms' major foreign competitors and that the frequency with which government and industry find themselves at cross-purposes is a serious obstacle to strategic and organization change in individual U. S. firms.[16]

Beginning with the Civil Rights Act of 1964, and subsequently reinforced by innumerable statutes, court decisions, and administrative rulings, employers have been ordered to provide designated minorities with at least equal access to jobs and promotions; to remove gender specifications from jobs and promotions; to provide job opportunities for physically and mentally handicapped persons; to provide evidence of nondiscrimination in hiring, termination, and promotion with respect to gender, sexual preference, marital status, pregnancy and certain illnesses; to provide equal pay for equal work to all these categories of employees; and to modify requirements for hiring or promotion that have the effect of discriminating against any of them. Additionally, they are required to refrain from hiring illegal aliens, to abolish mandatory retirement, to prevent sexual harassment in the workplace, to advertise job openings, to provide health care and pension plans that do not unduly favor some categories of employees, to install accountable grievance procedures, and to maintain drug-free workplaces.

The modest Personnel Department of yesterday became today's Human Resources Management Division as the regulatory requirements expanded. Its responsibilities were further enlarged by the growth of fringe benefits during the same period. The aggregate cost of the fringe benefits paid by American employers increased by nearly 900 percent between 1960 and 1979,[17] and that figure includes only those benefits that add a precise dollar value to wages or salaries. Many other fringe benefits—vacations, paid holidays, employee discounts, subsidized commuting, supplemental retirement plans—expanded at the same time.

A bureaucratic employment system of normal form is not designed to maximize productivity. Its table of organization forms a steep pyramid with the greatest number of employees at the lowest levels. As Jaques pointed out in the paper cited above, that distribution is incongruent with the normal distribution of human abilities, which follows the familiar bell-shaped curve and puts most of the population near the middle. By defining its rank-and-file positions as low-level and assigning duties to them which can be performed by workers of less than average ability, the bureaucratic employment system wastes much of the potential productivity of its work force. Moreover, the table of organization of a bureaucratic employment system has a built-in tendency to favor seniority over merit. Seniority can be rewarded by scheduled increments within a pay range, or by promotion at a predictable time to the next higher position, while appropriate rewards for merit call for unequal increments of pay awarded at unpredictable times in disregard of established ranges, or for promotions to positions that may not be vacant at the time the promotion is earned.

Regulations against discrimination, while socially valuable, have the unintended effect of further weakening the connection between performance and pay. The thrust of these regulations is to ensure the equal treatment of employees in any given category. Any attempt to reward outstanding performance by preferential pay is likely to be attacked as discriminatory as is any attempt to dismiss unproductive employees who are otherwise well-behaved. The Yankelovich and Harman proposal to bring individual pay into closer alignment with individual performance is probably impracticable under existing circumstances, but there are other measures that can accomplish the same purpose. The most important of these are participatory management, job enlargement, and administrative pruning.

Participatory management is a concept that is rediscovered every few years and given a new name: human relations, group dynamics, Theory Y, upward management, the Type Z organization, quality circles, networking, self-management. A popular writer on social change described it this way in 1982:

> ... the new management style will be inspired by and based on networking. Its values will be rooted in informality and equality; its communication style will be lateral, diagonal, and bottom up ...[18]

Fifty years earlier, Elton Mayo, the pioneer of human relations research in industry, expressed similar expectations.[19]

The perennial insights of the perennial movement towards participatory democracy are these:

- Workers know more about their jobs than supervisors and are in a better position to devise improvements in work processes.
- Consultation is a more effective way of eliciting cooperation from subordinates than ordering and forbidding.
- Workers are more easily influenced by peers than by supervisors.
- The improvement of productivity is best accomplished by giving rank-and-file peer groups the primary responsibility for planning, implementing and monitoring changes in work processes.

This cluster of ideas was reinforced after 1970 by the widely held belief that participatory management was a major element in the competitive achievements of Japanese industry. But despite numerous successful experiments, participatory management has never really caught on in the United States. The quality circle movement, patterned directly on Japanese experience, was estimated to involve about 1,000 American companies at its height in 1982, while about 100 companies were exploring more advanced forms of participatory management, and about 500 had installed plans that allowed workers to share in productivity gains.[20] These figures reflect wide interest but not a major trend.

There is a clear tendency for U. S. companies to abandon even the most successful experiments in participatory management because of the extra burdens they impose on management and the strain they put on bureaucratic procedures.

The same conclusions hold, in a general way, for job enlargement, also called job sharing and job enrichment. There are two overlapping insights here: (1) that workers become more productive when they are given larger, more diversified and more responsible tasks; and (2) that groups become more productive when they are assigned relatively large tasks and allowed to plan and coordinate the division of effort among their members.[21] The concept is nearly as old as participatory management, to which it is closely related, and its history is similar. Many companies have experimented with such plans, most of the experiments were successful, most of them were eventually discarded as inconvenient. A typical sequence of events is that the manager who introduces a job-enrichment program is rewarded for its success by a promotion and the project is quietly shelved by his successor.

An indirect method of increasing worker motivation, raising productivity, and breaking the iron grip of the bureaucratic employment system has been tried by a number of high-technology manufacturers, by a few old-line companies emerging from bankruptcy, and by some innovative investment firms. It involves a drastic reduction in the number of management positions, forcing the few remaining managers to delegate responsibility, abandon unproductive tasks, and streamline those they retain. Intel is a well-known example, and the MIT Commission described the case of the Chaparral Steel Company where

> there are almost 1,000 employees, and yet there are only four job levels. Production workers are responsible for identifying new technologies, training, meeting with customers and maintaining equipment. Foremen and crews install new equipment. Security guards are trained as emergency medical technicians, and they update computer records while on their shift.[22]

It is again the case that most of the reported experiments have been very successful in raising productivity and fostering high morale.

But, like more direct approaches to participatory management and job enrichment, administrative pruning is a marginal phenomenon rather than a general trend and is likely to remain marginal, since very few enterprises are configured so that anyone has both the inclination and the power to reduce the number of managers and management levels.

Several hundred firms, most of them small, are owned and controlled by their employees and in several thousand others, employees hold substantial minority shares. More than a million Americans work in the United States for foreign employers and that number is growing rapidly as Japanese, French, British, Dutch, West German, and Arab investors use their trade surpluses to buy up American firms. But although working for employee-owned or foreign-owned firms may feel a little different, most of them assume the normal form, and display the usual problems, of bureaucratic employment systems.[23]

NOTES

1. Based on *SAUS88*, Tables 609 and 626; and Roger Penn, "Where Have All the Craftsmen Gone? Trends in Skilled Labor in the United States since 1940," *British Journal of Sociology.* 37 (1986): 569–80.
2. Based on *SAUS88*, Table 711; and Sara Rix, ed. *The American Woman, 1990–91* (Washington, D.C.: Women's Research and Education Institute, 1990).
3. See James P. Smith and Michael P. Ward, *Women's Wages and Work in the Twentieth Century* (Rand Corporation, 1984), Table 10.
4. Amy O'Leary, "Necessary Choices: Dual Earner Couples' Time Spent in Housework" (Ph.D. diss., University of Virginia).
5. Roger Penn, 573; and *SAUS88*, Table 627.
6. Based on *SAUS89*, Tables 680 and 1185; and *SAUS79*, Table 1324.
7. Theresa Diss Greis, *The Decline of Annual Hours Worked in the United States since 1947* (Philadelphia: Wharton School, 1984).
8. Bureau of Labor Statistics, *Bulletin 2217*, June 1985; and Associated Press, March 1989.

9. Based on *SAUS80*, p. 429; and *SAUS88*, Tables 641 and 665.

10. Based on *SAUS88*, Table 662 and 668.

11. See Steven M. Bloom and David E. Bloom, "American Labor at the Crossroads," *American Demographics*, September 1985.

12. Richard Hamilton and James Wright, *The State of the Masses* (New York: Aldine, 1986).

13. Daniel Yankelovich and Sidney Harman, *Starting with the People* (Boston: Houghton Mifflin, 1988).

14. Suzanne Berger, Michael L. Dertouzos, Richard K. Lester, Robert M. Solow, and Lester C. Thurow, "Towards a New Industrial America," *Scientific American*, 200, no. 6:39–47. See also Michael L. Dertouzos et al., *Made in America: Regaining the Productive Edge* (Cambridge, MA: MIT Press, 1989).

15. Elliot Jaques, Paper presented at the meeting of the American Sociological Association, Washington D.C., 1985.

16. Berger et al., 43.

17. Yung-Ping Chen, "The Growth of Fringe Benefits: Implications for Social Security," *Monthly Labor Review*, 104 (November 1981): 3–10.

18. John Naisbitt, *Megatrends: Ten New Directions Transforming Our Lives* (New York: Warner Books, 1982), 198.

19. Elton Mayo, *Human Problems of an Industrial Civilization* (New York: Macmillan, 1933). Other notable works in this tradition include Kurt Lewin, *Resolving Social Conflicts* (New York: Harper, 1948); Harriet O. Ronken and Paul R. Lawrence, *Administering Change: A Case Study of Human Relations in a Factory* (Cambridge, MA: Harvard Graduate School of Business Administration, 1952); Alvin W. Gouldner, *Patterns of Industrial Bureaucracy* (Glencoe, IL: Free Press, 1954); Douglas McGregor, *The Human Side of Enterprise* (New York: McGraw-Hill, 1960); Rensis Likert, *New Patterns of Management* (New York: Macmillan, 1961); Peter Drucker, *Management: Tasks, Responsibility, Practices* (New York: Harper and Row, 1974); Robert E. Cole, *Work, Mobility and Participation* (Berkeley: University of California Press, 1979); and Christopher Eaton Gunn, *Worker Self-Management in the United States* (Ithaca, NY: Cornell University Press, 1984).

20. Thomas A. Kochan, Harry C. Katch, and Nancy R. Mower, *Worker Participation and American Unions: Threat or Opportunity* (Cambridge, MA: Upjohn Institute for Employment Research, 1984). See also Hy Kornbluh, "Work Place Democracy and Quality of Work Life: Problems and Prospects," *Annals of the American Academy of Political and Social Science*, 473 (1984): 88–95.

21. Frederick Herzberg, "One More Time: How Do You Motivate Employees?" *Harvard Business Review*. 5 (1987): 109–120.

22. Berger et al., 45.

23. See the illuminating accounts of the reactions of U. S. workers to Japanese bosses in a special section of the *Los Angeles Times*, 10 July 1988.

10

TRENDS IN LEISURE

Leisure is variously defined as voluntary activity, pleasure-seeking activity, free as opposed to constrained activity, play as opposed to work.[1] Work and leisure are supposed to be more sharply separated in modern than in traditional societies and that is probably the case for blue-collar workers in factories and clerical workers in offices, who are tightly scheduled, work by the clock, arrive and leave at set times, are confined to the workplace, and have no job obligations outside of working hours. But even in these tightly supervised occupations, there is some mingling of work and leisure on the job. Many different forms of recreation can be observed in any American enterprise during work hours: touch football on the shop floor, social gossip in the storeroom, light reading at the reception desk.

The leisure component is typically greater in occupations that are not confined to a workplace. Police officers, messengers, building inspectors, repairmen, and outside salesmen usually develop customary evasions for leisure during work hours. In many higher-ranking occupations—among company presidents or elected officials, for example—work and play are combined in two important ways: first, the work is so gratifying that it may be said to be performed for its own sake; second, a great deal of business is transacted in leisure settings. There is no reason to think that work and leisure were combined otherwise for Roman politicians or Renaissance merchants. All things considered, it is doubtful that work and leisure are more clearly separated in our own era than in earlier times or that their meanings are very different for us than they were for our ancestors. However, modernization has important, continuing effects on patterns of leisure. As modernization advances,

1. Leisure activities are continually diversified, elaborated, and expanded.

2. Stratification based on the division of leisure diminishes much faster than stratification based on the division of labor.

3. Advanced industrial societies undergo periodic "leisure explosions," marked by sharply increased participation in both active and passive leisure activities.

The typical mode of diversification involves adding new activities without abandoning old ones. When radio was introduced in the U. S. around 1920, newspaper readership increased instead of declining. When television arrived around 1945, it did not interrupt the growth of the radio audience. The invention of the outboard motor did not discourage the continued development of inboard motors or of sailboats and canoes.

At the same time, the options within each category become more numerous. Cable television is offered as an alternative to broadcast television and the rental of films for VCR playback is an alternative both to television and to the cinema. Nearly all sailboats were made of wood before 1950; they are now more commonly made of synthetic materials, but wooden boats are still being built.

Another aspect of diversification is the finer and finer subdivision of interests: from garden shows to flower shows to lily shows to daylily shows, each with its own infrastructure and its own specialized public. A newspaper survey of leisure in one small city mentions medical alert service, skydiving, recycling, wine tasting, clog dancing, skateboarding, windsurfing, stitchery, ceramic collecting, rock climbing, horsebreaking, and monster truck competitions as leisure activities promoted by well-organized local groups, along with scores of more familiar sports and hobbies.[2]

Numerical growth can be taken for granted in nearly every leisure domain. Of more than two dozen active sports in the U. S. whose followers can be counted from 1960 to 1990, only billiards declined in popularity.

Any stratification of a population by class, wealth, or power may be expected to affect leisure patterns. People of high status always engage in more leisure activities than those of low status whether or not they have more free time. The reservation of certain leisure activities to persons of high status was for centuries a key element in Western social structure.[3] Robin Hood's yeomen were legally ineligible to hunt deer or to fence with swords. Eighteenth-century peasants never danced the minuet or sat down to a table of whist. Factory workers did not play croquet in 1890 or golf in 1930.

Contemporary studies of American leisure activities in many different settings[4] show that there is still a positive correlation between the status of individuals and families and the number and intensity of their leisure activities, but that the correlation is much lower than it used to be and continues to decline. No important leisure activity is entirely reserved to people of high status. Blue-collar workers in the United States now play golf, go skiing, and attend symphony concerts, although less frequently than white-collar workers. The new pattern is clearly revealed by a survey of leisure activities that we carried out in Middletown in 1983.[5] Business-class and working-class respondents engaged in approximately the same activities, although the former reported more travel, attendance at spectacles, and athletic participation, and the latter reported more hunting, fishing, and camping. While more business-class than working-class respondents had visited certain distant places—San Francisco, Paris, Athens—the rank orders were identical for the two groups, and it was not at all unusual for working-class people to travel abroad. When we compare the Middletown of 1924, or even of 1960, with today's Middletown, we discover significant convergence in vacation schedules, reading habits, club membership, drinking patterns, sports interests, and hobbies. The partial equalization of leisure patterns has not been accompanied by any significant equalization of income or occupational status, either in Middletown or in the United States as a whole.

The reduction of class differences in leisure patterns has been paralleled, especially since 1960, by the reduction of gender, age, and ethnic differences. Although there is still considerable differentiation between men and women in overall leisure patterns, nearly all the activities that were formerly typed as masculine or feminine have recently attracted devotees of the opposite sex. Men do quilting and gardening. Women lift weights and hunt deer. Similarly, differentiation by age persists but is less obligatory than it used to be. There has been a steady rise in the proportion of elderly people who engage in active sports and in the proportion of adolescents who practice crafts in a serious way.

An even more striking change has been the disappearance, since 1960, of the color bar that excluded black athletes from participation in major league sports, with the result that black athletes nearly monopolize professional and intercollegiate basketball and track sports, nearly dominate professional and intercollegiate football, and figure prominently in baseball, too. Although blacks are not much involved in tennis or golf, or in winter sports like hockey and skiing, none of these have audiences remotely comparable to those of football, baseball, and basketball. Scarcely a generation ago, nearly all of America's star athletes were white; today, most of them are black.

There was a leisure explosion in the United States in the 1920s, marked by the extremely rapid spread of automobiles, radio, golf, boating, and domestic tourism. It was not matched in other countries. A second leisure explosion, involving the whole range of electronic and print media, active and passive sports, domestic and international tourism, recreational vehicles, second homes, and spectacles of all kinds, occurred between 1960 and 1975. It *was* shared with other industrialized countries[6] and its impetus has not yet been exhausted. Table 10–1 tells part of the story. Note the loss of momentum in some, but not all, of these activities after 1975.

TABLE 10–1   THE LEISURE EXPLOSION IN THE U. S.

	1960	1975	1986
	(in millions)		
Golfers	4	13	20
Tennis players	5	29	18
Visitors to national parks	79	239	365
Major league baseball attendance	20	30	46
College football attendance	20	32	36
Horseracing attendance	41	79	71
	(in thousands)		
New books published	15	39	43
Opera performances	4	6	11

SOURCE: Based on *Statistical Abstract of the United States 1979*, Tables 398, 406, 407, 997; and *Statistical Abstract of the United States 1988*, Tables 357, 368, 372, 373, 383, 414.

Because of the intricate division of leisure into many distinct domains, from rodeos to rare books, the entire panorama is not easy to see, but large increases have occurred in each of the following major categories since 1960: recreational reading, audiovisual entertainment, musical and theatrical performances, music and dance, spectator sports, participant sports, vacations and travel, hunting and camping, boating, cultivating and collecting, sedentary games, and voluntary social service.[7] This remarkably broad trend raises the puzzling question of where the time came from. As we noted in the previous chapter, the length of the workweek has not decreased significantly since 1960, while the proportion of the adult population in the labor force has increased (from 56 percent to 61 percent) due to the mass entry of women. On the other hand, the length of the work year has declined by 10 to 15 percent and the number of active and healthy retired people has been increased by the combined effects of earlier retirement, demographic succession, and the improvement of life expectancy. The time devoted to child care has been somewhat reduced by declining family size and earlier school entry and the time given to household chores has been cut by the improvement of appliances, fabrics, and grocery products, and the expansion of fast-food outlets. These factors have somewhat increased the average citizen's discretionary time but not nearly enough to account for the leisure explosion. The time required for the new leisure activities seems to come principally from what used to be idle time—the hours that were formerly spent in desultory conversation or in doing nothing at all.

The most important stimulus to the leisure explosion appears to be the steadily rising educational level of the population. Education itself is an activity that combines work and leisure in interesting ways. The student role resembles an occupation in many respects: assigned tasks, fixed schedules, regulated career advancement, institutional discipline. But it also resembles a leisure activity in being performed ostensibly for its own sake. Formal education prepares students for future leisure by teaching recreational skills directly, by encouraging the formation of new leisure interests, and by providing the intellectual background for such activities as reading history or listening to classical music.

There are strong interactive effects among the numerous upward trends combined in the leisure explosion. In recent decades, the growth of any leisure activity seems to have encouraged the growth of related activities. The great increase of television viewing that occurred between 1950 and the present was accompanied by an increase of recreational reading, instead of the reduction that common sense might lead us to expect. The extraordinary growth of spectator sports in the 1960s and 1970s ran parallel to the even sharper growth of participant sports. The geometric increase of air travel did not interfere with the continued growth of long-distance automobile travel.

These interactive effects are most striking in the mass media. The percentage of U. S. households with television sets increased from under 10 percent in 1950, all black and white, to 98 percent in 1980, mostly color sets, with more than one set in most households. In 1960, television was on in the average household for five hours per day; that figure rose to seven hours in 1982 before stabilizing. From 1960 to 1988, the number of radios in use increased by half, the number of cable TV subscribers rose from 650,000 to 42 million. In eight brief years, from 1980 to 1988, the proportion of households with VCR's rose from 1 percent to 51 percent. While all this was going on, the per capita circulation of newspapers decreased only slightly.[8]

No large population in history has ever spent so much time being entertained. The almost incredible volume of television viewing invites us to search for social and psychological effects. It is an article of popular belief that the depiction of violence on television fosters violent crime, but the extensive research that has been conducted on this question has produced inconclusive results.[9] The unkindest theory about the effects of television on American viewers is advanced by a French observer, Jean Baudrillard, who claims that Americans have lost the capacity to distinguish between authentic and simulated experience.[10] But that too is difficult to prove.

Some of the leisure activities which have exhibited spectacular growth since 1960 reflect technological innovations: electronic music, video games, home computing, recreational vehicles. But other activities—participant sports like tennis and jogging are notable examples—show very steep growth with only minor technological improvements. Still others, like recreational reading, have increased without any help from technology.

Along with many innovations, there are astonishing continuities in leisure patterns. The rules of baseball, for example, have not changed significantly during this century. The players and commentators are continuously aware of the long past enshrined in the record book and computers have made the comparison of present and past performances much easier than before. The conventions of filmmaking—plot, stars, scenery and costuming, background music, special effects—have not changed appreciably since the first sound films appeared 60 years ago. The arrival of the home videorecorder around 1980 led to the development of a parallel network for the distribution of films, with thousands of retail outlets renting films for home viewing, but it had little or no effect on the conventions of film production and surprisingly little effect on the existing network of movie theatres. The conventions of broadcast television—the half-hour programming module, the interruption of programs by carefully spaced clusters of commercials, the programming mix of serials, news, game shows, talk shows, sitcoms, soap operas, dramatic specials, and sports events, sprang into existence full-blown in the first few years of television, and have remained almost unchanged for four decades. Tennis rackets and golf clubs are continually improved but the rules of those games are set in stone. Today's gardens are produced with improved tools, machines, plant materials, and chemicals but they look very much like yesterday's gardens. The practitioners of archaic rituals like square dancing and fox-hunting, the builders of pipe organs and birch bark canoes, the bow-and-arrow hunters, the restorers of old houses and antique furniture, take infinite pains to avoid technological improvements.

When totally new leisure activities are devised with the aid of new technologies, their patterns of use develop almost overnight and are then likely to remain fixed. This has been the case for snowmobiles and sailboards, home computers and audio systems, aerobic dance and hydraulic exercise machines, ultra-light aircraft and mobile homes.

In recent years, the principal changes in the organization of leisure activities have been monetary rather than cultural. The dollar value of advertising in the mass media has risen more than 2,000 percent since 1960. This has interesting effects on the major spectator sports, where public interest has partly shifted from the athletic to the financial aspects—the extraordinary salaries and bonuses of players and coaches, their contract negotiations, their sponsorship deals, the high-pressure recruitment of college athletes, the disciplinary proceedings, and lawsuits to which these transactions give rise.

In newspaper and magazine publishing, the increase of advertising revenue has encouraged the merger of metropolitan dailies and the acquisition of important magazines by outside financial interests. In television news, the leading anchorpeople enjoy unprecedented earnings. The net effect has been to make the news media less accountable and more influential than ever before.

The smaller leisure domains have been monetarized too by the manufacturers of specialized equipment and the purveyors of specialized services. This has the invariable effect of raising the cost of participation but also, quite commonly, the number of participants and the quality of what they do. In a single recent year, 131,000 new swimming pools were built in the U. S., at a cost of nearly $5 billion.[11]

This last point reminds us that leisure and work combine in many ways and that any increase of a leisure activity, like attendance at major league baseball games, implies an increase of employment opportunities for those who get their living out of the game as players, coaches, managers, trainers, officials, secretaries, grounds-men, guards, accountants, cameramen, designers, manufacturers, suppliers, salesmen, brokers, and so forth. In every leisure domain, the activity that is a moderately expensive pleasure for most parti-cipants provides employment for some of them and high incomes for a few.

In some ways recent trends in leisure run parallel to recent trends in work. The mechanization of leisure, the progressive spe-cialization and differentiation of leisure activities, the substitution of institutional for personal services, and the spectacular increase in the sheer volume of leisure activity resemble the mechanization of work, occupational specialization, the depersonalization of produc-tion, and the continuous expansion of output associated with mod-ernization. But the differences between the division of leisure and the division of labor are as important as the similarities.

The division of labor is essentially coercive. The occupational choices available to a given worker at a given time fall within a narrow range, which usually becomes narrower in the course of a career. Entrance to privileged occupations is closely guarded. Occupational statuses fall into a single hierarchy that includes the entire labor force. Occupational earnings and other rewards are not very respon-sive to the wishes of individuals.

By contrast, access to a leisure domain is generally open. No-body is actively prevented from playing tennis or collecting stamps. Most leisure domains eagerly recruit new participants. Participation in one leisure domain is not ordinarily a bar to entering another. And although leisure performances confer prestige, and the prestige earned in a leisure domain is exportable to some extent, there is no consistent hierarchy of leisure activities. There is no recognized way to rank a marathon runner against a fly fisherman or an organ builder against a gardener.

Above all, leisure activities are intrinsically pleasant, which much work is not. Needless to say, the pleasures of the activity itself are inseparable from, and often subordinate to, the attraction of sociability.[12] Insofar as the distinction is tenable, people are more likely to play games in order to be with their friends than to join their friends in order to play games. Serious leisure performances are al-most always associated with intense sociability.

What happens in a leisure explosion is that great numbers of consumers are suddenly able to obtain equipment, like boats and second homes, that gives them access to new networks of sociability. The increase in collective happiness is appreciable.

NOTES

1. Stanley Parker, *The Future of Work and Leisure* (New York: Praeger, 1971); Neil H. Cheek, Jr., and William B. Burch, Jr., *The Social Organization of Leisure* (New York: Harper & Row, 1976); and John R. Kelly, *Leisure Identities and Interactions* (London: Allen and Unwin, 1983).

2. *Daily Progress*, Charlottesville, VA, 23 February 1990, Sec. 1–4.

3. See John Armitage, *Men at Play* (London: Frederick Wayne, 1977). Speaking of the division of play between rich and poor, Armitage writes that, "before the results of the Industrial Revolution had time to have effect, the division was a question of level. If a man held land he played; if he held a great deal of land he played even harder" (p. 14). He cites Joseph Strutt's early nineteenth-century book on *The Sports and Pastimes of England*, which had a section on "Rural Exercises Practiced by Persons of Quality," and another section on "Rural Exercises Generally Practiced."

4. Extensive, although slightly outdated evidence, is found in Richard F. Curtis and Elton F. Jackson, *Inequality in American Leisure* (New York: Academic Press, 1977).

5. Theodore Caplow and Bruce A. Chadwick, "Inequality and Life-Styles in Middletown, 1920–1978," *Social Science Quarterly*, 60 (September 1979): 367–86.

6. See, for France, Jean-Daniel Reynaud, Yves Grafmeyyer et al., *Français, Qui Êtes Vous?: Des Essais et des Chiffres* (Paris: La Documentation Française, 1981), and Henri Mendras, *La Seconde Revolution Française 1960–1985* (Paris: Gallimard, 1988); for Britain, Kenneth Roberts, *Contemporary Society and the Growth of Leisure* (London: Longmans, 1981), and Jonathan Gershuny, "The Changing Work/Leisure Balance in Britain 1961–1984," *Sociological Review*, 33 (1987): 9–50; for the Soviet Union, Joffre Dumazedier, *Sociology of Leisure* (Amsterdam: Elsevier, 1974).

7. For this last category, see "The New Volunteers," *Newsweek*, 10 July 1989, 36–39.

8. Richard Gertner, ed., *International Television and Video Almanac*, 33rd ed. (New York: Quigley Publishing Company); and *SAUS88*, Tables 887, 888, 889, 891, 892, 896.

9. See Paul F. Secord and Carl W. Backman, *Social Psychology*, 2nd ed. (New York: McGraw-Hill, 1974), 159–63.

10. Jean Baudrillard, *America*, trans. Chris Turner (New York: Verso, 1989).

11. Robert J. Samuelson, "Sporting Life," *Washington Post*, 30 August 1989, A23.

12. Rhona Rapoport and Robert L. Rapoport, *Leisure and the Family Life Cycle* (London: Routledge and Kegan Paul, 1975); and Peter Davis, *Hometown: A Contemporary American Community* (New York: Simon & Schuster, 1982).

11

TRENDS IN GOVERNMENT

The American system of government has been profoundly altered since 1960, although the only amendments added to the Constitution since then (on presidential voting in the District of Columbia, poll taxes, and presidential disability) had nothing to do with the important changes that occurred.

The most important of these changes was the expansion of federal authority into areas formerly reserved to state, local, and private authorities: education, health care, workplace conditions, the regulation of sexuality, crime control, the preservation of historic structures, the encouragement of the arts, the care of the handicapped, the design of automobile engines, and scores of other new interventions. In most instances, federal controls were superimposed on the existing state and local controls.

This constitutional transformation was achieved by a number of devices, of which the most important were judicial rulings that justified the new powers as necessary for the protection of long-established but newly expanded rights or in some cases, of newly discovered rights not explicitly mentioned in the Constitution. Thus, for example, federal rules mandating special facilities for handicapped pupils in public schools were imaginatively grounded on the equal protection clause of the Fourteenth Amendment, and the assertion of federal authority over contraception and abortion was based on a right to privacy that was said to be implied by, although not mentioned in, the Bill of Rights. Another method of obtaining new powers was by attaching conditions to the money that the federal government distributes to states, localities, public and private institutions, and individuals, on an ever-increasing scale; when President Nixon wanted to establish a national speed limit in response to the 1972 oil crisis, the authority to do so was created by threatening to withhold highway funds from noncomplying states. In a similar way, federal control of state and private universities was established originally by threatening to withhold the research grants and student loans on which the universities had come to depend, but the vast regulatory structure that has grown up over the years is by now self-sustaining.

With this multifaceted expansion, the federal government has acquired much more domestic power than it had before. Nearly all national issues are ultimately resolved in Washington. About half of all American families receive some form of payment from the Treasury.

The proliferation of functions since 1960 has affected every part of the government structure. In the executive and legislative branches, it is reflected by increases in the size of supporting staffs, and the shifting of many responsibilities from elected officials to the anonymous staff members who act in their names. The 535 members of the Congress presently employ more than 25,000 aides. The exact size of the President's office is concealed by ingenious budgetary arrangements, but it occupies as much space as the State and Treasury Departments together required during World War II. A parallel overgrowth of staffs has occurred in campaigning. A political commentator writes bitterly that,

> The obvious decline in political courage in recent years has been in direct proportion to the increasing role played in campaigns by consultants, tacticians, pollsters. Increasingly our politics is defined by pseudo-scientific amorality. The increasingly sophisticated use of political ads, the demonstrated effectiveness of negative campaigning, makes it decreasingly likely that politicians will do anything unpopular.[1]

The style of the American presidency seems to become more regal with every administration. The 1990 replacement of the President's specially equipped Boeing 747 and its backup plane came to $391 million, excluding maintenance.

The expansion of functions is reflected by a dramatic increase in federal budget outlays, from $92 billion in 1960 to $196 billion in 1970 to $591 billion in 1980 to about $1,500 billion in 1989.[2] But, contrary to general belief, the number of federal employees has increased only moderately during this same period, from 2.2 million in 1960 to about 2.9 million in 1990.[3] Indeed it has *declined* in relation to the national population. The armed forces grew from 2.5 million on active duty in 1960 to a peak of 3.5 million in 1969, declined to 2.2 million in 1974, and have remained in that neighborhood ever since.[4] The extraordinary ballooning of federal expenditures since 1960 has been accomplished in other ways than by adding new government employees, for example: by federal subsidies to state and local governments for purposes like school lunches and water purification; by third-party payments to health care providers and real estate operators; by procurement of the most expensive and complicated weapons systems ever devised; by the payment of benefits to farmers, college students, food stamp recipients, job trainees, railroad workers, and veterans on an ever-increasing scale; by payment of the huge interest costs attached to the ever-rising federal debt; and by the indexing of social security, civil service, and military pensions to keep pace with inflation. The approximately $3,000 spent by the national government for each resident of the United States in 1986, excluding interest payments on the national debt, was distributed as follows:[5]

Federal payroll	$ 453
Grants to state and local governments	405
Military procurement	739
Direct payments to individuals	1,359

The American version of the welfare state is unusual in three respects—the lateness of its development, the peculiar division of responsibility among the three levels of government, and the high incidence of program failure.

The assumption of welfare responsibilities by the federal government began in the first Roosevelt administration (1933–1937), with the Social Security retirement system, unemployment insurance, the United States Employment Service, government guarantees of bank deposits and home mortgages, income support for families with dependent children and for the blind, the distribution of surplus food to low-income families, public low-rent housing, the encouragement and supervision of collective bargaining, the establishment of a minimum wage, and direct subsidies to farmers—all of which became permanent—as well as programs of price control, industrial planning, and work relief that were later discontinued.

The second wave of innovation occurred from 1964 to 1966 in the presidency of Lyndon Johnson; the major legislative enactments included the Economic Opportunity Act, the Civil Rights Act, the Social Security Amendments of 1965, the Elementary and Secondary Education Act, and the Model Cities Act. More than 100 new federal programs were established under these statutes, furthering such goals as the encouragement of minority-owned businesses, social services for migrant workers, subsidized health care for the elderly, the suppression of gender and race discrimination in private employment, legal services for the indigent, emergency food distribution, family planning services, special education for handicapped and bilingual children, and a Community Action Program which supported thousands of local agencies with all sorts of purposes.

Many of the smaller Johnson programs faded away in later administrations but the major programs continued to expand their coverage, increase their benefits, and come more firmly under federal control. The process continues to this day. The growth of federal welfare expenditures from 1960 to 1986 is shown in Table 11–1. The rate of growth was very steep in every category:

TABLE 11–1   **FEDERAL SOCIAL WELFARE EXPENDITURES, 1960–1986 (billions of dollars)**

	1960	1986
Social Insurance	$19	$390
Public Aid	4	103
Veterans	6	27
Education	18	179
Housing	0.2	12

SOURCE: Based on *Statistical Abstract of the United States 1988*, Table 565. The "Health" category partly overlaps the "Social Insurance," "Public Aid," and "Veterans" categories.

Many of the federal programs alleviate the problems they were intended to resolve. Many do not. Hundreds of programs have been added to the government's repertory in the past 30 years in response to perceived needs, political expediency, bureaucratic initiatives, organized lobbying, and other short-term stimuli. The legislative measures that establish new programs, or modify old ones, are drafted and debated *ad hoc* without much attention to their interaction with existing programs or to their probable effects in the real world. When the intentions of a measure are obviously worthy, questions about practicality tend to be waved aside. As a result, the failure rate of recent federal programs has been high; some—such as Medicare— seem to aggravate the problems they were intended to resolve.

Medicare is the largest of a class of federal programs that pay third parties for services to the program's beneficiaries. Others are Medicaid, subsidized rental housing, and the burgeoning child care program. None of these programs has effectively controlled the prices charged by providers. The usual result of pumping government money into a service market is a dramatic rise in the price of services which enriches the providers and puts unreasonable burdens on taxpayers, on unsubsidized users, and eventually on beneficiaries. In the 17 years between 1970 and 1987, government payments to third parties for personal health care rose from $40 billion to $288 billion, but the health care expenses paid by individual citizens rose about as much, from $43 billion to $260 billion. In the same 17-year period, the aggregate after-inflation cost of physician services increased by 222 percent and of hospital services by 424 percent,[6] without much improvement in the average level of care. Twenty years after the introduction of Medicare, persons over 65 were paying a *larger* proportion of their own incomes for medical care than before the program was introduced.[7]

A similar escalation of costs has afflicted educational programs. From 1960 to 1985, public expenditures for education at all levels increased by 871 percent while enrollments showed an overall increase of barely 10 percent.[8] The consensus of expert opinion is that there was no commensurate increase in educational quality.

Aside from the tendency for entitlement payments to escalate out of control, American welfare programs suffer from a severe lack of coordination. As early as 1972, a congressional staff study reported that:

> It is no longer possible—if indeed, it ever was—to provide a convincing rationale for the programs as they exist in terms of who is covered and who is excluded, benefit amounts and eligibility conditions. No coherent rationale binds them together as a system. Additionally, the programs are extraordinarily complex, and the eligibility provisions lack uniformity even among programs with similar objectives and structures.[9]

The poor coordination among federal welfare programs has worsened in the intervening years and new problems have developed, notably the unintended transfer of wealth from younger to older cohorts of the population through the operations of the Social Security system.[10] By 1990, poverty had been almost wiped out among elderly Americans, but the number of children in poverty had risen sharply, and the economic prospects of young adults were gravely threatened by the inequities unintentionally created by the Social Security system.

The expansion of federal functions and expenditures has not resulted in a contraction of the 50 state governments or of the 81,000 local governments in the United States. Taken together, they spend more than half as much as the federal government and borrow a third as much.[11] These ratios are relatively stable so that the spectacular increase in federal expenditures after 1970 was closely tracked by increases in the expenditures of state and local governments. In a similar way, state and local government expenditures keep pace with each other. For no apparent reason, the national total of local government expenditures is always very close to the total of state government expenditures. There are good reasons, however, for the general trend of expenditures at the three levels of government to run in parallel; state and local governments receive massive subventions from the federal government, as do local governments from state governments.

In contrast to the rapid expansion of functions that occurred at all levels of government between 1960 and 1990, the political structure exhibited considerable stability during this period. The composition of the Republican and Democratic parties changed somewhat as the Democratic solid South dissolved and the Republicans discovered a blue-collar constituency, but the two-party system encountered no serious challenge during this period. Except for weak and temporary flurries of third-party activity in the presidential elections of 1960, 1968, and 1980, the two major parties garnered practically all the votes cast in state, local, and national elections. Of the eight presidential elections from 1960 to 1988, three were won by Democrats and five by Republicans, but Democrats controlled the House of Representatives during the entire 30 years and the Senate in all but six of those years. At the lower levels of politics, most of the safe enclaves formerly controlled by Democrats or Republicans were invaded by the other party. The balance of Democratic and Republican controlled state houses oscillated continually. The best Republican year was 1972 when 32 state governors were Republicans. The best Democratic year was 1984, when 35 governors were Democrats, although a Republican president was reelected in the same year by an overwhelming margin.[12]

This pattern reflects the decline of straight-ticket party voting. The proportion of respondents in national surveys who considered themselves to be political independents rose from 20 percent in 1958 to 30 percent in 1968 to 37 percent in 1978, since when it has been approximately level. The percentage of strong party identifiers decreased correspondingly, from 40 percent in 1958 to 30 percent in 1968 to 22 percent in 1978, with a slight increase in the 1980s.[13] However, the proportions of the electorate who attend political meetings and rallies, volunteer for party work, or contribute money to candidates show no definite trends since 1958—about 15 percent of the electorate is involved to some extent in political campaigning.[14]

Other important trends in national politics from 1960 to 1990 were: (1) a slow but steady decline in voting participation; (2) a sharp increase in the number of blacks elected to office and a moderate increase in the number of women elected; (3) the commercialization of election campaigns; (4) a worsening of the incumbency problem in the U. S. Congress—the difficulty in voting incumbents out of office; and (5) a sharp increase in the incidence of corrupt practices in both the executive and legislative branches of the federal government.

The percentages of eligible citizens who voted in the presidential elections of 1960 to 1988 are shown in Table 11–2:

TABLE 11–2   Voting Participation of Eligible U. S. Citizens

1960	63%
1964	62
1968	61
1972	55
1976	54
1980	53
1984	53
1988	50

SOURCE: Based on *Statistical Abstract of the United States 1989*, Table 433.

The off-year elections for Congress show a parallel but lower trend. In 1986, only a third of the eligible voters appeared at the polls. This trend is often viewed with alarm, as reflecting the alienation of citizens from politics, but it can also be interpreted more cheerfully as a self-screening whereby uninformed and indifferent voters improve the quality of electoral choices by abstaining.

There were only a handful of black elected officials in the United States in 1960. After the reenfranchisement of the black population in the Johnson era, there were 1,474 blacks holding office in 1970, 4,963 in 1980 and 6,703 in 1988,[15] distributed through all levels of government and all regions of the country, although more numerous in the South. The early black candidates were supported principally by black voters, but popular black politicians eventually garnered substantial support from white voters; 1989 saw the election of a black governor of Virginia and a black mayor of New York by predominantly white constituencies. The political engagement of hispanics progressed in parallel; about 4,000 hispanics held elective office by 1988. The number of women elected to office during this period increased, too, but at a much slower pace. There were 10 women members of Congress in 1960 and only 25 in 1990.

The commercialization of election campaigns has involved a dramatic escalation of campaign costs, a shift from amateur to professional management, the increasingly blatant packaging of candidates and issues, heavy reliance on television commercials, sophisticated polling, and a vast fund-raising apparatus that efficiently extracts money both from the general public and from "special interests" wanting favorable treatment in return. The cost of presidential campaigns increased from under $20 million in 1960 to over $200 million in 1988, after a primary campaign that also cost more than $200 million.[16]

The average cost of running for Congress rose from about $25,000 in 1960 to more than $500,000 in 1988, with some contenders spending millions. Most of this money went for 30-second television commercials, designed to sell candidates with the same techniques that sell diapers and detergents. The attempt to reform the financing of federal elections by means of the Federal Elections Campaign Act of 1971 and its 1974 and 1976 amendments had the unintended effect of creating more serious abuses than existed before. The new system prohibited large individual contributions but encouraged the formation of political action committees (PACs) representing trade associations, labor unions, and other interest groups. Beginning in 1974, when only a few hundred of these committees had been formed, the number increased to almost 5,000 in 1988, while their relative share of congressional campaign expenditures mounted from a small fraction to about 90 percent. Moreover, a quirk in the law for a time allowed candidates to carry campaign contributions over from one election to the next and to convert these accumulated funds to personal use when they left office. In effect, the system allows groups like the dairy industry, the Teamsters Union, and the National Rifle Association, to buy votes on legislation that touches their interests.

The incumbency problem in the U. S. Congress is directly related to the PAC system. About seven times as much PAC money is contributed to incumbents as to challengers. This advantage, added to those that incumbents enjoy through the franking privilege and access to the news media, has made it very difficult for challengers to unseat incumbents. In 1988, more than 98 percent of the incumbents who ran were reelected—a situation not fully compatible with the theory of democratic representation.[17]

The use of public office for private gain is no novelty in the United States. There were major financial scandals in the Grant and

Harding administrations and corruption is endemic in some state and local governments, but federal officeholders have generally held to higher ethical standards. President Eisenhower's chief of staff, Sherman Adams, was forced to resign merely for having accepted a vicuna coat and a home freezer from persons having business with the government. Very few high federal officials were convicted of criminal malfeasance in the half century between Presidents Harding and Nixon, but beginning with the trial of Vice President Spiro Agnew, the conviction of senior officials for perjury, bribery, influence-peddling, and other abuses of office, became commonplace. More than 100 Reagan appointees earned prison sentences, and many others appeared to profit personally from the diversion of housing and urban development grants, surreptitious operations in support of the Nicaraguan contras, the looting of thrift institutions, and the sale of procurement information to defense contractors. The Democrats were similarly afflicted. The speaker and majority leader of the House of Representatives were forced out of office in 1989 when their financial dealings came to public attention. Six senators of both parties were implicated in the worst of the savings and loan failures. The bribery of procurement officials is too common to attract much attention. The number of federal officials indicted and convicted for corrupt acts rose dramatically—from 9 in 1970 to 123 in 1980 to 596 in 1986.[18]

Public confidence in government as surveyed in 13 Harris polls from 1966 to 1988 showed a sharp downward trend from 1966 to 1976 and a slight rebound thereafter. The percentage of respondents expressing "a great deal of confidence" in "the people in charge of running" parts of the federal government is shown in Table 11–3:

TABLE 11–3   PUBLIC CONFIDENCE IN GOVERNMENTAL LEADERS

	1966	1976–78	1986–88
Executive Branch	41%	17%	18%
Congress	42	12	19
Supreme Court	50	29	31
Military	61	26	35

SOURCE: Louis Harris, "Confidence in Institutions Down, Led by Sharp Decline in Trust in White House," *The Harris Poll*, no. 37, 8 May 1988, 2.

These figures are quite volatile from year to year but the public's low esteem for Congress and the executive branch has become chronic. The decline of confidence in government from the 1960s to the 1970s was part of a broader decline in public confidence in all major institutions including business, higher education, the news media, medicine, law, religion, and labor. But 1987 data from the National Opinion Research Center's *General Social Survey* suggest that all of these institutions, except organized labor and the news media, now enjoy more public confidence than the executive and legislative branches of the federal government.[19]

The trends affecting the defense sector of government deserve separate consideration. Until the beginning of the cold war, the United States never maintained more than skeletal forces in peacetime. The large armies mobilized for every major war from the Revolution onward were disbanded as soon as the shooting stopped, leaving only a cadre of professional soldiers to await the next conflict. The Navy, although somewhat less elastic, expanded and contracted in a similar way. Cincinnatus rather than Caesar was the ideal; a distrust of standing armies was part of the national creed. Thus, in the two years following the Civil War, the number of military personnel on active duty in the Union forces declined by 93 percent; it continued to decline for another ten years, reaching a low of 34,000 in 1877. In the two years after World War I, the decline was 89 percent and that decline too continued for several more years until the number of military personnel stabilized around 250,000. In the two years after World War II, the decline was 87 percent—from 12.1 million to 1.6 million. Then, during the Korean War, the armed forces more than doubled, to 3.6 million, and remained above 2 million for the next four decades.[20] It should be noted, however, that under current arrangements, the size of the defense sector is greatly understated by a count of military personnel. In 1988, there were 2.2 million soldiers, sailors, airmen, and marines on active duty, but an additional 1.7 million civilians were employed by the Department of Defense, and 3.4 million workers held defense-related jobs in industry, for a total of 6.7 million, about the same level as during the Vietnam War.[21]

Direct outlays for national defense (in constant 1982 dollars) increased from $192 billion in 1960 to $255 billion in 1968 at the height of activity in Vietnam, declined to $164 billion in 1980, and rose again to $289 billion by 1990.[22] Real military expenditures in the late 1980s, an exceptionally peaceful period, ran slightly higher than in the late 1960s, when the nation was engaged in a bloody and protracted war in southeast Asia.

As of fiscal 1989, this level of expenditure paid for the deployment of 14 aircraft carriers, 1,000 intercontinental nuclear missiles, 100 nuclear submarines, 372 heavy bombers, more than 4,000 fighter

planes, and innumerable smaller weapons; the maintenance of occupation armies in West Germany, South Korea, and Japan; the operation of a worldwide system of overseas bases; and the most ambitious program of weapons research in history.[23] These forces were
designed to counter the threat of a Soviet invasion of western Europe
and to block the projection of Soviet power elsewhere in the world.[24]
Developments in eastern Europe after 1988 seemed to make these
missions obsolete and to call for new force structures.*

While today's armed services are nearly the same size as those of
1960 and stationed in many of the same locations, they are quite
different. The enlisted personnel of 1960 were mostly male, white,
and single. Because of conscription, they were a fair cross section of
the civilian population. The pay was low and the discipline severe
but military service was generally respected and postservice educational benefits were generous. Most servicemen were assigned to
nontechnical jobs: rifleman, truckdriver, medical corpsman. Many
officers and noncoms had combat experience in Korea; a good many
had fought in World War II. Drunkenness and AWOL were the usual
breaches of military law. Unit loyalty was strong and military values
were unchallenged.

The Vietnam War, with its confused goals and tactics, and its un-
profitable carnage, tore the services apart. One careful reporter, describing the condition of the U. S. forces in Europe in 1971, writes that:

> A wrecked Army it was, a "bored and ignored" Army that had
> been bled white to keep the U. S. war machine in Southeast Asia
> supplied with officers, experienced NCOs, materiel, and money.
> In some respects the 300,000 man American force in Germany
> was less an army than an armed savage mob of New World Vis-
> igoths. Standards had collapsed, morale was a farce; and disci-
> pline in many units resembled something very close to anarchy
> ... The list of crimes rolled on and on—murders, rapes, mug-
> gings and robberies by the thousands. Gangs of soldiers roamed
> the streets of Munich and Nuremberg while citizens cowed be-
> hind locked doors like the terrorized townsfolk in a Wild West
> melodrama ... Part of the Vietnam bequest was rampant drug
> addiction. As that war sputtered to a close, an estimated 10 to
> 15% of the American privates and corporals in Vietnam were
> heroin addicts ... As the epidemic spread to Europe, hashish
> became as common in many units as cigarettes or Life Savers ...

---

*Three former chairmen of the Joint Chiefs of Staff testified to that effect at congres-
sional hearings in January 1990.

The other cancer eating at the Army's vitals was racial hatred . . .
Court-martial boards sometimes acquitted AWOL soldiers, who
argued successfully that the barracks had become so dangerous
that sensible men had to flee for their lives . . . Lopsided brawls
in which a single white soldier or a single black was savagely
pummeled by a gang of the opposite race occurred so frequently . . .[25]

Recovery was achieved partly by the operation of time as the Vietnam
War receded and partly by the deliberate transformation of military
roles and obligations. The draft was abandoned to make way for an
"all volunteer force" attracted by career incentives and market wages.
Enlisted personnel assigned abroad were encouraged to bring their
families along, and the care and provisioning of dependents eventually became the principal activity of U. S. overseas commands.
Women were admitted to the services on equal terms and given limited combat roles. Minority recruitment and promotion was emphasized. Military law moved steadily closer to civil law. The benefits of
technical training were widely advertised by the services, and technical specialties became more numerous and important as the complexity of weapons systems increased.

The net effect of these changes was to erase many of the traditional distinctions between military and civilian culture. Increasingly, a military assignment could be viewed as a job with pay,
hours, and working conditions comparable to a similar job in private
industry. The reforms of the early 1970s "implied a redefinition of
military service away from an institutional format to one more and
more resembling that of an occupation."[26] There was even some interest in unionization and collective bargaining.[27]

Although discipline and good order returned to the services
with these reforms, a number of new problems appeared. Service
personnel became increasingly unrepresentative of the general population since the new economic incentives appealed especially to
those who were disadvantaged in the civilian labor market, either by
limited education or minority status. College graduates virtually disappeared from the enlisted ranks and technicians who qualified for
civilian employment tended to leave the service early.

Meanwhile, the maintenance requirements of sophisticated
weapons systems became overwhelming.

The fuel control system in a modern fighter jet has more than
5000 parts. . . . For every hour an F15 is airborne, the Air Force
spends an average of 53 hours maintaining the plane on the

ground. . . . the Air Force needs 166 different types of specialists to keep its planes aloft—a colossal headache in planning round-the-clock operations.[28]

One solution has been to incorporate contractor representatives into military units. When an aircraft carrier goes to sea, it carries a large contingent of civilian technicians, who are much better paid than their uniformed counterparts. Another solution has been to tolerate very high rates of equipment failure.

The effectiveness of the armed services is further hampered by intricate chains of command, complex bureaucratic procedures, an excessively intimate relationship between procurement officers and defense contractors, and above all, by interservice rivalry. The goal of parity among the services has probably weighed as heavily in the design of America's nuclear arsenal as the goal of parity with the Soviet Union. Each service is engaged in a continuous campaign to enlarge its functions at the expense of the others and each expects unswerving partisan loyalty from its officers.

The need for a thorough reorganization of U. S. forces to meet the strategic requirements of the post-cold war era was widely recognized even before the Persian Gulf crises of 1990.

NOTES

1. Elizabeth Drew, "Letter from Washington," *The New Yorker*, 31 July 1989, 77.
2. Based on *SAUS89*, Table 489; and 1990 press reports.
3. Bureau of the Census, *Public Employment in 1988*, Series GE-88-1, 1989.
4. Based on *SAUS89*, Tables 514, 543, 544. Total defense manpower, including military personnel, civilian employees of the Defense Department and defense-related employment in industry came to 6.7 million in 1988, almost the same as in 1960.
5. Based on a table prepared by Jeri Kristoff for *Washington Post* in 1987.
6. Based on *SAUS88*, Tables 135, 136, 138, 139.
7. *Ibid.*
8. Based on *SAUS89*, Tables 221, 228, 245, 247.
9. Quoted in Robert X. Browning, "Priorities, Programs, and Presidents; Assessing Patterns of Growth in U. S. Social Welfare Programs," in S. H.

Danziger and K. E. Portnoy, eds., *The Distributional Aspects of Public Policy* (New York: St. Martin's Press, 1988), 15.

10. Peter S. Peterson, *On Borrowed Time: How the Growth in Entitlement Spending Threatens America's Future* (San Francisco: ICS Press, 1988). A briefer explanation may be found in Subrata H. Chakravart and Katherine Weisman, "Consuming Our Children?" *Forbes Magazine*, 14 November 1988, 223–32.

11. Based on *SAUS89*, Tables 446, 447, 448, 449.

12. Based on *SAUS89*, Tables 411, 418, 425.

13. See Norval D. Glenn, "Social Trends in the United States. Evidence from Sample Surveys," *Public Opinion Quarterly*, 50 (1987):S109–S126.

14. Based on data in Michael E. McGerr, *The Decline of Popular Politics* (New York: Oxford University Press, 1986). The evidence presented in that work is not entirely consistent with its title.

15. Based on *SAUS89*, Table 429.

16. *Facts on File*, 8 September 1989, 658.

17. Incumbents, of course, always enjoy an advantage over challengers. The lowest reelection rate for incumbent congressmen after World War II was 79 percent in 1948. But since the campaign reforms of the 1970s went into effect, the reelection rate has run above 90 percent, and in the last three elections above 96 percent. See Congressional Research Service, *Reelection Rates of House Incumbents 1790-1988* (Washington, D.C.: Library of Congress, 1989).

18. Based on *SAUS89*, Table 312; and *SAUS79*, Table 319.

19. Based on *GSS87*, Items 181–184. The Gallup Poll, which words its question about institutional confidence somewhat differently, shows somewhat different numbers but very similar patterns. See *The Gallup Report*, no. 263, August 1987. The great loss of institutional confidence between the 1960s and 1970s was analyzed at length in Seymour Martin Lipset and William Schneider, *The Confidence Gap: Business, Labor and Government in the Public Mind* (New York: Free Press, 1983), but their identification of unemployment and inflation as causal factors has been somewhat overtaken by events, since institutional confidence did not improve very much as unemployment and inflation moderated in the 1980s.

20. Based on *Historical Statistics of the United States: Colonial Times to 1970*, Series Y 904–916; and *SAUS89*, Table 543.

21. *Ibid.*

22. Based on *SAUS89*, Table 526.

23. Frank C. Carlucci, *Secretary of Defense Annual Report to the Congress*, FY 1989.

24. A clear statement of these priorities may be found in the annual reports of Secretaries of Defense Weinberger and Carlucci for 1987, 1988, and 1989, which designate the Soviet Union and its Warsaw Pact allies as the adversaries against whom American military power is directed. "We recognize," says the 1987 report (p. 18), "that the Soviet Union threatens U. S. vital interests at many points across the globe . . . Maintaining the overall

military capability we must have over the longer term will require us to invest roughly as much in our defenses as our primary competitor invests in its forces."

25. Rick Atkinson, *The Long Gray Line* (Boston: Houghton Mifflin, 1989), 366–68.

26. Charles Moskos, "Making the All-Volunteer Service Work: A National Service Approach." *Foreign Affairs*, Fall 1981, 22.

27. David R. Segal, "Worker Representation in Military Organization," in F. D. Margiotta, ed., *The Changing World of the American Military* (Boulder, CO: Westview Press, 1978).

28. *Washington Post*, 18 August 1985.

29. Many scathing critiques of the U. S. military and of what President Eisenhower called the military-industrial complex have appeared in print. See, among others, Norman B. Augustine, *Augustine's Laws* (New York: Penguin Books, 1986); Richard Gabriel, *Military Incompetence: Why the American Military Doesn't Win* (New York: Hill and Wang, 1985); Gary S. Hart and William S. Lind, *America Can Win: The Case for Military Reform* (Bethesda, MD: Adler and Adler, 1986); Edward N. Luttwak, *The Pentagon and the Art of War* (New York: Simon & Schuster, 1984); and Louis Hicks, "A Report from the Field," *Armed Forces Journal International*, October 1987, 120.

12

THE INSTITUTIONAL MATRIX

The six major institutions discussed in the preceding chapters—family, education, religion, work, leisure, government—are so important in the study of social change that it is worthwhile to examine the influence of each institution upon the others during the period from 1960 to 1990.

This topic brushes the edge of an old sociological controversy. In Marxist theory it is axiomatic that the relations of production are fundamental and that changes in other institutions are always driven by changes in the institution of work. In the words of Friedrich Engels,

> The economic structure of society always furnishes the real basis, starting from which we can alone work out the whole superstructure of political and social institutions as well as of the religious, philosophical, and other ideas of a given historical period.[1]

Max Weber's studies of religion, beginning with *The Capitalist Ethic and the Spirit of Protestantism* and continuing with his later studies of Confucianism, Taoism, Hinduism, Buddhism, and Judaism, were intended in part to refute the foregoing theory. His aim in these works,

> ... was to characterize and explain the distinguishing traits of different kinds of religious belief and to trace the unintended, but nonetheless important consequences of different theological doctrines for the orientation that men bring to their economic activities.[2]

Religion, as Weber showed by examples drawn from half a dozen civilizations, was as likely to influence work as the other way around.

A few sociologists still accept the Marxist doctrine that work relationships account for everything else in a social system but the majority position is that the question of how much influence one institution exerts on another is best settled case by case in the light of empirical evidence. This leaves open the possibility that the influence of work or religion or government or the family on social change may vary with time and place, and indeed this is what the evidence seems to show.

The principal trends in the six major institutional sectors of American society between 1960 and 1990 were these:

In the Family

- Childbearing became elective, with the introduction of reliable oral contraceptives, sterilization, and legal abortion.
- The incidence of premarital sexual activity, extramarital childbearing, and households based on unmarried heterosexual and homosexual unions, all increased sharply.
- Large numbers of married women, especially the mothers of small children, entered the labor force.
- Large numbers of single women, especially black and hispanic women, raised their children without a man in the house.
- Government intervention into family relationships became more frequent and more pervasive.

In Religion

- Evangelical churches grew at the expense of the mainline Protestant denominations.
- The mainline Protestant denominations and the Roman Catholic Church shifted towards liberal positions on doctrine, morality, and social issues. Liturgies were modernized and democratized, and women were actively recruited to the Protestant ministry.

In Education

- Educational progress, as measured either by numbers or achievement, virtually ceased in the early 1970s, while costs continued to mount.
- The educational opportunities of minorities improved dramatically.
- Many new responsibilities were imposed on educational institutions, from the reduction of racial and gender prejudice, to the encouragement of bilingualism, the suppression of substance abuse, and the prevention of sexually transmitted disease.
- There was a vast expansion of the extracurriculum at every educational level, including the development of intercollegiate and interscholastic athletics as semicommercial enterprises.

In Work

- The proportion of women in the labor force increased sharply.
- The proportion of white-collar workers in the labor force increased sharply.
- The efficiency of the U. S. economy declined relative to foreign competitors.
- The long-term rise of real wages virtually ceased in the early 1970s.

In Leisure

- There was a great explosion of leisure activity, both active and passive.
- The differentiation of leisure patterns by social class, gender, ethnicity, and age, diminished.
- The amounts invested and earned in leisure activities increased dramatically.

In Government

- The functions and powers of the federal government expanded greatly.
- Expenditures at all levels of government increased dramatically.
- Serious operational problems developed in the welfare system, the political system, and the military.

It is evident at first glance that trends in the work sector did have some influence on trends in the other institutional sectors. The interrupted growth of real wages clearly stimulated the entrance of married women into the labor force. Families were not able to improve their living standards on the earnings of one breadwinner. But it is difficult to show that trends in work had much to do with the great changes in childbearing practices, household arrangements, and sexual patterns that were taking place simultaneously.

Since the loss of industrial momentum and the loss of educational momentum in the U. S. occurred at about the same time, it is tempting to look for a connection. But the connection is hard to find. The interruption of educational progress cannot fairly be charged to declining material support. On the contrary, expenditures for education skyrocketed after 1972, while enrollment and achievement ceased to advance.

The influence of trends in work on trends in leisure was minimal. Although the shortening of the work year by ten percent or so surely contributed to the leisure explosion, it hardly accounted for it. The shortening of the average male career by later entry into the labor force and earlier retirement would seem to favor the expansion of leisure activities, but that should have been more than offset by the increasing employment of women. It might be supposed that under the double burden of housework and paid employment, women would have decreased their involvement in leisure activities, but the evidence is all to the contrary.

The effect of trends in work on trends in government is difficult to assess, given the overlap between the two sectors. Approximately 18 million American workers are directly employed by public agencies[3] and many millions more are in jobs that depend on government contracts, grants, and subsidies. The government has been affected by the same trends as other employers and now has higher proportions of women workers and white-collar workers than formerly. And it can be argued that the growth of government debt is partly attributable to the productivity problems of the private sector. But, all things considered, the influence of economic trends on trends in government was less decisive in this period than in previous eras.

The government rather than the economy seemed to be the principal motor of social change after 1960; it acted partly in response to the demands of social movements and organized lobbies; partly on the initiative of ideological entrepreneurs in Congress, the courts, and the bureaucracy; partly for short-term political motives; and partly by accident. The random factor in public policy was enhanced by the growing complexity of government, the custom of disregarding the practical consequences of legislative acts and judicial decisions; and the cost-escalating mechanisms hidden in many government programs.[4]

The influence of government on trends in the family is apparent at first glance. Childbearing could not have become fully elective had not the Supreme Court removed the legal restrictions on contraception in 1964 (in *Griswold* v. *Connecticut*) and on abortion in 1973 (in *Roe* v. *Wade* and *Doe* v. *Bolton*). Planned Parenthood clinics and abortions for the indigent were publicly funded during much of this period, although that policy wavered with each political breeze.

The deregulation of sexual behavior, which was largely accomplished by the federal judiciary, accounted in large measure for the growth of nontraditional households, and presumably contributed to the increased incidence, as well as the increased visibility, of casual sex.

A wide range of government policies encouraged and facilitated the entry of married women into the labor force, including legislative, judicial, and administrative efforts to reduce gender discrimination in hiring and promotion, to open exclusively male occupations to women, to prohibit sexual harassment in the workplace, to establish maternity leave as a right, and to reduce the costs of day care for the children of working mothers by tax credits and grants.

The vast increase in unmarried childbearing that occurred during this period was related in a general way to the deregulation of sexual behavior, and more specifically to the extension of Aid to Families with Dependent Children and other public welfare benefits to unmarried mothers.

The influence of government on religion during this period was almost negligible. The line of separation between church and state, although frequently challenged by administrative agencies, was generally defended by the courts. The line became somewhat irregular in the course of these encounters without shifting very much. Except for such matters as employee benefits, accounting for tax exempt income, zoning, and fire laws, churches and other religious organizations remained exempt from government control, and trends in religion during this period were only remotely related to trends in government.

The same cannot be said of education. There were several important developments in the relationship between government and education after 1960: (1) the role of the federal government expanded greatly, putting a third layer of authority over the local and state agencies that controlled the public schools, improvising a regulatory structure for higher education, and extending jurisdiction to private schools; (2) most of the educational innovations of the period were either mandated or encouraged by the federal government, including desegregation, busing for racial balance, affirmative action in faculty and student recruitment, special education for the handicapped in regular schools, handicapped access, bilingual instruction, black studies, women's studies, the promotion of women's interscholastic and intercollegiate athletics, the codification of student rights, restraints on the disciplinary powers of teachers and principals, sex education, drug education, nutritional regulation in school cafeterias, the financing of higher education by student loans, and a host of other finely detailed initiatives; (3) there was a parallel reinforcement of state control over local school boards and the governing boards of public colleges and universities so that curricular and administrative decision making shifted from local to state authorities; and (4) the higher levels of government became increasingly responsible for the funding of public and private education at all levels from preschool through graduate school, with a complex array of capital and operating grants, tuition subsidies, tax incentives, bond guarantees, scholarships, direct and guaranteed student loans, work-study, and direct allocations for special programs.

In general, the educational and social improvements achieved by these efforts were somewhat less than had been hoped for. The burden of new responsibilities sometimes interfered with the schools' ability to perform their primary educational function; the substitution of distant for local control did not necessarily lead to better administration; and the shower of third-party payments had the usual effect of raising costs more than output.

The federal government also exerted a strong influence on the work sector during this period by means of its macroeconomic policies on the one hand and its assertion of authority over private employers with respect to such matters as workplace safety, environmental protection, discrimination in hiring and promotion, drug abuse, the employment of aliens, product liability, historic preservation, air pollution, asbestos removal, accounting standards, job classification, retirement policy, health insurance, retail pricing, highway load limits, pesticides, workplace smoking, sexual harassment, grievance procedures, affirmative action, the pricing of securities, and the design of pension plans, among other matters.

Nevertheless, the principal trends in work were only indirectly related to government actions. Whether flagging productivity growth and the consequent stagnation of real wages can be fairly attributed to the economic policies of the federal government is a highly debatable question,[5] and it is even more debatable whether the expansion of the federal presence in business and industry had a major effect on macroeconomic trends. Likewise, it is doubtful that either the great migration of women into the labor force or the enormous shift from blue-collar to white-collar work that occurred after 1960 were attributable to government actions or policies.

The effect of government on trends in leisure was not very significant during this period, except perhaps that the way in which television broadcasting was regulated by the Federal Communications Commission permitted the expansion of television advertising which was in turn responsible for the heavy monetarization of sports events like professional baseball, football, and basketball; collegiate football and basketball; professional golf and tennis; certain automobile and horse races; and the winter and summer Olympics. Network competition for the more popular spectacles generated enormous revenues* and made the business aspect of these sports as interesting to the public as the contests themselves.

The effects of trends in work on the other institutional sectors are much more difficult to discern. The increased involvement of women in the labor force had a relatively minor effect on the division of household labor and child care.[6] The increased proportion of white-collar workers in the labor force did not have much apparent influence on life-styles as blue-collar workers also took on a middle-class coloration. The flagging growth of productivity and real wages after 1970 did not check the long-term rise in living standards: consumers were more likely to consume their savings and go into debt than to curtail their expenditures, and the entry of wives into the labor force kept family income rising as real wages stagnated. But economic malfunctions did create new problems like those of homeless families and exacerbated old ones like the vulnerability of the family farm.

The effects of trends in work on trends in religion and leisure during this period were relatively insignificant.

The shift of a large part of the labor force from working with tools and materials to working with people and symbols should have had a massive impact on the educational system, since the new organization of work called for workers much more skilled in reading, writing, calculating, and reasoning. The rapidly rising educational level of the general population satisfied this demand to some extent, but the rising trends in high school completion and college enrollment upon which the rise in educational achievement depended, leveled off in the early 1970s just as the shift to white-collar work accelerated. The changes in primary and secondary curricula that the white-collar shift seemed to call for were frequently announced but somehow failed to occur. The reading and writing skills of pupils about to graduate from American elementary schools, and from American high schools, showed no significant improvement from 1971 to 1990.[7]

The influence of trends in work on trends in government must be sought at the macroeconomic level where faltering productivity

---

*In January 1990, CBS announced that advertisers would be charged $700,000 for each 30-second commercial aired during the 1992 Olympics.

and industrial competitiveness were largely responsible for the trade deficits which provided foreign nations with the capital to finance a large part of the U. S. public debt but had little to do with the growth of that debt, which resulted from the unwillingness of the government to limit its military and welfare expenditures.

The influence of trends in the family on other institutions is most marked in the case of religion. The rising incidence of premarital sexual activity, extramarital childbearing, divorce, homosexuality, and unmarried unions, forced the mainline denominations to choose between abandoning some of their traditional positions on sexual and family norms, or losing many of their communicants. They generally chose to keep the communicants.

The rise of Evangelical denominations was in part a reaction against this liberalization. Those who called themselves the moral majority, but were in fact a sizeable minority, chose to uphold traditional norms of monogamous marriage, sexual abstinence outside of marriage, and paternal and parental authority, as well as the absolute prohibition of homosexuality and abortion. They were ambivalent, however, about divorce.

The trend towards single-parent families helped to demoralize those parts of the educational system with a high concentration of pupils from such homes. Many of these children, being poor, undisciplined, and culturally deprived, made it hard for schools in which they predominated to function normally. Many schools gave up the effort to educate and limited themselves to custodial functions, indifferently performed.

The principal influence of the family on work after 1960 was the massive entry of married women into the labor force, followed by a considerable movement of women into occupations and jobs formerly reserved to men. The extent of this movement should not be exaggerated. Most of the married women who entered the labor force became office workers, machine operators, sales clerks, waitresses, schoolteachers. Only a few became airline pilots, police officers, stockbrokers, or corporate executives. But, in principle, nearly all occupations were open to women, and, in practice, a determined woman could pursue a career in almost any field, although not necessarily on equal terms with men.

Trends in the family had little apparent effect on trends in leisure during this period.

The influence of family trends on trends in government was somewhat less than expected. The greatly increased numbers of working mothers, single-parent families, children in poverty, and homeless families, seemed to call for government action. Most of the platform of the women's liberation movement became public policy. Women became a voting bloc with respect to women's issues and their votes were decisive.

But the response of government at all levels to the new social problems created by family trends was weak and hesitant. Having largely created the problem of single-parent families by means of the family-breaking incentives built into the welfare system and the extension of welfare eligibility to unmarried adolescent mothers, the federal and state agencies tinkered endlessly with their welfare regulations throughout the 1970s and 1980s* without making any effective changes. The average monthly number of recipients under the Aid to Dependent Children (later Aid to Families with Dependent Children) and the average monthly payments to families increased as shown in Table 12–1.

TABLE 12–1   AID TO FAMILIES WITH DEPENDENT CHILDREN (AFDC)

	AFDC Recipients (millions)	Average Monthly Family Payment
1960	3.1	$108
1970	9.7	190
1986	11.0	355

SOURCE: Based on *Statistical Abstract of the United States 1979*, Table 566; and *Social Security Bulletin Annual Statistical Supplement, 1988*, Table 9.G2.

Contrary to a popular impression, the level of support provided to children in poverty has not even kept pace with inflation, and the cost of this basic welfare program is a negligible fraction—well under 2 percent—of federal outlays. The relatively new problem of homeless families with young children has yet to be seriously addressed.

Trends in primary and secondary education had little apparent effect on trends in the family during this period, but the escalating cost of higher education created real—sometimes severe—hardships for middle-income families. The absence of any improvement in educational effectiveness was often blamed for flagging produc-

---

*There were experiments with a negative income tax during the Nixon administration, and with individualized job training and placement during the Reagan years; the experiments were moderately successful but led nowhere.

tivity in the work sector, as we noted in Chapter 8. At the same time, the rising level of educational achievement in the population, and the increasing volume of extracurricular activities in the schools, contributed directly to the leisure explosion. Trends in education had little or no effect on trends in religion. Although strong inverse correlations between educational level and religious practice have been observed in other countries, they cannot be found in the United States.

Trends in religion had little effect on trends in the family, in work, or in leisure during this period. They did have some effect on education as Catholic parochial schools were hard hit by the decline of the teaching orders while the private schools newly established by Evangelical denominations flourished. The growth of Evangelicalism affected government too, as the Evangelicals solidified into a right-wing political bloc which opposed abortion, welfare, flag-burning, gun control, affirmative action, and the deregulation of sexuality, and strongly supported nuclear weapons programs, the death penalty, school prayer, and the war on drugs. This so-called "moral majority" came to exert a disproportionate influence in national and state politics because of their propensity for bloc voting and their tactic of evaluating candidates by their positions on single issues.

Trends in leisure during this period had little effect on work, government, or religion. The old struggle between religion and leisure for the control of Sunday was finally settled for millions of Americans by reserving Sunday morning for church and the rest of the day for recreation. For intact families, the effects of trends in leisure were generally favorable. More and more leisure activities were restructured to permit family participation and the new instruments of electronic leisure—cable television, video recorders, audio systems, computer games—were home-centered and seemed to contribute to family solidarity. There were unmistakable increases in the amount of contact time between husbands and wives, between parents and adolescent children, and among related households.[8]

Education was also affected by trends in leisure during this period although the important effects were peripheral: the development of interscholastic and intercollegiate athletics as semicommercial activities, and the vast expansion of the extracurriculum at every level from the elementary school to the university. But it would be going beyond the available data to argue that the growth of the leisure functions of the educational system had much influence, favorable or unfavorable, on its primary function of transmitting knowledge.

NOTES

1. Friedrich Engels, "Socialism: Utopian and Scientific," in A. P. Mendel, ed., *Essential Works of Marxism* (New York: Bantam Books, 1961), 63.
2. Reinhard Bendix, "Max Weber" in *International Encyclopedia of the Social Sciences* (New York: Macmillan, 1968), vol. 16, 496.
3. Based on Bureau of the Census, *Public Employment in 1988*, Series GE-88-1, 1989, Table E.
4. For detailed descriptions of cost escalating mechanisms in federal welfare programs, see Peter J. Peterson, *On Borrowed Time: How the Growth of Entitlement Spending Threatens America's Future* (San Francisco: ICS Press, 1988); and Joseph R. Califano, Jr., *America's Health Care Revolution: Who Lives? Who Dies? Who Pays?* (New York: Random House, 1986). For an account of the federal government's institutionalized reluctance to examine consequences, see United States General Accounting Office, *Program Evaluation Issues*, November 1988.
5. For a comprehensive analysis of U. S. macroeconomic policies and their possible consequences since 1945, see Walter Russell Mead, "The United States and the World Economy," (in 2 parts), *World Policy Journal*, 6 (Winter 1988–89):2–45, and 6 (Summer 1989):385–468.
6. For a summary of the voluminous literature on this question, see Amy O'Leary, "Necessary Chores: Dual Earners' Time Spent in Housework" (Ph.D. diss., University of Virginia, 1989).
7. The "National Report Card" of the U. S. Department of Education, as announced to the press, 9 January 1990. The scores for black and hispanic pupils, however, did show some improvement.
8. See, among many other sources, T. Caplow, H. M. Bahr, and B. A. Chadwick et al. *Middletown Families: Fifty Years of Change and Continuity* (Minneapolis: University of Minnesota Press, 1982), Chapters 6, 7, and 9.

13

TRENDS IN MONEY

Prices rose continuously during the three decades after 1960 and, after 1970, the rate of inflation exceeded anything seen in this country since the last days of the Confederacy. In relation to what the consumer's 1960 dollar would buy in the basket of commodities measured by the Consumer Price Index (food, beverages, housing, clothing, transportation, medical care, personal care, and entertainment) the 1970 dollar was worth 85 cents, the 1980 dollar was worth only 38 cents, and the 1990 dollar was down to about 26 cents.[1] To put it another way, inflation from 1960 to 1989 came to 285 percent.

Per capita personal income rose from $2,201 in 1960 to $4,051 in 1970 to $9,919 in 1980 to about $17,500 in 1989, far exceeding inflation in the 1960s, barely keeping up with it in the 1970s, and gaining a little ground in the 1980s. The increase for the entire period was 695 percent.[2] This was more than twice the rate of inflation so that, in real terms, most ordinary commodities now cost the consumer less than half of what they cost in 1960.

These large percentages pale next to the increase in the money supply. The total money supply, including currency, travelers' checks, bank deposits, money market funds, short-term Treasury obligations, and commercial paper, leaped from $319 billion in 1960 to $4.8 trillion in 1989, an increase of more than 1,400 percent.[3] The country was awash in dollars[4] and they circulated with unprecedented velocity. Much of the new money was created by borrowing as government, corporate, and consumer debt rose to previously unknown levels. Much of it was attributable to the superinflation of tangible assets like real estate, precious metals, and objects of art. Some was generated by financial manipulation, black markets, the savings and loan bubble, and the expansion of world trade. These categories overlap, of course.

Ordinary inflation, which ranged from about 100 percent for telephone service to about 500 percent for fuel oil from 1960 to 1989 was driven by such factors as public and private borrowing, the abrupt rise in the cost of energy accomplished by the OPEC cartel in 1973, the importation of more goods than were exported, and the willingness of American families to spend more than they earned.

Superinflation, which ranged from about 1,000 percent for grand pianos and college tuition to more than 20,000 percent for Old Master drawings and the largest malpractice awards, appeared during this period in third-party payment plans, in the markets for several kinds of scarce goods, and as a consequence of litigation, speculation, and other money games. Considerable superinflation occurred throughout the industrialized world, but the superinflation attributable to third-party payments, litigation, and defense contracting was more conspicuous in the United States than anywhere else.

Unlike other modern welfare states, the U. S. government elected to subsidize health care, higher education, and housing, not by operating these services and making them available at low cost, or by reimbursing consumers, but by third-party payments to providers—physicians, hospitals, colleges, real-estate developers, landlords—at prices set by the providers. The providers responded rationally by continually raising their prices. In health care, this escalatory mechanism was reinforced by a vast system of third-party payments by private insurers. By 1990, a successful cardiac surgeon could earn more than a million dollars a year in fees and a single week's dosage of an exotic prescription drug for a single patient might cost more than $1,000, while in the humdrum backstretch of health care, a three-minute interview with a physician might be billed at $40 and an overnight hospital stay at $1,500.

Among the numerous markets for scarce goods, the real estate market is the largest and most important. Realtors like to remind their customers that "land is a good investment because they aren't making any more." In some rural areas near metropolitan cities, the price per acre of undeveloped land jumped from under $200 in 1960 to more than $15,000 in 1990. In coastal and mountain resort areas, the increases were much steeper. The price of the average one-family house rose from about $10,000 in 1960 to about $125,000 in 1989, but in some places, like Washington, New York, Boston, and San Francisco, prices were two to four times higher than average. One effect of the real estate boom was a massive transfer of wealth to the age cohort over 55, who had acquired their homes at low prices, and from the cohort under 35, whose rent or house payments often took half their incomes.

The most extreme rates of superinflation occurred in the markets for "collectibles"—a variegated category that includes art of museum quality, antique furniture, stamps and coins, gems, guns, fine musical instruments, classic automobiles, prize cattle, and racehorses. In each of these markets, the pressure of demand on a limited supply rose steadily as hordes of new millionaires, domestic and foreign, rushed to acquire the visible symbols of affluence. In these categories, prices commonly doubled or tripled from one auction to the next.

The upward price trend for collectible items was powerfully reinforced by a feature of the U. S. tax system which, until 1986, permitted the owner of a valuable object who donated it to a museum or other charitable institution, to deduct its appraised market value from his income. (The tax revisions of 1986 and subsequent years curtailed this privilege for some, but not all, taxpayers.) The recipient institution was allowed to sell donated objects after a short holding period; many art objects reentered the market and, when the price had appreciated further, were used again in the same way. Since the collectors, appraisers, and curators involved in these transactions all stood to gain from continuously rising prices, it was not surprising that prices continued to rise, sometimes by huge increments. In one famous episode, the director of the Metropolitan Museum of Art in New York paid $1 million for a Greek vase when the previous record price for vases had been $50,000. The appraisable value of hundreds of Greek vases in private and public collections instantly jumped to the new level, providing a stronger incentive for collectors to donate their Greek vases to museums and for curators to "de-acquisition" them a little later.

Another large market for scarce goods was artificially generated by defense procurement practices, which granted monopolies to major contractors and allowed them to attach very imaginative prices to the components and spare parts of complex weapons. It is routine for the government to be charged hundreds or thousands of dollars each for humble items like toilet seats, hammers, and coffee pots, while the prices of highly technical items reach such fantastic levels that a single plane has been priced at $850 million.

Gambling was another important source of superinflation. As of 1960, two types of gambling were available to Americans. Speculation in stocks, bonds, and commodities was legal and reputable. Lotteries, games of chance, and betting on sports events, were, with minor exceptions, illegal and disreputable. The exceptions were in

the state of Nevada, where games of chance were licensed and encouraged; the game of bingo, tolerated in many places because of
church or charitable sponsorship; and pari-mutuel betting at a small
number of race tracks. Off-track betting and betting on other sports
was available everywhere through local bookmakers, but was illegal
everywhere. An illegal lottery called "The Numbers" had a huge following among the poor in metropolitan cities and was the leading
income source for organized crime.

Between 1960 and 1990, every type of gambling was expanded
and diversified, and most of the disreputable kinds were legalized. In
every case, the prizes or possible gains were superinflated. In the
financial markets, the average daily volume of trading on stock and
commodity exchanges rose steadily throughout this period, but the
increase of trading in stocks and commodities was overshadowed by
the explosive growth of the bond, options, and futures markets and
the invention of a wide assortment of new financial instruments:
stock index options and futures, currency options and futures, real
estate trusts, mortgage pools, zero-coupon bonds, junk bonds, and
many others. Futures markets were created for commodities not
previously traded, and commodity indexes and options were added
to widen the opportunities for speculation. The same period saw the
growth of foreign financial markets, especially the Tokyo market,
which became the largest in the world. The development of international computer links made it convenient for Americans to speculate
in foreign markets without leaving home.

The expansion of lower-status gambling kept pace. By 1990, almost half of the states were operating public lotteries, offering prizes
as high as $50 million. Pari-mutuel betting was legal wherever horses
were raced commercially. Reno and Las Vegas had lost their monopoly of legal casinos; New Jersey, Florida, and several other states were
in active competition. Illegal bookmakers were still taking bets on
sports events but the great volume of gambling money now flowed
through legal channels.

There were many other money games that contributed to superinflation during this period. Revenues and costs were superinflated in
the major professional sports and, to a lesser extent, in intercollegiate
sports. The flood of money generated by television advertising permitted million-dollar player salaries and hundred-million-dollar
franchise prices. But that was trivial compared to the superinflation
induced by the corporate mergers and acquisitions frenzy of the
mid-1980s, which created more large personal fortunes than any

previous period of American business history while greatly swelling the volume of corporate debt. The insider trading that accompanied these maneuvers was spectacular. Michael Milken, the most prominent of the merger and acquisition experts, drew a personal income of more than $500 million from the brokerage firm of Drexel Burnham Lambert in the single year of 1987.

Litigation became a money machine too. As the number of lawsuits grew, damage awards climbed into unexplored territory. In a New York malpractice case, a jury awarded $8 million for an infant death blamed on medical negligence. In a Texas suit for breach of contract, damages of $11 billion were assessed against an out-of-state corporation. Hundreds of millions of dollars were awarded to claimants in class action suits against companies like Johns-Manville, and A. H. Robins, which had manufactured unsafe products. Even libel awards climbed into the millions: in May 1990, a Pennsylvania jury awarded a former public official $34 million in libel damages against a newspaper that had accused him of nepotism. The costs of litigation escalated correspondingly: legal fees of $10 or $15 million in a single case became commonplace.

The flood of new millionaires made ostentation a spectator sport. The costliest production car available in 1960 was a Rolls-Royce at $14,000. A new sports car announced for 1990, with a top speed of over 200 miles an hour, was priced at $560,000. For many brand name luxury goods, like Vuitton bags and Rolex watches, an exorbitant price was the principal selling point; they were used to display one's affluence to strangers.

At higher levels of ostentation, it became possible to rent a New York apartment at $50,000 per month, and to buy a yacht for $25 million. Nothing, in this era, succeeded like excess.

Racketeering of the conventional kind declined sharply after 1960, partly because it was brought under federal jurisdiction and vigorously prosecuted, but also because the legalization of gambling removed the crime syndicates' main source of income. The conventional rackets—protection, extortion, the numbers game, controlled prostitution— were largely, but not entirely, replaced by the lucrative activities associated with the illegal drug trade that provided American consumers with the staples of marijuana, heroin, and cocaine, as well as faddish products like LSD, mescaline, and angel dust, and illegal versions of tranquilizers, steroids, and amphetamines. As increasingly stringent enforcement ratcheted up the prices of these commodities, the profits became huge, and nearly everyone involved in the trade—from street dealers to international smugglers—joined the ranks of the newly rich. The street dealers bought Rolexes and Cadillacs. The international smugglers bought ocean villas and racing stables. Street prices fell as smuggling overwhelmed enforcement. Prisons filled to the eaves. And the money kept rolling in.

The editor of a national magazine summed up the national mood that accompanied these trends:

> Although money has always occupied an exalted place in the American imagination, never in the history of the Republic has that place been raised so high as in the years of the Reagan ascendancy . . . By 1985 the new style had congealed into a tasteless opulence expressed in fur coats for Cabbage Patch dolls and advertising copy that read, "Feel gloriously rich," "Satisfy her passion with gold," "It comes in 23 colors, including envy green," . . . The media, both electronic and print, dote on the iconography of wealth. The magazines glisten with the displays of opulence, the lists of best-selling books, both trade and mass market, attest to the public obsession with the beauty and power of money—who has it, how to groom and cherish it, what to wear in its presence, why it is so beautiful, where it likes to go in the summer.[5]

All these forms of superinflation ran counter to a fundamental trend of modernization—the continuous decline of real prices (prices expressed in work-hours). Ordinary inflation conceals the tendency of real prices to fall year after year, as the purchasing power, measured in goods, of the average hourly wage, measured in money, grows without apparent limit. Fourastié and Bazil[6] have documented the steady decline of real prices in France since the beginning of the eighteenth century, with particular attention to recent years (up to 1983). Ordinary inflation masks this tendency, so that most people are unaware of the perpetual downward movement of the real prices of nearly all goods and services under the impulse of technical progress. The only "normal" exceptions are goods and services whose supply is not increased by technical progress, and those whose prices are arbitrarily set by the state or by a monopoly. We have no comparable study of U. S. prices, but even a superficial sampling of the prices of ordinary goods and services shows the same long-term downward trend.

The real prices of most of the everyday items of consumption that enter into the consumer price index declined in the usual way in the United States between 1960 and 1990. But there were an unusual number of exceptions, and some of them—like medical care and utility charges—were important components of the average family budget. There seem to have been many more instances of real prices actually rising in the United States during this period than in the previous 30 years, or in the 30 years before that. Middle-income families confronted a particularly formidable set of rising real prices for suburban real estate, college tuition, liability and property insurance, fuel oil, health care, household and automobile maintenance, and vacation travel—items that bulked large in middle-income budgets. Lower down the income scale, some families in high-rent areas could find no affordable housing at all and became homeless, sleeping in cars or public shelters.

The ebullience of money in high places had no measurable effect on the overall pattern of income inequality, which remained astonishingly stable through good times and bad, as Table 13–1 shows.

TABLE 13–1   INEQUALITY OF U.S. FAMILY INCOMES, 1949–1984

	Percentage of Total Family Income Going to:				
	First Quintile (poorest)	**Second Quintile**	**Third Quintile**	**Fourth Quintile**	**Fifth Quintile (richest)**
1949	5%	12%	17%	24%	43%
1969	6	12	18	24	41
1984	5	11	17	24	43

SOURCE: Based on Frank Levy, *Dollars and Dreams* (New York, Russell Sage Foundation, 1987), 14.

As of this writing, national statistics on income distribution are not yet available for the years after 1984. The extraordinary stability shown in the above table may have been jarred by the tax reforms of 1981 and 1986, which made federal income taxes much less progressive, and by the Social Security reform of 1983, which set steeply rising rates for the regressive Social Security payroll tax. In 1990, according to one careful calculation, an investment banker earning $200,000 a year would pay $280 in federal taxes on $1,000 of additional income; an automobile mechanic earning $27,000 would be taxed $357 on the same amount of additional income, and a plumbing contractor earning $86,000 would pay $483. The 1986 tax law contained the strange feature called the "bubble," whereby the marginal tax is 33 percent for an income of $90,000 but only 28 percent for an income of $190,000.[7] It is hard to explain why these inequities have been so feebly protested.

The extraordinary long-term stability of the overall income distribution conceals the enormous variation of income by family composition, as shown by the following estimates of 1984 average income for four types of families:[8]

Husband–wife families, age 45–54, both working	$42,100
Husband–wife families, age 25–34, only husband working	23,450
Families headed by woman under age 26	5,200
Husband–wife families, over age 64	18,600

Ethnicity too has a major influence on family income. 22 percent of white families had incomes over $50,000 in 1986, compared to 9 percent of black families and 10 percent of hispanic families. At the lower end of the scale, 30 percent of black families and 23 percent of hispanic families had incomes under $10,000, compared to 10 percent of white families.[9] The overall ratio of black to white average family incomes rose appreciably from 1960 to 1973, and declined slightly thereafter to the present level of about .55.

The proportion of the population in poverty has fluctuated much more than income shares, partly because of periodic changes in the official definition of poverty. The proportion of the population below the poverty line declined sharply from 1959 to 1982, remained near 11 percent until 1979, and then rose again, reaching 15 percent in 1983, with much higher percentages, 32 percent and 26 percent respectively, for blacks and hispanics.[10] There was a very slight decline in poverty between 1983 and 1987.[11]

While the influence of ethnicity on poverty was relatively constant during this period, the influence of age increased, largely due to the workings of federal entitlements which, as we noted in Chapter 12, are generous for old people and niggardly for children. Peterson and Howe calculate that federal benefit outlays in 1986 averaged $9,137 for persons over 64 and $811 for persons under 18.[12]

As a result of this discriminatory treatment, which resulted from indexing retirement pensions to the cost of living after 1972, and failing to index the welfare programs affecting children and adolescents, the proportion of American children living in poverty increased from 14 percent in 1973 to 20 percent in 1987 (43 percent of black children), while the proportion of old people living in poverty declined from 25 percent to 12 percent during approximately the same interval.[13]

The distribution of wealth is much more unequal than the distribution of income. Whereas the richest 20 percent of the population receive about 43 percent of total income, the richest 1/2 percent probably own more than 50 percent of all financial investments.[14] It seems almost certain that inequality in the distribution of American wealth increased sharply in the 1980s, when the marginal tax rate on very high incomes was reduced from 70 percent to 28 percent, estate tax exemptions were raised sharply, and windfalls of all kinds proliferated. But it is quite impossible to get accurate measures. Most of the wealth of the truly rich is composed of financial assets, and no one knows precisely how these are distributed. The surveys are few and far between, the truly rich are not numerous enough to be captured in survey samples, and both the rich and the poor are secretive about their assets.[15] The usual method of estimating assets is to analyze estate tax returns but that method does not take account of the innumerable devices that wealthy people use to avoid inheritance taxes, and it covers only that small fraction (fewer than 5 percent) of estates for which tax returns are filed. Nevertheless, we know enough to see that the differences are truly spectacular—from a small number of individuals and households whose assets are measured in billions to a great multitude whose net worth is negative, since they owe more than they own.

Age, family composition, and ethnicity have powerful effects on the distribution of wealth as does education and—in a somewhat circular way—home ownership. In 1984, the latest year for which this information is available, households with heads over age 60 had a median net worth of $60,266 while the median net worth of households with heads under age 35 was only $5,754—a startling difference. With age disregarded, white households had a median net worth of $39,135. The corresponding figures for black and hispanic households were pitiful: $3,397 and $4,913 respectively. Households headed by a married couple had a median net worth of $50,156 contrasted with $9,883 for those headed by an unmarried woman. The median net worth of households headed by college graduates was twice as high as that of households headed by high school graduates, and the median net worth of homeowners, taken as a group, was 33 times as high as that of renters![16] Because equity in a home is the only large asset held by the majority of U. S. households, the trend of home ownership is one of the best available indicators of economic well-being. Following a sharp rise after World War II, home ownership rose only slightly from 62 percent in 1960 to 64 percent in 1980; since then it has declined slightly.[17] But the superinflation of real estate prices during the 1980s created substantial wealth for homeowners already in possession.

Has the gap between rich and poor been increasing, as is often alleged? The question is not easy to answer. At the upper end of the money scale, there are many more millionaires but their money buys less advantage than ever before.* Very few of the new millionaires have full-time servants or stately mansions. Nearly all luxury goods and services are conspicuously superinflated and many high-income families cannot afford the conventional appurtenances of wealth.

At the lower end of the scale, most of the elderly poor were rescued from poverty in recent years by increasingly generous Social Security checks, but their places have been taken by the new underclass of unmarried—mostly black and hispanic—mothers and their children. The differences between poor farmers and rich farmers widened but most of the poor farmers found other jobs. There were local economic crises in many parts of the country as industries like steel, rubber, oil, automobiles, and textiles painfully adjusted to foreign competition. Unemployment soared in the late 1970s and early 1980s, but very few workers became permanently unemployed. Rates of social mobility did not change very much, but social class differences in household equipment, clothing, speech habits, leisure patterns, religious practices, education, and health care continued to diminish.

In comparison with other industrialized countries, the trends at the top of the money scale were not extraordinary. West Germany and Japan had relatively more new millionaires. Conspicuous consumption was no less conspicuous in France.

But great differences developed at the bottom. Between 1960 and 1990, poverty was virtually eliminated in the other leading industrial countries, even among "guest workers" and recent immigrants, while in this country, after some improvement in the 1950s, the incidence of poverty increased, and the economic hardships of some groups—migrant farm workers, the mentally retarded, homeless families, welfare families, urban Indians—became visibly more severe. The United States was unique among modern welfare states in being unable—as of 1990—to provide minimally adequate health care, housing, education, and police protection for its poorest citizens.

---

*In the late 1980s, real estate agents in New York and Washington used the term "millionaire" to refer to somebody with an annual *income* of at least $1 million.

NOTES

1. Based on *SAUS89*, Table 748, extrapolated to 1990.

2. Based on *SAUS79*, Table 730; and *SAUS89*, Table 701.

3. Based on *SAUS79*, Table 882; and *SAUS89*, Table 821. The 1960 and 1989 measures are not exactly comparable, but the order of magnitude is correct.

4. The world too was awash in dollars, but the complicated story of international monetary relationships is not considered here. In 1986, more than $330 billion dollars were traded in foreign exchange markets daily, according to C. Michael Abo and Marc Levinson, *After Reagan: Confronting the Changed World Economy* (New York: Council on Foreign Relations, 1988). That essay provides one of the best available accounts of how the dollar's relationship to other currencies changed between 1960 and 1988. See also Evan Luard, *The Management of the World Economy* (New York: Macmillan, 1983).

5. Lewis H. Lapham, *Money and Class in America: Notes and Observations on Our Civil Religion* (New York: Weidenfeld and Nicolson, 1988), 39–40.

6. Jean Fourastié and Beatrice Bazil, *Pourquoi les prix baissent?* (Paris: Hachette, 1984). The underlying theory was set forth by Fourastié much earlier in *The Causes of Wealth*, trans. and ed. by T. Caplow (Glencoe, IL: Free Press, 1960).

7. Paul Taylor, "Tax Policy as Political Battleground," *Washington Post*, 18 February 1990, A1–A13.

8. Lapham.

9. Based on *SAUS88*, p. 427.

10. Quoted in Robert X. Browning, "Priorities, Programs, and Presidents; Assessing Patterns of Growth in U. S. Social Welfare Programs," in S. H. Danziger and K. E. Portney, eds., *The Distributional Aspects of Public Policy* (New York: St. Martin's Press, 1988), 15.

11. Based on *SAUS89*, Table 734.

12. Peter G. Peterson and Neil Howe, *On Borrowed Time: How the Growth in Entitlement Spending Threatens America's Future* (San Francisco: ICS Press, 1988), 156, Figure 4–2.

13. Based on *SAUS89*, Tables 737 and 738.

14. Lars Osberg, *Economic Inequality in the United States* (Armonk, NY: M. E. Sharpe, 1984).

15. For a fuller discussion of the problem, see Eugene P. Erickson, "Estimating the Concentration of Wealth in America," *Public Opinion*, 52 (1988): 243–53.

16. Based on *SAUS89*, Table 747.

17. Based on *SAUS89*, Table 1243.

14

TRENDS IN SEX

The 30 years after 1960 saw extraordinary changes in the erotic attitudes and practices of Americans and in the laws and mores concerning these matters.

The introduction of nearly infallible oral contraceptives around 1960 and the legalization of abortion in 1973 made childbearing elective for women and thereby transformed the relationship between lovers. Previously, even a brief affair was potentially dangerous for both parties. The woman might find herself pregnant; the man might incur unwanted obligations. Being risky, sexual relationships were treated seriously by most people. Women who took them casually were despised. Men who did so were feared. All this changed when childbearing became elective.

One of the things that happened in apparent response to this new condition was the deregulation of voluntary sexual relations between consenting adults, which was discussed in Chapter 6. The right to privacy discovered by the Supreme Court in 1964 was promptly used by lower courts to nullify the statutes that prohibited oral sex and other bedroom exercises, and to decriminalize fornication, seduction, cohabitation, and adultery. State legislatures followed suit and, although a few such laws still remain on the books, no attempt is made to enforce them.[1] An even more important development, from a practical standpoint, was the repeal or nullification of laws that permitted civil suits for adultery, seduction, and alienation of affections and the introduction of no-fault divorce, beginning with the 1966 New York statute that permitted divorce by mutual consent after a separation. Within two decades, no-fault divorce became available throughout the United States, and the courts ceased to discriminate between innocent and guilty (adulterous) spouses in awarding custody, setting alimony, and dividing marital property. "Marital fidelity," writes Carrier, "is no longer of great interest to the law, either in adjudicating divorce or otherwise."[2]

The informal suppression of nonmarital sexual activity by private moralists melted away as the legal structure changed. Cohabitation became almost as respectable as marriage. By 1985, an unmarried couple could rent an apartment or buy a house almost anywhere in the U. S. on the same terms as a married couple and were not likely to be shunned by anybody. Their children would not encounter any particular disadvantage; bastardy was no longer penalized either by law or by public opinion.

The laws that prohibited homosexual activity were slightly more resistant to change. Gay activists were shocked in 1986 when the Supreme Court upheld a Georgia sodomy law in apparent disregard of the privacy doctrine. Nevertheless, most states had by then repealed their sodomy statutes, several states had enacted gay rights legislation, and there were no longer any serious obstacles to homosexual cohabitation. Although homosexual marriage is not legal anywhere, some official agencies have begun to treat homosexual couples like married couples, and some courts are willing to enforce cohabitation contracts involving couples of the same sex. Homosexuals are no longer subject to blackmail, ostracism, and dismissal from responsible jobs. The ranks of avowed homosexuals now include congressmen, civic leaders, bishops, professors, corporate executives,and other notables whose careers would formerly have been destroyed as soon as their sexual preferences became known.

Both as a cause and an effect of sexual deregulation, there has been a great increase in the sexual activity of unmarried women, a smaller but appreciable increase in the sexual activity of unmarried men, and a reduction in the average age of sexual initiation. These trends began earlier, but accelerated after 1960, as Table 14–1 suggests.

TABLE 14–1   **PREMARITAL SEXUAL EXPERIENCE AMONG TEENAGE WOMEN**

Women Reaching Age 18 in	Proportion Having Had Premarital Intercourse
1956–58	23%
1962–64	23
1971–73	43
1980–82	54

SOURCE: Based on Sandra L. Hofferth, John R. Kahn, and Wendy Baldwin, "Premarital Sexual Activity Among U.S. Teenage Women over the Past Three Decades," *Family Planning Perspectives*, 19 (1987): 49.

The proportion who became sexually active before they were 15 increased from 3 percent to 13 percent during the same interval. Black women reported higher rates of sexual activity at every age.

Another study charts the increase of "heavy petting" among students at a southern state university between 1965 and 1980. The proportion of women claiming to engage in that behavior increased from 34 percent to 73 percent; the proportion of men from 71 percent to 87 percent.[3] Their attitudes changed in step with their behavior. The proportion of the college women in the samples strongly agreeing that premarital sexual intercourse is immoral declined from 70 percent in 1965 to 25 percent in 1980 and the proportion of men with the same opinion from 33 percent to 17 percent.[4]

Such trends are so impressive that they are commonly exaggerated. According to the available studies, the majority of American adolescents, male and female, white and black, are virgins at 17, and a sizeable minority are still virgins at 20. But those who want sexual experience can easily find a willing partner and do not encounter much social pressure to abstain.

The style as well as the incidence of sexual activity changed after 1960. It was no longer conventional to make love in the dark or partly clothed. The "missionary position" was scorned by couples who studied and practiced the 72 modes of embrace described in the Kama Sutra. Orgies became moderately popular. Anal intercourse was added to the virtuoso repertory. Popular manuals prescribed, and readers practiced, all sorts of ingenious titillations, like covering a partner with whipped cream and licking it off. The trend is difficult to capture statistically, but we can get a sense of it from one set of figures. In the monumental Kinsey studies, published in 1948 and 1951, and describing the sexual activities of married couples in the previous decade, fewer than half of the married men in the sample and only 15 percent of those without a college education, admitted to practicing fellatio or cunnilingus with their wives. In a 1983 study by Blumstein and Schwartz, 90 percent said they practiced both.[5] Oral-genital play had become as American as apple pie.

Along with the increasing incidence and variety of sexual activity came a dramatic equalization between men and women, whereby women became more like men in their sexual behavior and attitudes. Until about 1965, studies of adolescent sexual activity invariably showed many more boys than girls to be sexually experienced at any given age. But when Coles and Stokes surveyed a national sample of adolescents in the early 1980s, they found slightly more male than female virgins.[6] Similarly, a much higher proportion of husbands than of wives admitted to adulterous affairs in the earlier studies while the numbers are substantially equal in more recent ones. The double standard that held women more accountable than men for breaches of sexual norms, and regarded promiscuity as enviable in men and despicable for women, nearly disappeared between 1960 and 1990. Many women took to using in mixed company the four-letter words that had formerly been taboo to them, flaunted casual liaisons, and frequented male prostitutes without embarrassment. But these unconventional gestures were trivial compared to the great shift in attitudes towards female sexuality. Both men and women abruptly abandoned beliefs unquestioned for generations which held that most women had weaker sexual appetites than men, took little pleasure in the sexual act, and had no physical need for sexual gratification. Men and women came to be regarded by many or most Americans as equal sexual actors with the same claims to sexual independence and the same obligations to spouses and lovers.

There was also some sexual equalization during this period with respect to social class, ethnicity, and age. The sharp differences between the sexual practices of college graduates and those of high school graduates recorded by the Kinsey studies around 1950 had vanished by 1980.[7] The wide differences between blacks and whites recorded about the same time had considerably narrowed.[8] And at both ends of the age scale, below 18 and over 65, there was evidence of increasing sexual awareness and activity.

Another prominent feature of the sexual liberalization that occurred after 1960 was a vast increase in vicarious sexual activity and of erotic themes and images in books, magazines, films, plays, and advertising. Bahr remarks that:

> ... the media have been the primary source of sexual information and role models ... Thus, with the exception of the invention of the contraceptive pill, most milestones of the "sexual revolution" have been media events, including the publishing of the Kinsey reports, Supreme Court decisions which permitted the dissemination of sexually explicit material, and the application of contemporary communications technology—telephones, communications, satellites, television, video-cassette recorders, computers—to "sex businesses."[9]

The commercialization of sex took a number of forms. X-rated films became available to the general public in the 1970s after the courts had struck down obscenity statutes or made them unenforceable. In large cities the films were viewed by predominantly male, middle-aged audiences in "adult theaters" but in smaller cities and towns, they were shown at drive-ins or at special late shows, mostly to young couples. A distinction soon developed between "hard porn," which depicted exotic forms of copulation with multiple partners of both sexes and with sado-masochistic embellishments as graphically as possible, and "soft porn," which took a more romantic approach to the same material and eschewed genital closeups. The early films in this genre were technically crude but within four or five years, the production of erotic films became a major industry with its own stars and directors and high technical standards. The rapid adoption of videorecorders by U. S. households in the 1980s greatly expanded the market for erotic films[10] by making them accessible in private to millions of viewers who would not have been comfortable at a public showing of the same material: middle-aged and elderly couples, notables and officials, single women, and of course, children and adolescents.

The rise of the videorecorder spelled the end of the sex shops that sprang up all over the country in the 1970s. These retail establishments sold erotic books, magazines, souvenirs, and paraphernalia but principally offered "adult" films for viewing on the premises. They disappeared as quickly as they had appeared. Meanwhile, the limits of permissible images in conventional films and television widened steadily; from the naked female bosom in the late 1960s to frontal male nudity—at a distance—in the late 1980s. Permissible subject matters were extended even further. By 1990, network television was building dramatic episodes around bisexuality, gang rape, pedophilia, sex changes, artificial insemination, female masturbation, and other topics formerly unmentionable in public. Along with these video developments came an odd little audio industry that sold erotic recordings—with much panting and moaning—to millions of telephone subscribers.

Parallel changes occurred in the print media, where classic eighteenth-century works like *Justine* and *Memoirs of a Woman of Pleasure*,* which had been accessible to Americans only at certain Parisian bookstores and in the locked collections of research libraries, were dusted off and reissued as paperbacks after a 1966 Supreme Court decision effectively nullified all obscenity laws. Hundreds of contemporary works were hastily written for the same

---

*It was the Supreme Court's decision to vacate a ban on this particular work that opened the floodgates.

market. As with film, two categories of pornographic literature—hard and soft—promptly developed, and at the same time, the taboos on sexual (and scatological) language and the depiction of sexual encounters were greatly relaxed in conventional fiction.

A content analysis of best-selling novels from 1959 to 1979 by Abrahamson and Mechanic showed a steady increase in sexual content and ingeniously discovered a decrease in the length of time that characters were acquainted before going to bed together. Another study showed an increase in the sexual content of mass-circulation magazines from 1950 to 1980, as well as a shift from conservative to liberal attitudes on sexual matters.[11]

But the most conspicuous pornographic vehicles in the print media were the mass-circulation sex magazines. The prototype was *Playboy*, founded in 1953 and operated for a time in conjunction with a chain of night clubs. Its circulation rose from under 1 million in 1960 to a peak of 6 million in 1974, the highest circulation of any American publication. By then it encountered competition from *Hustler*, *Penthouse*, and more than 100 other magazines that featured glossy full-color photographs of female nakedness in fine pubic detail, uninhibited articles on sexual topics, and cartoons and advertisements to match. The young woman chosen each month for the *Playboy* centerfold became an instant celebrity. Both boys and girls in Middletown high schools in 1978 listed the three leading sex magazines among those they regularly read. *Playgirl* and some of its imitators, designed symmetrically for female readers, also achieved mass circulation, although at a much lower level; women readers seemed to prefer the pornography designed for men. The aggregate circulation of sex magazines remains very high today, despite their repetitive content and the greater impact of videotapes.

The mass marketing of erotic fantasies in the U. S. after 1960 was a phenomenon unmatched in previous history. Its gigantic scale seemed to portend important consequences. In 1973, 53 percent of the respondents interviewed in the *General Social Survey* of the National Opinion Research Center agreed that pornography "leads to the breakdown of morals" and "leads people to commit rape" and both these majorities increased significantly through 1987. A staggering 95 percent of the 1987 sample agreed that there should be laws against the distribution of pornography to persons under 18.[12] The 1986 Report of the Attorney General's Commission on Pornography expressed the same opinions in more sophisticated language.[13] But there is less than meets the eye in these vigorous condemnations.

The *General Social Surveys* have also found solid majorities agreeing that pornography "provides information about sex," and "provides an outlet for bottled-up impulses."[14] It is impossible either to prove or to disprove the proposition that pornography encourages rape. There was a rather sharp rise in the number of forcible rapes reported to the police between 1965 and 1980, which roughly matched the rising volume of pornography, but that was also a time when the victims of rape were systematically encouraged to come forward, and when the penalties for rape were much reduced. Studies of violence against women in pornographic magazines and films find no upward trends and one study found much less of it in X-rated than in R-rated films.[15] Even more uncertainty attends the counterproposition that pornography provides an outlet for suppressed impulses that might otherwise burst out in violent acts.[16]

Whatever ultimate influence the recent diffusion of erotic themes and images may have on the American character, the most clearly demonstrable effect so far is the removal of sexual ignorance. At the time of the Kinsey studies, sexual ignorance was widespread among American men and women. Many of them grew up with only the haziest information about the anatomy of the opposite sex or about coitus. A large percentage of married women were totally uninformed about conception and contraception. A large percentage of married men had no useful knowledge about the sexual responses of women. Their erotic techniques were limited, and it appears that many sexually active women never experienced an orgasm.

This particular set of social problems may now be regarded as solved. American children are bombarded with sexual information of all kinds, abundantly illustrated, as soon as they learn to read. No sexual topic, however bizarre, is excluded from public discussion. The short, Anglo-Saxon terms of sexual reference that, as recently as 1960, were unprintable, unrepeatable in mixed company, and supposed to be unfamiliar to respectable women, are now admitted to print and to general conversation, although still considered obscene. The Latin terms of sexual reference that were once understood only by doctors and lawyers are now used freely by sixth graders.

The trends of sexual liberalization were so conspicuous between 1960 and 1990 as to obscure some important continuities, and some powerful countertrends. While restraints on premarital sex were abandoned, and adultery was decriminalized, extramarital sex continued to be disreputable in most circles, and divorce was an appropriate reaction to the discovery of an extramarital affair. A large majority (78 percent) of the adults interviewed in the *General Social Survey* of 1989 perceived extramarital relations as "always wrong" while only 2 percent checked "not wrong at all."[17] The level of disapproval has risen in recent years.*

While homosexuality came under official protection, public opinion remained intolerant of it. The *General Social Survey* shows a slow but unmistakable increase from 1973 to 1988 in the proportion of respondents agreeing with the statement that homosexuality is always wrong.[18] And although sexual relations between whites and blacks no longer provokes either legal sanctions or personal violence, the portrayal of interracial love-making is still taboo in the popular media, and black-white marriages continue to be exceedingly rare—about 1 in 300—in the U. S.[19]

Prostitution is another sexual pattern almost untouched by liberalization. In 1990, prostitution remains illegal in every state except Nevada and the laws are enforced by repeated arrests of streetwalkers and other lower-class female prostitutes; call girls and escort services are occasionally prosecuted and more often required to buy immunity from arrest. There are no national statistics on female prostitution, but its incidence and organization do not seem to have changed very much since 1960. Male prostitution, both homosexual and heterosexual, is much more visible than it used to be. It is very rarely prosecuted.

The most powerful countertrends to sexual liberalization involved incest, pedophilia, marital rape, and sexual harassment, each of which aroused public concern and massive government intervention between 1975 and 1990. The common element in these phenomena seems to be the lack of consent. Martha Chamallas explains the legal rationale:

> As the liberal view of sex began to permeate the law, consent of the parties simultaneously emerged as the crucial determinant of the lawfulness of sexual conduct. Because consent replaced marriage as the legitimating force in many contexts, the extent of the legal control of sexual conduct often depended on the definition given to "consent" in the particular setting.[20]

---

*In the in-depth interviews of married couples conducted as part of the Middletown III study, the idea that adultery might be excusable under some circumstances was emphatically repudiated by most respondents. No vestige of the traditional double standard whereby adultery by husbands was less culpable than adultery by wives can be detected in recent U. S. surveys.

This legal viewpoint was reinforced by a feminist agenda that called for resistance to male exploitation and new legal protections for single and divorced women.

Incest has always been severely penalized by American courts. The commonly prosecuted form of incest was between fathers and adolescent daughters; it was concentrated in certain white ethnic communities, the mother was the usual complainant, and long prison sentences were meted out.[21] Until the 1980s the prosecution of adults for sexual or quasi-sexual relations with their own preschool children were unheard of. Sigmund Freud himself had pronounced that the incidents of sexual molestation in early childhood recalled by many adults are normal fantasies. But feminist doctrine now insists that they are not. The number of prosecutions of fathers and stepfathers rose briskly in the 1980s, usually on the complaint of wives or ex-wives, and often joined to a custody battle. The popular excitement was so great that rules of due process were brushed aside. Courts routinely denied adults accused of child abuse the right to confront their child accusers, in order to protect the latter from psychological damage. And they gravely accepted the testimony of four-year-olds who had been repeatedly interrogated about events months in the past. Although some of the accusations were substantiable, the scope for error was unusually great. In one Minnesota town, a large group of parents had their children taken away and were subjected to a long and painful trial on the thinnest of accusations. Sexual blackmail became an easy option for malicious children.*

Along with the concern about incest, there was a public outcry about child abuse in day care centers. The McMartin trial in Los Angeles, in which the staff of a day care center were accused of multiple molestations of preschool children, is said to have been the longest criminal trial in American history and to have cost $15 million. The defendants were acquitted in January 1990 because the jury thought that the child witnesses had been too carefully coached. But the public continued to feel uneasy about babysitters and nursery school teachers. Since children are held to be incapable

---

*News items like the following became commonplace. "Clearwater, Florida—An 11-year-old girl who recanted testimony that she was raped by her mother's boyfriend had fabricated her story after watching a televised dramatization of a rape, lawyers said. Her testimony, given when she was nine, helped convict Ivie Cornell Norris, who spent 513 days in Pinellas County Jail and could have faced life behind bars. Her recantation freed him ... The girl's mother told the judge that the girl admitted a couple of months ago she had fabricated the story with the idea of getting Norris out of the way ..." *Washington Post*, 28 January 1990, A18.

of giving consent, any form of pedophilia is now considered criminal and is punishable under federal as well as state law.

The legal view of rape has also been changing rapidly, although rather confusingly, and the rape statutes of nearly every state have been rewritten in recent years. On the one hand, rape has become a less serious offense. Whereas sentences for adult rape were formerly on a par with those for murder, they are now about the same as for car theft. But the definition of rape has been considerably broadened and it is much easier than it used to be to show lack of consent. Victims no longer have to prove either physical coercion or physical resistance. The victim's prior chastity or lack of it is no longer admissible in evidence. In the early 1980s, many states rewrote their laws to allow married women to charge their husbands with rape, in effect repealing the blanket consent to sexual relations that had long been implied by the marital contract. Prosecutions for homosexual rape increased sharply about the same time, and precedent was further shattered in a few cases in which women were charged with raping men. Towards the end of the 1980s, there was extensive discussion of "date rape" in the media and there was a movement to further widen the definition of the offense. The number of rapes reported to the police increased from 14 per 100,000 of the population in 1967 to 36 in 1980 and then leveled off.[22]

The most innovative new regulation of sexuality was the prohibition of sexual harassment in the workplace. This new offense, unknown before 1975, was enacted into law by judicial opinions and administrative rulings which held that the sexual harassment of women workers or students violated their civil rights. The theory was ratified by the Supreme Court in the 1986 case of *Meritor Savings Bank* v. *Vinson*. Meanwhile, lower courts upheld a number of civil verdicts assessing damages against employers for maintaining workplaces in which sexual harassment occurred.

This development underscores the central importance of consent in current views of sexual relations. Various courts have ruled that sexual harassment need not involve physical contact, public embarrassment, or threatened loss of employment, although cases involving these elements are obviously stronger. At the minimum, any sexual advance towards an employee by a supervisor or colleague that is not welcomed is an act of harassment; it may be impossible to tell in advance. The presumption of harassment is stronger in the case of a supervisor than a colleague.

Beginning about 1988, the new concept was enthusiastically extended to faculty-student relationships in colleges and universities.

Sexual liaisons between faculty and students, which had been facilitated by the abandonment of *in loco parentis* obligations by academic authorities some years earlier, became highly suspect and potentially actionable. Solemn administrative directives cautioned
faculty members to be circumspect in their behavior when alone
with a student of the opposite sex. The following incident was cited
with apparent seriousness in a student magazine in 1989 to illustrate
the abuse of sexual power on campus:

> A freshman at a large midwestern university began receiving
> persistent phone calls from the female graduate student who
> was teaching his history seminar. As seemingly harmless as the
> invitations to football and basketball games appeared, the fresh-
> man felt growing pressure to accept them for fear of academic
> retaliation. Although the relationship never developed into a
> sexual one, he fears the "A+ with Distinction" he received as a
> final grade would have been jeopardized had he refused the
> teaching assistant's advances.[23]

Another kind of check to sexual liberalization was supplied by
the herpes epidemic that began in the mid-1970s and continued
through the 1980s and the AIDS epidemic that became visible in 1981
and threatened to continue indefinitely. The classic venereal diseases, syphilis and gonorrhea, were still present, of course, along
with new nuisances such as chlamydia and trichomoniasis, but being more or less curable, and concentrated among the poorest and
least educated sector of the population, they did not inhibit sexual
freedom among the affluent and educated. The inhibiting effect of
herpes was greater; that disease, although not life-threatening, was
painful, apparently incurable, and very contagious. Anyone with
multiple partners had a fair chance of contracting it. AIDS, or HIV
infection, was much worse, not only painful and incurable, but invariably fatal.* By the time it was identified in the early 1980s it had
already spread like wildfire through the homosexual communities of
New York, San Francisco, Los Angeles, Houston, Washington, and
other large cities.[24] By 1988, something like half of the gay men in
those places were infected with the HIV virus.[25] Patterns of casual
gay promiscuity that had flourished in the tolerant climate of the

---

*In the early years of the epidemic, most victims died within a few months of being
diagnosed. As better treatments were introduced, and otherwise healthy but nevertheless infected people were tested, the average term of survival after diagnosis
increased and as of this writing, although the life-expectancy of AIDS patients remains
very short, "invariably fatal" may no longer be strictly accurate.

previous two decades became untenable. And although very few cases of AIDS in the U. S. (as opposed to Africa) were attributable to heterosexual intercourse, the possibility clearly existed and the horrors of the disease were so intimidating that many formerly promiscuous men and women became wary of sex with strangers.

By 1990, there were signs that the trend of sexual liberalization was tapering off but the structural changes that had taken place in the law and the mores with respect to such matters as premarital sex, single parenthood, female sexuality, and the emphasis on consent, were unlikely to be reversed.

NOTES

1. Achsah Carrier, "A Sexual Revolution? Changing Sex Laws in the Twentieth Century," University of Virginia, Comparative Charting of Social Change Project, 1988. I am much indebted to Dr. Carrier for her careful investigation of this topic.
2. *Ibid.,* 6.
3. Ira E. Robinson and Davor Jedlicka, "Changes in Sexual Attitudes and Behavior of College Students from 1965 to 1980: A Research Note," *Journal of Marriage and the Family,* 44 (1982): 238.
4. *Ibid.,* 239.
5. Philip Blumstein and Pepper Schwartz, *American Couples: Money, Work, Sex* (New York: Morrow, 1983), 236.
6. Robert Coles and Geoffrey Stokes, *Sex and the American Teenager* (New York: Rolling Stone Press, 1985).
7. Gail Elizabeth Wyatt, Stefanie Doyle Peters, and Donald Guthrie, "Kinsey Revisited, Part I: Comparisons of the Sexual Socialization and Sexual Behavior of White Women over 33 Years," *Archives of Sexual Behavior* 17: (1988) 201–239; "Kinsey Revisited, Part II: Comparisons of the Sexual Socialization and Sexual Behavior of Black Women over 33 Years," *Archives of Sexual Behavior* 17: (1988) 289–332.
8. *Ibid.*
9. Howard M. Bahr, "Forms of Exotic Expression," a trend report for the International Research Group on the Comparative Charting of Social Change, October 1988, 4. The Bahr report has been a major source for this discussion.

10. The report of the Attorney General's Commission on Pornography, is-
    sued by the Department of Justice in July 1986, estimated that "as many
    as half of all the general video retailers in the country include within
    their offerings some material that . . . would commonly be conceded
    to be pornographic." The quotation is from p. 288. The estimate is proba-
    bly low.

11. Paul R. Abrahamson and Mindy B. Mechanic, "Sex and the Media: Three
    Decades of Best-selling Books and Major Motion Pictures," *Archives of
    Sexual Behavior*. 12 (1983): 185–206; Joseph E. Scott, "An Updated Longi-
    tudinal Content Analysis of Sex References in Mass Circulation Maga-
    zines," *Journal of Sex Research*, 23 (1987).

12. *GSS80*, Item 162; and *GSS87*, Item 220.

13. Attorney General's Commission on Pornography.

14. *Ibid.*

15. Joseph W. Slade, "Violence in the Hard-Core Pornographic Film: A His-
    torical Survey," *Journal of Communication*, 1984, 148–61; Joseph E. Scott
    and Steven J. Cuvelier, "Violence in *Playboy* Magazine: A Longitudinal
    Analysis," *Archives of Sexual Behavior*, 16(1987): 279–88; and also Bahr.

16. As eloquently argued by Alain Robbe-Grillet, "A Voluptuous Tomorrow,"
    Saturday Review, 20 May 1972, 44–46. "The moralist," he wrote, "does not
    destroy the passions he judges to be unhealthy (indeed, how could he
    manage that?) but merely imprisons them behind a wall of silence, a
    blindfold over the eyes; a system even more pernicious than that of judi-
    ciary condemnation, for it has been shown to lead to underground pro-
    liferation and uncontrollable outbursts . . . Instead of repressing his im-
    pulses to a dim unconscious that will someday oblige him to commit
    some quite material atrocity (the habitué of pornography) gradually
    learns to name them and to take pleasure in them. In a word he achieves
    a catharsis of his own violence."

17. *GSS87*, Item 218.

18. *Ibid*, Item 219.

19. *SAUS89*, Table 55.

20. Martha Chamallas, "Consent, Equality and the Legal Control of Sexual
    Conduct," *Southern California Law Review* 61(1988): 777–862.

21. A 1938 study found more than a hundred of such offenders in the Joliet
    penitentiary in Illinois at that time. See Svend Riemer, "A Research Note
    on Incest," *American Journal of Sociology*, 45(1940): 566–75.

22. Based on *SAUS89*, Table 283; and *SAUS79*, Table 291.

23. Miriam Arond, Madeline Hutchinson, and Ann O'Reilly, "Power Play:
    Sexual Politics on Campus," *CV*, April 1989, 34.

24. A superb account of the early years of the AIDS epidemic and of societal
    reactions to it is given by Randy Shilts, *And the Band Played On* (New York:
    St. Martin's Press, 1987).

25. *Report of the Presidential Commission on the Human Immunodeficiency
    Virus Epidemic*, June 1988.

15

TRENDS IN HEALTH

One good indicator of the general health of a national population is "life expectancy at birth"—a complicated measure that is often misinterpreted. For a given year, it is the median age at which the cohort of infants born in that year would die if the specific death rates for every age group recorded in that same year persisted without change throughout the lives of the cohort. It is not intended to predict the actual longevity of those babies, since the specific death rate for every age will change before they arrive at that age. Life expectancy can also be measured from any later age, from 5 or 20 or 100.

The life expectancy of a national population is always substantially increased by modernization, because of such factors as a more varied and abundant diet, improved sanitation, purified milk and water, and immunization against childhood diseases. In the United States, life expectancy at birth rose from 47 in 1900 to 70 in 1960. But, as in other countries, almost all of the improvement was due to the reduction of infant mortality—deaths in the first year of life—which declined from about 150 per 1,000 births in 1900 to 26 in 1960. The improvement in life expectancy at age 65 was very modest—from 12 years in 1900 to 14 years in 1960.[1] Between 1960 and 1985, life expectancy at birth increased at a slower rate, from 70 to 75, but most of the improvement now occurred at the elder ages. Life expectancy at age 65 increased from 14 to 17 years.[2]

Something strange happened along the way. The life expectancy advantage of women over men increased from one year in 1900 to six years in 1960 and to more than seven years in 1985.[3] No one is quite sure why. There are relatively more widows in the population now than ever before.

Meanwhile, the rest of the industrial world was catching up and passing the United States. In 1987, when this country's life expectancy at birth was just over 75, Canada, Japan, the Netherlands, Spain, Sweden, and Switzerland had passed 77; Portugal was the only country in western Europe that was clearly behind the United States, although the per capita expenditure on health care in the U.S.

($1,926 per capita in 1987) far exceeded that of any other country, in some cases by absurd margins. Greece, with a life expectancy of 77, spent $157 per capita on health care; Japan, with a life expectancy of 78, spent $702.[4] The U. S. infant mortality rate, which stood at 11 in 1988, contrasted unfavorably with France and the United Kingdom at 9, West Germany at 8, Canada at 7, and Japan at 6.[5] Although the life expectancy of blacks is about five years lower than that of whites and their infant mortality is almost twice as high, excluding blacks from the U. S. averages does not change the comparative picture; the life expectancy of the U. S. white population taken alone is significantly lower than that of Japan and most of western Europe and its infant mortality is higher. The world's most expensive and technologically advanced health care system is not fully competitive with the less expensive and less elaborate health care systems of other industrial nations.

Data from national surveys seem to confirm that the enormous growth of the health care system and of medical technology since 1960 have not been as beneficial for the general health of the population as was hoped. The proportion of respondents in national surveys who describe their own health as "excellent" decreased somewhat from 1957 to 1988 while the proportion describing their health as "fair or poor" increased slightly.[6] A more objective measure, the number of workdays lost because of illness or injury, shows no distinct trend since 1960.

Between 1960 and 1985, the childhood diseases for which effective immunization was available—diphtheria, measles, German measles, mumps, infantile paralysis, and whooping cough—virtually disappeared, while the incidence of chickenpox increased. Tuberculosis and syphilis greatly declined. Salmonella infections, and gonorrhea greatly increased. Rates of heart disease and stroke declined sharply. Cancer, diabetes, and hypertension increased. And the AIDS epidemic appeared; the number of known cases rose from none in 1980 to 15,000 in 1985 and 100,000 in 1990.[7]

The relationship between the general health of the population and the workings of the health care system is rather slippery. Medical procedures that make sick patients more comfortable do not necessarily prolong their lives, indeed may shorten them. The successful treatment of one life-threatening condition may not prevent the patient's dying of another. And medical treatment is itself hazardous. The Harvard study of hospitalization outcomes in New York State in 1984 found that 99,000 patients, 3.7 percent of the total, were injured in the course of hospital treatment during that single year.[8]

Many of the new prescription drugs, diagnostic devices, and surgical procedures introduced since 1960 carry serious risks for patients, which the most careful physician may not have enough information to assess. And high-technology medical efforts are heavily concentrated on elderly patients with multiple pathologies, who are not likely to survive very long even with intensive treatment.[9] Finally, it should be remembered that professional health care is only one of the many factors affecting the general health of a population and is seldom if ever the most important factor.[10] The most influential nonmedical factors affecting the health of American adults today seem to be obesity and cigarette smoking, both of which are significantly correlated with cardiac and pulmonary disorders, and inversely correlated with life expectancy. Despite widespread enthusiasm for exercise and dieting, the incidence of obesity remained about the same among men from 1960 to 1980 and increased among women. Cigarette smoking, which was found in the 1970s to be a much more lethal habit than had previously been supposed, increased sharply from 1960 to 1970, held level through the 1970s, and declined somewhat during the 1980s but not nearly as much as the danger seemed to call for. The average consumption of cigarettes by the nearly one-third of U. S. adults who smoked in 1987 was 1.4 packs per day.[11]

The enthusiasm for exercise was relatively new. The proportion of respondents in national samples who reported exercising daily rose from 24 percent in 1961 to 59 percent in 1984;[12] some respondents may exaggerate, but the trend is consistent with the leisure explosion described in Chapter 10. Dieting and weight reduction programs also flourished in the 1970s and 1980s. Nutritional fads and a preoccupation with body weight have been idiosyncratic features of American culture since the nineteenth century.[13] The campaign to lower blood cholesterol levels by diet almost displaced other nutritional cults in the late 1980s; it was fervently supported by the National Institutes of Health and by the American Heart Association, which advised all American adults to follow low-cholesterol diets and to have their cholesterol levels continuously monitored by physicians, although the empirical studies on which these recommendations were based did not seem to show that the risk of heart disease was much affected by a low-cholesterol diet.[14] Even before the height of the cholesterol campaign, an FDA decision to permit the advertising of health claims for food products had led to the extensive redesign of commercial foods and beverages to take advantage of nutritional fads; extraordinary claims were made on the thinnest of evidence for what were alleged to be health foods, generally low-fat, low-salt, low-sugar, or high-fiber versions of common groceries. They captured large market shares. Meanwhile, fast food chains were threatening to sue health care professionals who "libeled" the wholesomeness of burgers, fries, and shakes.

There were obvious linkages between the exercise and nutritional cults and a number of trends described elsewhere in this volume: the sexual revolution, the deferral of entry into the labor force, the greater economic independence of women, the growing number of active elderly people, and the relative affluence of the elderly compared to the young. The net effect has been to prolong the erotic behaviors and attitudes of early adulthood into later stages of the life cycle. Cosmetic plastic surgery, generally undertaken to restore a youthful appearance to aging faces, boomed in the 1980s. According to a press report, 477,000 of these operations were performed in the single year of 1984.[15]

The improvement of life expectancy at the later ages that occurred after 1960 did not signify any lengthening of the life span, that is, of the maximum age to which people can survive under favorable conditions. That remained where it had always been—a few years above the age of 100 for a tiny fraction of the population. The possibility of extending the life span by genetic engineering or other procedures has been much discussed in recent years but no discernible progress has been made so far. In the meantime, the large share of health care resources devoted to the treatment of elderly patients with degenerative conditions produces rather meager benefits. As a matter of routine, American hospitals attempt to delay the death of terminally ill patients without much regard to cost, "The single most expensive medical bill is the last week in tertiary care hospitals with a terminal illness."[16] The medical expenses of Medicare beneficiaries in the last year of life run about seven times as high as for other beneficiaries.[17]

Most of the available technology for diagnosing and treating the principal kinds of degenerative disease—cancer, heart disease and other organ failures—has been developed since 1960. The new diagnostic equipment made it possible to observe the functioning of internal organs and to measure physiological processes in great detail. The new treatments included procedures for replacing defective hearts, kidneys, livers, and pancreases; repairing eyes, ears, and brains; installing artificial joints and limbs; transferring physiological functions to external machines and using radiation, shock waves, magnetism, chemical implants, bone marrow, and genetic material for various therapeutic purposes. The necessary equipment is enormously expensive, difficult to operate, and subject to rapid obsolescence. The procedures are enormously expensive, difficult to perform, and often risky. All of these innovations were added very rapidly to a health care system already superheated by vast infusions of public money, the overbuilding and overstaffing of hospitals, the exploitative practices of insurers and manufacturers, and jagged imbalances between supply and demand. The result was a semipermanent crisis, which began to be noted around 1970, when the following was written:

> Much of U. S. medical care, particularly the everyday business of preventing and treating routine illnesses, is inferior in quality, wastefully dispensed, and inequitably financed. Medical manpower and facilities are so maldistributed that large segments of the population, especially the urban poor and those in rural areas, get virtually no care at all—even though their illnesses are most numerous and, in a medical sense, often easy to cure.
>
> Whether poor or not, most Americans are badly served by the obsolete, over-strained medical system that has grown up around them . . .[18]

The health care costs that seemed so excessive in 1970 have been dwarfed by subsequent increases. In Chapter 11, we noted the extraordinary rise of government payments for health care after 1970. The aggregate figures shown in Table 15–1 are even more impressive.

TABLE 15–1   **AGGREGATE U. S. HEALTH EXPENDITURES, 1960–1990 (billions of dollars)**

1960	$ 27
1970	75
1980	248
1990 (est.)	578

SOURCE: Based on *Statistical Abstract of the United States 1979*, Table 143; and *Statistical Abstract of the United States 1989*, Table 136. The estimate for 1990 was obtained by extrapolating the observed annual increments from 1983 to 1986 as given in the latter table.

By 1990, the cost-containment efforts of federal and state agencies, and of private insurers like Blue Cross-Blue Shield, had greatly reduced the autonomy of physicians with respect to the choice of treatment for a given condition, the decision to hospitalize a patient, the length of hospitalization, and the setting of fees. All of these professional decisions were now subject to cumbersome rules and guidelines that varied from one insurer to another, and from one locality to the next. The new rules produced mountains of inaccurate paperwork without, however, achieving any effective control of medical fees and hospital charges, which continued to rise at about three times the rate of ordinary inflation.

Cost containment was difficult for a number of reasons. Both public and private systems of health insurance in the U. S. originally allowed health care providers to set their own "usual and customary" fees, which were paid without objection by third-party agencies more closely related to providers than to patients. Under this beneficent regime, physicians became accustomed to very high earnings and hospitals to very high staffing levels which they are very reluctant to reduce. Federal programs encouraged the overbuilding of hospitals and the overutilization of medical services by the marginally ill; the resulting patterns are not easily reversed. The prescribing monopoly of physicians—more extensive in the U. S. than anywhere else—barred consumers from choosing pharmaceutical products on the basis of price and made it possible for the manufacturers of patented prescription drugs to set monopoly prices that had no visible relation to production costs.* Despite the enormous expense of promoting prescription drugs to physicians and hospitals, the ethical pharmaceutical manufacturers enjoy wider profit margins than any other American industry.

When cost containment is applied to specific procedures in the physician's office, he or she responds rationally by ordering more diagnostic tests or by undertaking more procedures. When cost containment is applied to hospitals by limiting the number of hospital days allowed for a given condition, the hospital responds by cramming more billable tests and procedures into each hospital day.

Besides the largely ineffective drive for cost containment, a number of other developments impinged upon the economic structure of the health care system in the 1970s and 1980s, notably the malpractice crisis, the growth of the physician population, the coming of the health care corporation, and a consumer movement that achieved limited success.

---

*There was a movement towards generic prescribing in the 1980s, but generic versions were only available for older drugs that had outlived their patent protection, and there were justifiable doubts about the quality of some of these.

THE MALPRACTICE CRISIS   Very few medical malpractice suits were brought in the U. S. before 1960 and they were rarely successful. Physicians customarily refused to testify against each other and it was considered unethical for nurses to testify against physicians. This began to change during the turbulent 1960s as the political solidarity of the medical profession weakened and expert witnesses became available to claimants. Nearly four times as many malpractice claims were filed between 1965 and 1970 as during the previous half-century, 16,000 in 1970 alone. By 1984, the most recent year for which there are national estimates, 74,000 malpractice claims were closed, 43 percent with compensation to the claimant. The median payment was around $18,000 but the mean payment was much higher, more than $80,000, because of a few very generous awards. Insurers reported legal defense costs of $807 million.[19]

Malpractice insurance premiums soared and malpractice concerns became obsessive in the health care community. In the 1970s, medical associations and insurance carriers sponsored a movement for tort reform that elicited legislation in nearly every state to limit the number of claims and cap the amount of awards. Many of these statutes were eventually nullified in the courts. Those that survived had the unintended effect of raising the duration and cost of litigation. The volume of claims fell off somewhat between 1975 and 1980 but the dollar value of malpractice awards increased sharply during that interval and after 1980, the number of claims climbed again for several years and then apparently declined.*

The malpractice system that has evolved in the United States during the past 30 years is, among other things, a battleground between the two leading professions of law and medicine, which are well organized, politically influential, and mutually distrustful. The conflict is increasingly overt. Many lawyers see the incompetence and carelessness of some physicians and the failure of the medical profession to police itself as the basis of the malpractice crisis. Physicians commonly ascribe malpractice litigation to the greed and chicanery of lawyers.

The burden of the current system is imposed directly on health care providers by increased insurance premiums, and indirectly on

---

*Statistics on malpractice in the U. S. are too fragmentary to trace national trends. Statewide studies carried out in recent years in North Carolina, West Virginia, and New York suggest that the burden on insurers has been systematically exaggerated.

health care consumers by increased fees, and by defensive medical practices that involve the multiplication of tests and procedures or the withdrawal of services. Malpractice insurance premiums were negligible before 1960 but increased tenfold between 1965 and 1975 and as much again between 1975 and 1990, by which time a physician practicing a high-risk specialty in a high-risk area, like an obstetrician in Dade County, Florida, might be charged as much as $200,000 a year. Whether these charges are justified by the insurers' costs is a much debated question, but they have led many physicians in high-risk specialties to retire from practice. Between 1982 and 1989, the proportion of qualified obstetricians who refused to perform normal deliveries rose from 17 percent to 28 percent; in New England, more than half abandoned the field.[20]

The Harvard study of medical injury in the hospitals of New York state in 1984 estimated that $894 million would have been enough to pay the medical expenses and compensate the lost income of the hospital patients in that sample who were killed or disabled, with or without negligence, during hospitalization. Instead, physicians and hospitals in New York paid about $1 billion that year in malpractice premiums but fewer than 1 in 60 of the injured patients received any compensation.[21]

The obsession with malpractice causes great anxiety to physicians and other health care providers and creates an atmosphere of mutual suspicion in the doctor-patient relationship. Nevertheless, it confers real benefits on both providers and consumers. The multiplication of precautionary tests and procedures to avoid malpractice liability makes it easy for providers to evade cost-containment measures.[22] And the pervasive concern about malpractice undoubtedly protects patients against careless treatment at a time when the rapid progress of medical technology has greatly increased the probability that practitioners will make use of procedures they do not fully understand.

The current malpractice system does not begin to achieve either of its stated purposes: it does not effectively deter the minority of incompetent practitioners, and it does not equitably compensate the victims of medical injury. Unlike other insurance premiums, malpractice premiums are not based on the experience of individuals, so that a physician who repeatedly injures patients is not automatically penalized. The system has no provision at all for compensating the hundreds of thousands of patients who are nonnegligently injured in the course of treatment and virtually no way of compensating those whose injuries, although attributable to negligence, are only moderately severe. The cost of preparing a malpractice suit in most states in 1989 was in the neighborhood of $30,000; since malpractice lawyers are customarily paid by contingency fees of 30 to 35 percent of the amount recovered, and the probability of success is less than 50 percent, a $100,000 injury is probably too small to be litigated. In the small fraction of cases that do qualify, outcomes are so unpredictable that the system is commonly compared to a lottery.

GROWTH OF THE PHYSICIAN POPULATION As the U. S. health care system grew throughout the first half of the twentieth century, the number of physicians barely kept pace with the growth of the population, and did not begin to match the growth of hospital facilities.

> As demand for house staff grew, competition among hospitals intensified. Between 1940 and 1950 the proportion of approved house staff positions that hospitals were unable to fill rose from 10 to 30 percent. The house staff shortage, of course, resulted directly from the decision to expand hospitals without expanding medical school enrollments. By 1967 hospitals were looking for more than 12,000 interns annually but American medical schools were graduating fewer than 7,000 students a year . . .[23]

The shortage was partly met by the importation of foreign medical graduates who, after 1960, came predominantly from underdeveloped countries—Korea, India, the Philippines, Jamaica. The restrictive admission policies of U. S. medical schools, ostensibly intended to maintain high standards of professional competence, paradoxically allowed thousands of exotic doctors trained in less demanding systems to practice in this country. The strict limitation of medical enrollment eventually yielded to public pressure, as Table 15–2 shows.

TABLE 15–2   **U.S. PHYSICIANS PER 100,000 POPULATION**

1900	157
1930	125
1950	134
1960	148
1970	166
1980	211
1990 (est.)	281

SOURCE: Based on *Statistical Abstract of the United States 1989*, Table 149; and *Historical Statistics of the United States: Colonial Times to 1970*, Series B275–290. The 1990 estimate was obtained by extrapolating the rate of growth from 1980 to 1985.

The effects of the rapid recent growth of the medical population have begun to be felt in the reappearance of doctors in small communities, the resumption of house calls here and there, and a renewed interest in family practice, now designated as a specialty. Competent applicants are again available for salaried medical positions in government, industry, and health maintenance organizations. But the escalation of medical fees has not so far been checked by this new abundance. The price-setting mechanisms of the health care system have been remarkably insensitive to supply and demand in the short run.

> The dynamics of the system in everyday life are simple to follow. Patients want the best medical services available. Providers know that the more services they give and the more complex the services are, the more they earn and the more they are likely to please their clients ... The obvious defect is the absence of any effective restraint.[24]

THE RISE OF HEALTH CARE CORPORATIONS The twin cornerstones of the American health care system in the twentieth century have been the independent practitioner and the community hospital. In the 1970s, these began to give way to corporate organizations of various kinds. Hundreds of community hospitals were absorbed into large hospital chains operated for profit; hundreds of others became part of nonprofit chains operated along business lines. Although some economies of scale were achieved, operating costs generally rose under these new managements.[25] Another new corporate form that appeared in the 1970s was the Health Maintenance Organization (HMO) which provided comprehensive health services to subscribing families for a fixed annual fee. Patterned after a small number of earlier plans developed by industrial firms for their employees, federally sponsored HMOs were proposed during the Nixon administration as an answer to escalating costs. The concept was strongly opposed by the medical lobbies and the project took off rather slowly but by 1986, there were 623 plans in operation with 26 million subscribers and enrollment was growing by more than 20 percent a year.[26] HMOs do seem to generate lower costs than the conventional combination of independent practitioners and hospitals; their personnel are salaried and fully utilized and they are able to emphasize preventive care.

Meanwhile, independent practice has increasingly come to mean group practice. Group practices vary from a simple partnerships of two or three physicians in the same specialty to sizeable organizations that offer comprehensive health care, including dentistry and physical therapy, and operate their own pharmacies. The most rapidly growing form of group practice is the walk-in clinic, which offers quick medical service at fixed prices and welcomes comparison with fast-food restaurants. Some of them are owned or franchised by chains. Another new type of corporation is the dialysis center, often owned by physicians, which performs a single expensive procedure for profit. Similar centers that provide diagnostic services have begun to appear; some of them operate out of mobile trailers.

THE CONSUMER MOVEMENT IN HEALTH CARE   The consumer movement in health care was concentrated in the single decade of the 1970s, but it had far-reaching effects on the legal framework of health care and on public attitudes. The movement had several loosely connected themes: (1) the assertion of a general right to health care; (2) the assertion of special rights for the handicapped; (3) an effort to diminish the power of physicians vis-à-vis patients; (4) a feminist protest against the dominant role of male physicians in obstetrics, gynecology and pediatrics; (5) an attempt to demedicalize birth and death; (6) an insistence on the legitimacy of alternative therapies like herbal medicine and acupuncture.

The general right to health care was sufficiently conceded so that health insurance became an obligatory fringe benefit of most permanent full-time jobs. The new rights of the handicapped—convenient access to public places and events, special vehicles and parking privileges, equal opportunity in the workplace—were widely if not perfectly implemented. The imbalance between physicians and patients was partly corrected by the new requirement of informed consent, which assigned the final responsibility for treatment decisions to patients and required physicians to give patients enough information for rational choice. The principle is more honored in the breach than the observance[27] but it does have some practical effects.

The most visible result of the feminist protest was a sharp increase in the number of women in medicine. About one third of current medical graduates are women compared to 5 percent in 1960.[28] There has also been a sharp increase in the number of nurse-midwives, a weak movement towards home births, and a somewhat more successful effort to remove the dying from hospitals to hospices. Nonmedical therapists—osteopaths, homeopaths, chiropractors, psychologists—have achieved considerable respectability and all sorts of exotic therapies can be practiced without interference provided that they do not infringe on the prescribing monopoly of physicians. The 1980s also saw a boom in medical self-care, marked by the development of a large consumer market for medical instruments like stethescopes and manometers and for diagnostic tests and equipment.[29]

The changes described above were important but they had virtually no effect on the underlying problems of runaway costs and inequitable distribution. The most commonly cited figure is that 30 million Americans* have no health insurance coverage at all,[30] but this number is misleadingly low since very few insurance plans, public or private, cover *all* health care expenses and most U. S. families are not protected against financially catastrophic illness. Millions of families, insured or not, have been priced out of the market for routine medical care; their only recourse is the hospital emergency room:

> For many poor people, squalid hospital emergency rooms have taken the place of doctors' offices, leaving emergency-room physicians with little time for genuine emergencies. Increasingly, people with mild heart attacks or gunshot wounds must compete with patients whose minor distress easily could have been treated in lower-cost clinics . . . Patients with ear infections or other easily treated maladies continually pack emergency rooms that look and smell like kennels. Facilities designed to handle about 20 patients often hold 100. Patients wait for hours or days on pallets, wrapped in hospital gowns with their possessions stuffed into plastic garbage bags. Interminable waits have become so routine that hospitals provide food services for the emergency rooms. For those who need to use bedpans, privacy is beyond hope.[31]

The problem has been exacerbated by the growth of the commercial hospital chains and the development of business-oriented group practices. These organizations are continuously concerned about reducing their unit costs and maximizing their profit margins; they are understandably reluctant to treat indigent patients, whom they refer or transfer as quickly as possible to the only available alter-

---

*The exact number has been much debated. The official estimate of the Department of Health and Human Services as of July 1989 was 31.1 million, including 6.8 million children and 12.3 million persons in poverty or near poverty. The majority of uninsured families were neither poor nor unemployed. See *Washington Post*, 1 July 1989, A5.

native—the emergency room of a publicly supported hospital. But since publicly supported hospitals have a high proportion of non-paying patients, they suffer from chronic financial pressure, and are seldom able to expand their facilities to meet increasing demand. Moreover, they suspect that any improvement of their emergency rooms would attract additional patients rather than alleviate over-crowding. The problem is likely to worsen as present trends continue.

NOTES

1. Based on National Center for Health Statistics, *Health: United States, 1985*. CPHW 86-1232, 1986; National Center for Health Statistics, *Trends and Current Status in Childhood Morality, United States 1900-1985*, PHS 89-1410, 1989; and *Historical Statistics of the United States: Colonial Times to 1970*, 1975, Series B 148. The infant mortality figure for 1900 is an estimate based on Massachusetts data.
2. Based on *Health: United States, 1985*; and *SAUS89*, Table 109.
3. *Ibid.*
4. Based on *SAUS89*, pp. 817, 818, 821.
5. Based on *SAUS89*, Table 1405.
6. Based on Richard G. Niemi, John Mueller, and Tom W. Smith, *Trends in Public Opinion: A Compendium of Survey Data* (New York: Greenwood Press, 1989), Table 15.3.
7. P. M. Golden, *Charting the Nation's Health: Trends Since 1960*, National Center for Health Statistics, August 1985. These summary figures conceal many diverse trends and tendencies. See also National Center for Health Statistics, *Health, United States, 1987*, PHS 88-1232, March 1988, and press reports for 1990 AIDS total.
8. *Washington Post*, 1 March 1990, A3.
9. Lockhart B. McGuire, "A Long Run for a Short Jump: Understanding Clinical Guidelines," Cardiology Division, (unpublished paper, University of

Virginia, 1990). The phrase in the title refers to a proposed coronary by-pass operation for a 79-year old man who had survived two myocardial infarctions, had variably compensated congestive heart failure, slowly progressing kidney failure, and a previous cerebrovascular accident.

10. For documentation of this point, see Thomas McKeown, *The Role of Medicine: Dream, Mirage, or Nemesis?* (Princeton, NJ: Princeton University Press, 1979).

11. Based on *SAUS89* Tables 190, 192, and 1290.

12. Based on *SAUS89*, Table 211.

13. Hillel Schwartz, *Never Satisfied: A Cultural History of Diets, Fantasies and Fat* (New York: The Free Press, 1986).

14. The research evidence on diet, cholesterol levels, heart disease and life expectancy is nicely summarized by Thomas J. Moore, "The Cholesterol Myth," *Atlantic Monthly*, September 1989. Similar waves of enthusiasm have swept the federal medical establishment from time to time, as described by Diana B. Dutton, *Worse than the Disease: Pitfalls of Medical Progress* (Cambridge, MA: Cambridge University Press, 1988).

15. *Newsweek*, 27 May 1985.

16. Kenneth R. Crispell and Carlos P. Gomez, "Proper Care for the Dying—A Critical Public Issue," University of Virginia Health Sciences Center, 1989.

17. Victor R. Fuchs, *The Health Economy* (Cambridge, MA: Harvard University Press, 1986), 318. This work is the best available source of information on current economic issues in the U. S. health care system.

18. *Business Week*, January 1970.

19. General Accounting Office, *Medical Malpractice: Characteristics of Claims Closed in 1984* (Washington, D.C.: Government Printing Office, 1987), Publication No. HRD-87-55.

20. Based on a table provided by the American Medical Association, *Washington Post*, 12 October 1989, A25.

21. Reported in the *Boston Globe*, 1 March 1990, 9.

22. Patricia M. Danzon, "The Effects of Malpractice Litigation on Physicians' Practice Patterns," (unpublished paper, University of Pennsylvania, June 1989).

23. Paul Starr, *The Social Transformation of American Medicine* (New York: Basic Books, 1982), 360. See also Joseph A. Califano Jr., *America's Health Care Revolution* (New York: Random House, 1988).

24. Starr, 386–87.

25. Fuchs, Part II.

26. National Center for Health Statistics, *Health United States 1987*, 4.

27. For a description of how informed consent works in practice, see Sharon Butler Wyatt, "Conflict of Responsibility: Legal Rules of Consent in Pediatric Emergencies" (Ph.D. diss., University of Virginia, 1988).

28. Based on *SAUS89*, Table 268.

29. Brad Edmondson, "The Market for Medical Self-care," *American Demographics*, 7 (1985): 25.

30. Based on a 1984 survey published in 1987. National Center for Health Statistics, *Health Care Coverage by Sociodemographic and Health Characteristics, United States 1984*, PHS 87-1590, November 1987.
31. *Washington Post*, 11 February 1990, A14.

16

TRENDS IN INTOXICATION

The effort by government to suppress the consumption of certain euphoriant drugs—especially marijuana, heroin, and cocaine—has recently repeated the Prohibition experiment (1920–1933) on a larger scale. Between 1968 and 1990, the annual federal expenditure in the "war on drugs" increased from $60 million to $7.9 billion. "All of us agree," said President Bush in a September 1989 address, "that the gravest domestic threat facing our nation today is drugs."[1] And most of us did. A national survey published the same week reported that 53 percent of the public would support sending U. S. troops to Colombia to prevent the exportation of cocaine.[2] An army of drug enforcement agents, border patrolmen, FBI agents, and police officers were already engaged in the interdiction effort. Their efforts yielded thousands of felony convictions for drug offenses in 1988, accounted for more than 40 percent of the inmates of federal prisons, and destabilized a dozen foreign governments, without appreciably reducing the availability of the forbidden substances to the American consumer.

As in the case of Prohibition, the enforcement effort is what makes the illegal drug trade so lucrative and competition among dealers so deadly. Because of the personal risk and the absence of legal protection, the drug trade is governed by violence, and the profits are large enough to support sophisticated organization and armament. The retail price of cocaine in the U. S. is about 25 times the price paid by importers; for heroin, the profit margin is even greater. The direct effects of illegal drugs seem to be less serious than the effects of enforcement. Marijuana, heroin and cocaine do not ordinarily induce violent behavior, although they may cause vehicles and machinery to be carelessly operated. The sustained use of any of these substances seems to be less hazardous to the user's health than the sustained use of alcohol or tobacco. Overdosage is a grave risk with both heroin and cocaine and addiction may interfere with job routines. But it is the enforcement effort which make drugs so expensive that users are driven to crime and prostitution to support their habits, and so degrading that they are prevented from leading normal lives. It supports a criminal underworld, overloads the criminal justice system, corrupts public officials, and demoralizes communities. Even the health effects of the enforcement effort seem to be more severe than those inherent in the drugs. Because there is no surveillance of product quality, much of the product is adulterated and toxic, and the dosage is unpredictable. Illicit drug users sharing needles in basements and alleys infect themselves with hepatitis and AIDS. So far, at least, the war on drugs, like the war on alcohol two generations ago, has been self-defeating.[3]

The mood-changing substances consumed by contemporary Americans fall into several major categories, based on symbolic rather than chemical attributes. They are (1) the sociable drugs: alcohol and tobacco; (2) the innocent drug: caffeine; (3) the major abominable drugs: marijuana, heroin, and cocaine; (4) the minor abominable drugs: hashish, methadone, LSD, mescaline, MDMA, and many others; (5) the medical mood-changers: analgesics, barbiturates, amphetamines, tranquilizers, antidepressants; and (6) consumer versions of medical mood-changers, especially barbiturates and amphetamines. These substances differ in physiological action, potency and duration, side effects, toxicity, tolerance, and addictiveness, but none of these characteristics account for their placement in one or another of the symbolic categories. The sociable drugs are more addictive and much more harmful than most of the others, but they were incorporated into the consumption habits of the general population before their dangers were fully appreciated. The consumption of sociable drugs by children is prohibited, although not criminal; adult usage remains entirely respectable. Caffeine is moderately addictive and has occasional serious side effects, but its social image is so innocuous that it is freely administered to infants. The major abominable drugs vary greatly in potency and addictiveness. They are not, on the whole, very hazardous to the health of users, but they are associated in the public mind with disreputable minorities, deviant life-styles, social disorder, and uncontrolled violence. The possession of a minute quantity of an abominable drug is often more severely punished than armed robbery. At least a third of the total effort of the U. S. criminal justice system is currently dedicated to the suppression of abominable drug use. In the abominable drug market, products rise and fall in cycles of fashion as in other luxury markets. At any given time, a rack of obsolete drugs are going out of use while new products are being advertised by the mass media under the guise of warning the public.

The mood-changing drugs prescribed by physicians for the relief of depression, anxiety, and other emotional complaints vary from mild muscle relaxants with little demonstrable effect to the powerful drugs used in the treatment of schizophrenia and the alleviation of acute pain. A large number of prescriptions for tranquilizers, antidepressants, and sedatives are written for patients with no definite illness, often at the patient's request and commonly renewable on demand. Drug use sanctioned by a prescription is by definition reputable. The consumer market for prescription mood-changing drugs covers a gamut of practices from the resale of prescribed products by patients to the illicit manufacture of prescription products for direct sale to consumers. The market is dominated by barbiturates and amphetamines, often in high dosages. Runaway prescription products are legally classified with the abominable drugs, but are viewed much less seriously by the enforcement agencies.

SOCIABLE DRUGS   The per capita consumption of alcoholic beverages increased sharply from 1960 to 1980 but declined somewhat in the 1980s, as shown in Table 16–1:

TABLE 16–1   **U. S. CONSUMPTION OF BEER, WINE, AND DISTILLED LIQUOR (gallons per capita)**

	Beer	**Wine**	**Hard Liquor**
1960	24	1	2
1970	29	2	3
1980	37	3	3
1987	34	3	2

SOURCE: Based on *Statistical Abstract of the United States 1979*, Table 1431; and *Statistical Abstract of the United States 1989*, Table 196.

The recent decrease in the consumption of beer and hard liquor has been plausibly attributed to the diminishing proportion of young adults in the population, the raising of the legal drinking age from 18 to 21, and the campaign against drunk driving. It is too soon to know whether the upward trend in alcohol use has been permanently checked. Between 1972 and 1982, the proportion of young adults of both sexes who had some experience with alcohol rose from 82 percent to 95 percent but the proportion of heavy drinkers fell slightly.[4]

Alcohol is an important element in American rituals of sociability. The great majority of American adults and a smaller majority of adolescents drink on appropriate occasions in the company of their friends and relatives. Most of them take no particular harm from it, but five to ten percent become physically addicted to alcohol with deleterious consequences for their health, their work, and their family relationships and a similar fraction of them engage in antisocial actions like drunk driving and impulsive assault. A study by the National Center for Disease Control estimates that 105,000 Americans died in 1987 from the effects of alcohol, about a third of them from drunken injuries and the remainder from alcohol-related diseases like cirrhosis of the liver.[5] A substantial proportion of drunken injuries are suffered by sober persons who get in the way of a drunk driver or of someone on a binge. The incidence of alcohol-related highway crashes has, however, declined significantly since 1970.[6]

Cigarette smoking, the principal form of tobacco consumption in the United States, has come under increasing regulatory pressure in recent years. Cigarette advertising was dropped from television and radio in 1971. Smokers began to be segregated in restaurants, hotels, and common carriers around 1983. By 1990, smoking was banned on commercial aircraft and in thousands of offices and stores. During the previous two decades, a growing mass of evidence showed tobacco to be by far the most toxic drug in common use. Lung cancer and other obstructive pulmonary diseases that are highly correlated with smoking account for more than 200,000 deaths in the U. S. each year; cardiovascular disease, also closely associated with smoking, causes nearly 1 million deaths each year.[7] The life expectancy of heavy smokers is significantly lower than that of moderate smokers and very much lower than that of non-smokers.[8] Smoking by pregnant women induces fetal disorders. The dangers of smoking have been energetically publicized by the federal health agencies. Tobacco usage has declined rather slowly in response to the pressure of adverse publicity; the 37 percent of U. S. adults who smoked cigarettes in 1970 fell to 30 percent in 1985, but there was no change in smokers' average consumption.[9] Tobacco appears to be more addictive than any other drug; there are very few occasional users. And it is closely linked to other addictions:

> Of the pack-a-day cigarette smokers [among high school seniors in 1986] 95% have used an illicit drug . . . Current marijuana use is eight times as high among pack-a-day smokers as non-smokers . . . Daily use of some illicit drug other than marijuana is 13 times as high.[10]

Despite the fearsome side effects of cigarette smoking, and the widening campaign to discourage the habit, it remains entirely legal and reputable.

THE INNOCENT DRUG   Caffeine, the active ingredient in coffee, tea, and cola drinks, is a mild and slightly addictive stimulant. Its principal side effects are headache, nervousness, and insomnia. The per capita consumption of coffee in the U. S. declined steadily from 1960 to 1990 and much of the current consumption is in decaffeinated form. The per capita consumption of tea increased slightly during the same period. The per capita consumption of cola drinks approximately doubled.[11] Except in certain religious sects, caffeine is not a social or political issue.

THE MAJOR ABOMINABLE DRUGS   The three drugs in this category have very different properties and histories. Marijuana (Indian hemp or *cannabis*) is a weed that can be grown almost anywhere; its dried leaves and flowers are smoked or eaten for euphoriant effect in many parts of the world, especially in Islamic countries where alcohol is forbidden. Although never unknown in the U. S., it was not widely used until the 1960s, when huge quantities were brought into the country by soldiers returning from Vietnam and it became symbolic of the counterculture and linked to rock music. Marijuana never acquired much of a following among people born before 1950; about two-thirds of those born between 1950 and 1965 had some experience of marijuana before the age of 25; very few of them continued with it as they grew older.[12]

Heroin is a derivative of the opium poppy that is inhaled or injected. It was introduced into the U. S. around 1900 as a nonaddictive replacement for morphine just as methadone was introduced around 1960 as a nonaddictive replacement for heroin. The mix of euphoric, analgesic and sedative effects varies somewhat among these related narcotics, but they are all highly addictive and all of them require increasing dosages with prolonged use. It is generally agreed that there were relatively more narcotics addicts in the U. S. in 1880 than in 1980; most of them were elderly whites and the habit was then entirely legal. The long sequence of federal statutes outlawing the recreational use of narcotics began with the Harrison Act of 1914; in recent years, the restrictions and penalties have become steadily more severe. Around 1960, young blacks and Puerto Ricans living in New York and Chicago were overrepresented in the addict population, but there were many white and/or rural and/or elderly users.[13] In the following decades, the volume of heroin use slowly declined and the addicted population came to be composed almost exclusively of young urban blacks and hispanics. The use of heroin by school children declined sharply, and it became customary for heroin addicts to "mature out" before reaching middle age.[14]

Cocaine was rarely seen in the United States before 1975; it was occasionally used to enhance the effect of heroin. The coca leaves from which cocaine is extracted have been chewed since time immemorial by the people of the Andean highlands. The active agent was isolated in 1860 and was long regarded as benign. Cocaine was and is used in surgery as a topical anesthetic in the nose and mouth. It induces a temporary feeling of well-being and alertness; as with alcohol, only a minority of users become addicted. Cocaine is usually prepared as a fine powder and inhaled, but a smokable form of cocaine called crack began to spread throughout the United States in 1985. The astonishing growth of the cocaine market is reflected in the amounts seized by federal drug agencies,[15] shown in Table 16–2.

TABLE 16–2   FEDERAL COCAINE SEIZURES (kilograms)

1960	3
1967	20
1980	2,000
1988	90,000

SOURCE: William Bates and Betty Crowther, *Drugs: Causes and Circumstances and Effects of Their Use* (Morristown, NJ: General Learning Press, 1973); and White House, *National Drug Control Strategy* (Washington, D.C.: Government Printing Office, 1989), 75.

The rise of cocaine has been so sudden and recent that it is difficult to obtain an accurate picture of users or usage patterns. Initially, and to some extent still, cocaine sniffing appeared to be a "yuppie" (young, upwardly mobile professional) fad. It was also widespread in certain stressful and fatiguing occupations like long distance truck-driving and filmmaking. The advent of crack opened a new and larger market among adolescents and young adults. Retail distribution in the larger metropolitan areas is largely in the hands of blacks; competition is violent—about 300 murders of drug dealers by drug dealers were reported in Washington, D.C. alone in 1989. But the majority of users are white and the traffic has spread into communities of every size. The U. S. Chamber of Commerce estimated total U. S. sales in 1989 at $110 billion; that looks implausible but there is no doubt that the market is very large and that the vast federal effort to interdict the importation of cocaine has not noticeably reduced the product's availability.

THE MINOR ABOMINABLE DRUGS   The minor abominable drugs resemble the major ones in that the possession, distribution, or use of any of them for recreational purposes can be prosecuted as a felony. They differ in having fewer users and attracting less media attention. Hashish is a Mideastern form of processed cannabis about six times as potent as ordinary marijuana. It has a small cadre of devotees. Morphine, frequently prescribed for the medical relief of pain, is the drug of choice for a sizeable population of addicted physicians and nurses. Methadone is used in drug rehabilitation programs as a supposedly nonaddictive replacement for heroin; some of it escapes into the illicit drug market. Of all the drugs in current use, the injectable form of methamphetamine called "speed" is the most likely to induce violent behavior. The synthetic hallucinogen, lysergic acid or LSD, enjoyed a great vogue among university students and other young people from 1965 to 1975, along with mescaline, psilocin, PCP, and similar products. The popularity of the hallucinogens has since declined but they have not gone completely out of style. There seem to be two types of users: generalized drug addicts for whom these drugs are part of an extensive repertory, and intellectuals who attach spiritual or aesthetic value to the experiences induced by the hallucinogens.

At any given time, there are one or more innovative products seeking a niche in the lucrative market for abominable drugs. In 1990, the leading new drug was an oriental import called shabu and marketed as "ice." It claimed to provide an effect similar to that of crack cocaine but lasting much longer. In the customary tones of shocked alarm, the mass media provided the new product with abundant free advertising, stressing its irresistible appeal, warning of its side effects, telling where to get it, how to use it, and what to pay for it.[16]

THE MEDICAL MOOD-CHANGERS   Most of the several hundred medical mood-changers that are currently prescribed were developed and introduced after 1960. The principal exceptions are morphine, which has been in the pharmacopoeia for more than a century; phenobarbitol, introduced in 1912; the amphetamines, which came into use in the 1930s; and the phenothiazine tranquilizers, which began to be administered to schizophrenic patients around 1954. The rest are more recent inventions, including scores of tranquilizers and antidepressants designed to produce emotional changes. Dependence on these products is not counted as drug abuse if they are prescribed by a physician for some medical purpose like the relief of anxiety, depression, or insomnia; but since emotional disorders exist whenever patients say they do and many prescriptions are written at the patient's request or are indefinitely renewable, there is little to prevent a patient's becoming permanently dependent on one or more of these psychotropic drugs. The amounts prescribed are staggering. In the heyday of the barbiturates around 1967, the legal sources of drugs were supplying about 17 barbiturate doses per year for every person in the United States over the age of ten. At the same time, it was estimated that 50 million Americans were regularly taking a meprobamate tranquilizer. A little later, even larger numbers were habituated to the antianxiety drugs Librium and Valium. At the beginning of 1990, physicians were writing 650,000 prescriptions every month for a new antidepressant called Prozac; patients were expected to continue with it permanently.[17]

THE CONSUMER MARKET FOR MEDICAL MOOD-CHANGERS   A large fraction of all the psychotropic drugs that are produced go directly to consumers by backdoor distribution, illegal importation, counterfeit prescriptions, theft from hospital dispensaries, the sale of samples, and so forth. Since the traffic is clandestine, it cannot be accurately measured, but the number of respondents in national surveys who say they have used medical mood-changers without a prescription is greater than the number who say they have used cocaine.[18]

To sum up the major trends of the past 30 years, the consumption of alcohol is higher today than in 1960 but has declined somewhat since 1980, especially in the form of hard liquor. The consumption of tobacco has declined steadily but almost a third of the adult population are still addicted to cigarettes. The consumption of marijuana increased dramatically from 1960 to 1975; since then it has declined. The consumption of heroin by high school and college students declined sharply; among other users, it has been relatively stable. The rapid expansion of the cocaine market that began after 1975 still continues. The consumption of the minor abominable drugs increased dramatically between 1960 and 1975; the aggregate volume shows no clear trend since 1975, although individual products rise and fall in response to changing fashions. The market for medical mood-changers seems to have followed a parallel track—a very steep rise from 1960 to 1975, followed by a trendless period with extensive shifting among products.

Spokespeople for the drug enforcement establishment currently take the position that abominable drug use has declined in response to their efforts. That claim rests principally on survey findings that the volume and incidence of marijuana smoking among high school and college students declined after 1985, and that heroin use by high school and college students has nearly disappeared. But it is conceivable that the intensification of the war on drugs has made survey respondents more reluctant to answer truthfully and the claim of declining drug use is further undermined by the apparent continued growth of the cocaine market. Cocaine is the first high-priced abominable drug to secure a mass market, marijuana being relatively cheap and heroin and the hallucinogens having relatively small clienteles. The dollar value of the cocaine now consumed in the U. S. almost certainly exceeds the combined dollar volume of all other illicit drugs. Moreover, there is reason to think that the national surveys that measure drug use understate the prevalence of cocaine because cocaine users do not respond to such surveys. Fragmentary data from other sources suggest that the increase of cocaine use outweighs the modest declines recorded for marijuana and heroin. Cocaine-related emergencies in hospital emergency rooms, which were negligible in 1980, rose to nearly 10,000 in 1984 and nearly 50,000 in 1988, but declined somewhat in 1989.[19]

The chief scientist of the Justice Department's Drug Use Forecasting program, testifying before a congressional subcommittee in March 1990, reported that 47 percent of all the criminal suspects arrested in 20 major cities in 1988 tested positive for cocaine, meaning that they had used cocaine within two or three days of being arrested.[20] More than twice as many people were sent to federal prisons for drug offenses in 1987 as in 1984, most of them for cocaine. They constituted 42 percent of all new prisoners.[21] The rising number of federal drug convictions more than doubled the federal prison population between 1980 and 1989; by the latter date, it was operating at 156 percent of capacity.[22] State prisons also were overcrowded by drug offenders; many of these jails were releasing old prisoners not yet eligible for parole to make room for the newly sentenced.

Opium is grown principally in Burma, Afghanistan, and Iran; the coca plant in Peru, Bolivia, and Colombia. Opium is converted into heroin in many countries. Nearly all coca is processed in Colombia, where relatively little is cultivated. Marijuana, which grows almost anywhere, comes into the U. S. in large quantities from Colombia, Mexico, and Jamaica. The wild marijuana that grows as a weed in this country and attracts so much enforcement effort, contributes almost nothing to the supply, but a great deal of cultivated marijuana is grown domestically. Although they neither grow nor process drugs, certain Bahamian and West Indian islands are active as shipping points. Some other countries that have relatively liberal drug laws, especially the Netherlands and Nepal, attract large numbers of American drug addicts. Still other countries—Panama, Switzerland, Canada—have sheltered the fortunes of drug dealers. In recent years, U. S. drug enforcement agents have been very active in other countries, with or without local consent.

The use of drugs to stimulate or soothe the emotions, to encourage sociability and sexuality, to evoke fantasies, to relieve fatigue and stress, to quiet the nerves and dispel depression, to ease the troubles of adolescence and the pains of menopause, to assert identity and to dilute the frustrations of everyday life, has become an integral part of the consumer culture of the advanced industrial countries. What makes the American situation distinctive is the extent and intensity of the effort to repress drug use by criminal sanctions and the resulting creation of a vast drug enforcement apparatus and of a vast criminal underworld.

It is generally acknowledged that inner-city blacks are the principal victims of this pattern. Drug dealing is far and away the best-paid occupation open to young black men without educational credentials, and drug money provides an economic base for the street gangs on which the same young men rely for emotional and physical security. But retail drug dealing is very hazardous for the participants—most of whom are eventually arrested and imprisoned—and for their neighbors, whose streets, schools, parks, playgrounds, stores, and apartment buildings become unsafe and anarchic under the influence of the drug trade.

Various theories have been put forward to explain the American preoccupation with abominable drugs, the military rhetoric that envelops it, and the indifference to experience that underlies the continued expansion of drug control programs that have invariably failed in the past.[23] The record so far suggests that interdiction measures are futile; that drug education in the schools may encourage students to experiment with drugs; that the danger and illegality of drug use is part of its attraction to young people; that drug treatment programs are only effective for a small fraction of users who voluntarily determine to quit; that most treatment facilities are not utilized to capacity; that addicts are seldom reformed by imprisonment; that prosecution is not an effective deterrent as long as drug dealing offers greater economic rewards than any alternative career. The official response to these dilemmas, strongly supported by public opinion, has been to double and redouble the interdiction effort, make drug education compulsory, establish more treatment facilities, increase the penalties for drug law violations, stage more raids, prosecute more zealously, and build more prisons. In recent years, the armed forces have been brought into the picture to aid in interdiction and to conduct search and destroy missions against marijuana and coca fields in Latin American countries. A proposed naval blockade of the Colombian coast to intercept drug shipments was reluctantly abandoned when that country protested. Police forces all over the U. S. are procuring military weapons for use in the drug wars. Obligatory drug-testing programs are spreading throughout industry and government. The confiscation of drug assets by enforcement agencies has become a major industry, without much oversight or due process. In the five years between 1980 and 1985, the most recent date for which the information is available, the volume of full-time employment in the U. S. criminal justice system increased by half, largely to cope with increased antidrug activity.[24] There are now hundreds of thousands of public employees whose careers depend to some extent on the continuation of the drug problem as presently defined. It is easy to understand why the suggestion that drug usage might be decriminalized is roundly denounced by drug enforcement professionals.[25]

The usual argument against decriminalization is that it would greatly increase the consumption of abominable drugs. There is no scientific way of assessing that prediction. It is conceivable that the removal of the financial incentives for drug dealing and of the thrill of illegality, would eventually diminish drug use but that is by no means certain. Even if the current demand for drugs is largely attributable to drug enforcement, as some experts believe, it does not follow that the abatement of drug enforcement would restore the status quo ante. In the near term, it is likely that the war on drugs will continue to escalate, that effective control of the market for abominable drugs will not be achieved, and that the social costs of both drug use and drug enforcement will continue to mount.

NOTES

1. Quoted in "Talk of the Town," *The New Yorker*, 18 September 1989; a nearly identical statement had been made by President Nixon in 1968. The federal expenditure for 1968 was found in a press release of the National Center for Marijuana and Drug Abuse; the FY 1990 figure is taken from the White House, *National Drug Control Strategy* (Washington, D.C.: Government Printing Office, 1989), Appendix B.

2. "Hitting the Drug Lords," *Newsweek*, 4 September 1989, 19.

3. The factual basis for this assessment was nicely summarized by Ethan A. Nadelmann, "Drugs: The Case for Legalization," *Washington Post*, 8 October 1989.

4. Judith Droitcour Miller, *National Survey of Drug Abuse: Main Findings 1982* (Washington, D.C.: National Institute on Drug Abuse, 1983). For evidence of a slight decline in alcohol experience from 1982 to 1988, see National Institute on Drug Abuse, *National Household Survey on Drug Abuse: Population Estimates* 1988, DHHS Publication no. ADM 89-1636, 1989.

5. Associated Press report, 23 March 1990.

6. M. D. Lawrence, J. R. Snortum, and F. E. Zimring, *Social Control of the Drinking Driver* (Chicago: University of Chicago Press, 1988).

7. Based on *SAUS89*, Table 117.

8. *Washington Post*, 1 March 1990, A3. A study reported a little later in the same year claimed to show an 18-year difference in actual longevity between smokers and nonsmokers: *Washington Post*, 13 May 1990, A4. Another large-scale survey is summarized thus: "If you are a twenty-five-year-old nonsmoking male, the odds are 7 to 2 in favor of your reaching the age of sixty-five. If you smoke one pack of cigarettes a day, the odds are only 3 to 2." John D. McGervey, *Probabilities in Everyday Life* (New York: Ivy Books, 1986), 192.

9. Based on *SAUS89*, Table 192.

10. National Institute on Drug Abuse, *National Trends in Drug Use and Related Factors among American High School Students and Young Adults, 1975-1986*, Publication no. ADM 87-1535, 1987, 249.

11. Based on *SAUS79*, Table 203; and *SAUS89*, Table 196, extrapolated.

12. Miller, 16.

13. William Bates and Betty Crowther, *Drugs: Causes, Circumstances and Effects of Their Use* (Morristown, NJ: General Learning Press, 1973).

14. Bruce A. Chadwick, "Consumption of Intoxicants," Quebec, Comparative Charting Group, Trend Report no. 13.8, 1988. See also National Institute on Drug Abuse, *Epidemiology of Heroin 1964-1984* (Washington, D.C.: Government Printing Office, 1985).

15. For additional evidence on the cocaine supply see National Narcotics Intelligence Consumers Committee, *The Supply of Illicit Drugs in the United States*, April 1988.

16. *Newsweek*, 27 November 1989, 37–40. Similar announcements appeared in the other leading newsmagazines and on the network news programs. The introduction of crack cocaine five years earlier benefited from the same type of unintended but highly effective advertising.

17. William J. Skinner, "Abused Prescription Drugs: Sources of Helpful Drugs that Hurt," in J. R. Wittenborn et al., eds. *Drugs and Youth* (Springfield, IL: C. C. Thomas, 1969), and Geoffrey Cowley et al., "The Promise of Prozac," *Newsweek*, 26 March 1990, 38–41.

18. Miller, Table 10.

19. Data from the National Institute of Drug Abuse, *Washington Post*, 12 December 1989.

20. *Ibid.*, 28 March 1990, A7.

21. Based on *SAUS89*, Tables 191 and 192.

22. Associated Press, 4 December 1989. If other abominable drugs are included, two out of three male arrestees in major American cities tested positive in 1988, according to *National Drug Control Strategy*, 18.

23. See, for example, Steven L. Nock and Paul W. Kingston, *The Sociology of Public Issues* (Belmont, CA: Wadsworth, 1990), 64–69.

24. Based on *SAUS89*, Table 299.

25. For a good selection of such denunciations see U. S. House of Representatives, Select Committee on Narcotics Abuse and Control, "Drug Legalization—Catastrophe for Black Americans," Washington, D.C., SCNAC-100-2-9, 1989. But see the statement of the Mayor of Hartford, CT in the same hearing for a contrasting view.

17

ETHNIC TRENDS

The meaning of the word "ethnic" in the American language has begun to change in recent years. It formerly denoted European immigrants and their immediate descendants who settled close together, preserved a distinctive culture, and acknowledged a common identity. The current meaning of the term is broader and denotes any social identification based on descent. In some recent sociological writings, "ethnicity" includes what used to be called "race." The newer usage implies that "white," "black," "hispanic," and "Asian" are cultural rather than biological categories. It can be argued that the criteria for these categories are not only cultural but capricious. A white, in the U. S., is a person of exclusively European ancestry who does not have a Spanish surname or speak Spanish at home. A black is a person who has any African ancestry whatever. (Since most American blacks have some European ancestry, the opposite and no less reasonable rule would classify them as white.) An hispanic is a person with a Spanish surname or who speaks Spanish at home; the criterion differs according to circumstances. Hispanics may have any mixture of European, African, or Indian ancestry without becoming white or black or Native American. A Native American is a person affiliated with an organized Indian tribe and claiming a stated minimum percentage of tribal ancestry. An Asian is a person of entirely Asian descent for some official purposes and of predominantly Asian descent for other purposes. Although the offspring of a white-black union is automatically black, anyone else whose parents belong to different groups has an ambiguous ethnic identity and is often able to decide which classification is preferable in a given situation.

The subjectivity of ethnicity meant that an increasing number of Americans became free to be as ethnic or as nonethnic as they chose to be, and also in some cases enabled them to choose from among different ethnic identities. There were about five thousand Cuban-Chinese in New York City and in nearby Hoboken, New Jersey, in the mid-1980s. One of them said, 'I am

Cuban, Chinese and American' . . . she worked as an administrative assistant in a midtown bank and was married to an American of Italian descent . . .[1]

The classification rules for white ethnic groups are not simple either. Ethnic identification is not exclusively based on national origin. Religion is a qualifying factor—Irish Protestants are ethnically distinct from Irish Catholics and Hungarian Jews from Hungarian Catholics. Religion rather than national origin is the primary identifier for Jews, but there are important national subdivisions within the Jewish population and many Jews who abandon their religion keep their ethnic identity. Some ethnic groups have a regional character; Italian-Americans are predominantly Sicilian; French Canadians are a coherent ethnic group in New England; English Canadians are not.

The extraordinary importance of ethnicity in the social structure of the United States is due to the way the population grew: by successive waves of voluntary immigration, and also by the importation of slaves and contract laborers. Among the voluntary immigrants, the advantages of earlier arrival could never be completely overcome by latecomers, so that ethnic groups were eventually stratified by date of arrival—the English and Scotch-Irish at the top, followed by the Germans, the Irish, the East European Jews, the Poles, the Italians, the Greeks, and the Puerto Ricans, with innumerable smaller groups—New York Dutch, Louisiana Creoles, Sephardic Jews, Minnesota Swedes, Slovaks, Slovenians, Armenians, Soviet Russians—fitted into local status systems according to their order of arrival, with some weighting for religion.

But for those who were not free immigrants, early arrival conferred no prestige at all, presumably because it did not enable them to accumulate property and power. Native Americans, the very earliest settlers, sank into rural poverty after a long and desperate resistance to the tide of white settlement. The Africans imported as slaves had virtually no chance of acquiring wealth or influence; the few blacks who were free before the Civil War were excluded by law and custom from civic equality. The abolition of slavery substituted collective servitude for individual servitude; that condition persisted for another century. The Chinese contract laborers brought into the country in the nineteenth century were treated harshly. Chinese immigration was forbidden altogether between 1882 and 1945. The Mexican contract laborers on whom agriculture in the West has depended from the beginning are not, even now, admitted to full social participation. Their low status has had a depressive effect on that of the old Mexican inhabitants of the Southwestern states and of the urban Mexican immigrants, legal and illegal, of recent decades.

In sum, ethnic stratification in the United States reflects the allocation of ethnic groups either to the main ethnic system, where the prestige of a group is largely determined by seniority, or to the minority system, where ethnic groups that were formerly subject to apartheid regulations, are now encouraged by government policy to improve their statuses, while still burdened by multiple disadvantages.

The dismantling in the southern states of the Jim Crow laws that formerly prohibited blacks from marrying whites or sharing public facilities with them and of the code of racial etiquette that required blacks to express deference to whites in every encounter and in the northern states, of the customs and regulations that excluded blacks from privileged residential districts, labor unions, supervisory jobs, hotels, restaurants, and churches, as well as from elite schools and colleges, major league teams, private hospitals and public office, was accomplished in about 15 years. The federal courts led the way, beginning with the *Brown* v. *Topeka* decision of 1954, which banned deliberate segregation in public schools, and then reaching out to abolish all the other "separate but equal" arrangements. The entire body of apartheid legislation was nullified by judicial decisions and the courts then went beyond legal discrimination to restrict administrative discrimination in schools, churches, hospitals, and charitable institutions by threatening the withdrawal of their tax exemptions; to forbid discrimination by retail and commercial establishments on the grounds of public policy, and to restrain discrimination by employers and labor unions under the interstate commerce clause. Beginning with the Civil Rights Act of 1964, these reforms were reinforced by a stream of federal and state legislation that gave black citizens effective access to the political process and enforceable sanctions against discrimination in employment, housing, education, and public services. By 1975, official discrimination had been effectively abolished. Black job and college applicants were more likely to receive preferential than discriminatory treatment. The number of black office-holders rose exponentially. The access of blacks to public facilities was effectively guaranteed.

The gaps between whites and blacks with respect to education, income, and health, which had begun to narrow earlier, continued to shrink. Blacks who completed their educations around 1930 had 3.9 years less schooling than their white contemporaries; by 1980, the difference had shrunk to 0.7 years.[2] The life expectancy of the black population, which was about nine years lower than that of the white population in 1930, is about four years lower now;[3] this relatively poor showing reflects the persistence of high infant mortality among blacks. The progress of blacks in income and occupation has been steady and significant. Black male wages as a percent of white wages advanced from 43 percent in 1940 to 73 percent in 1980; for new workers in the labor market, the 1980 ratio was 84 percent.

> ... the real story of the last 40 years has been the emergence of the black middle class, whose income gains have been real and substantial. The growth in the size of the black middle class has been so spectacular that as a group it outnumbers the black poor ... Nowhere were these changes more dramatic than when we focus on the contemporary economic elite. For the first time in American history, a sizable number of black men are better off than white middle-class America. During the last twenty years alone, the odds of a black man penetrating the ranks of the economic elite increased tenfold.[4]

The same authors present data to show that by 1980, a somewhat larger proportion of black employees than of white employees in the equal opportunity sector (public agencies and private enterprises with more than 100 employees) held managerial and technical positions.[5]

Other observers take a less optimistic view of recent developments, pointing out that black unemployment continues to run much higher than white unemployment, that the proportion of blacks completing four years of college did not increase faster than the proportion of whites completing four years of college after 1970, and that black family income—as distinct from individual earnings—lost a little ground in relation to white family income after 1975. These facts are cited in a recent report on minority participation in education and American life, which concludes that:

> In education, employment, income, health, longevity and other basic measures of individual and social well-being, gaps persist—and in some cases are widening—between members of minority groups and the majority population.[6]

A study widely publicized in 1990 estimated that 23 percent of all black men between ages 20 and 29 were in prison or on probation or parole.[7]

The reason why such disparate estimates of black progress and prospects are possible is that while inequality between whites and blacks has been decreasing, inequality has been increasing within the black population, especially between the educated, prosperous, intact black families who participate fully in the mainstream culture and the poor, badly educated, unmarried, and largely unemployed residents of black ghettos, who live in a squalid, disorderly, and dangerous world. In Chapter 6 on family trends, we looked at the rapid increase of illegitimate births and single-parent families in the black population. These trends have been reinforced by the rapidly increasing concentration of blacks in large cities.

The proportion of the U. S. population counted as black declined slowly and steadily from 19.3 percent in 1790 to 9.7 percent in 1930 and then began an equally slow and steady rise to about 12.4 percent today.[8] The trend of urbanization has been much more dramatic. In 1930, most of the black population were located in the rural South. Fewer than half of the black population live in the South today and only about 2 percent of those are engaged in farming. Today, blacks are overwhelmingly urban throughout the country.* Table 17–1 shows how their concentration in large cities has increased:[9]

TABLE 17–1   **BLACK POPULATION OF LARGEST U. S. CITIES, 1930–1980 (percent)**

	1930	1960	1980
New York	5%	14%	25%
Los Angeles	3	14	17
Chicago	7	23	40
Houston	22	23	28
Philadelphia	11	26	38
Detroit	8	29	63
San Diego	2	6	9
Dallas	15	19	29
San Antonio	8	7	7
Phoenix	0	5	5
Baltimore	18	35	55
San Francisco	1	10	13
Indianapolis	12	21	22
San Jose	0	1	5
Memphis	38	37	48
Washington, D.C.	27	54	70

SOURCE: For 1930 figures see: U. S. Bureau of the Census, *Negroes in the United States, 1920–32*, by Charles E. Hall, USGPO, 1935, (New York: Kraus Reprint Co., 1969), 54–55. For 1960, based on *Statistical Abstract of United States 1980*, Table 28.

---

*The proportion of the black population living in the South dropped below 50 percent in the 1980s, while the proportion living in metropolitan areas rose above 80 percent. Pending the results of the 1990 census, these figures are projected from tables in James P. Smith and Finis R. Welch, *Closing the Gap: Forty Years of Economic Progress for Blacks* (Santa Monica, CA: Rand Corporation, 1986).

This extraordinary concentration has both contributed to and detracted from progress towards equality. Black voters and office holders now dominate municipal politics in many of these cities. And since large cities often hold the balance between the two major parties in state and national elections, government agencies at all levels are protective of the interests, and sensitive to the concerns, of black voters. The other obvious advantage of being concentrated in large cities is superior access to economic opportunities and to such public services as higher education and hospital care.

The great drawback is continued segregation. Metropolitan cities tend naturally to be segregated by economic level—because the gradient of land values and rents is much steeper than in smaller communities—and by ethnicity—because ethnic neighborhoods are large enough to have their own institutions and to enjoy a measure of cultural autonomy. But in the case of poor blacks, and to a lesser degree hispanics, the tendency to segregation was powerfully reinforced after 1970 by the resegregation of urban public schools which followed the vigorous campaign by the federal courts to achieve desegregation by busing, redistricting, and the assignment of pupils to achieve racial balance. White parents seemed to accept school integration so long as a school held a majority of white pupils; when white pupils became a minority, they fled to the suburbs or shifted into private schools.[10] The process was hastened by continuing minority migration into the largest cities and by the relatively low fertility of urban whites. As the proportion of white pupils diminished, their rate of departure accelerated; in Washington, D.C. today, fewer than 1 percent of public school pupils are white. The resegregation of the schools automatically reinforced the existing pattern of residential segregation inherited from the past. But while before 1960 the black districts of metropolitan cities had included the entire black population, confined there by restrictive covenants and racial etiquette, today's segregated black districts are inhabited exclusively by the poor—affluent blacks having joined the white flight to the suburbs.[11]

Along with the dismantling of apartheid, there was a sharp decline of white hostility towards blacks, whether measured by responses to survey questions, by the incidence of racial epithets and stereotypes in casual conversation, or by interactional behavior. In 1948, the proportion of white respondents in a national sample who said they would object to a black neighbor was 63 percent; in a similar 1987 survey, it was only 13 percent.[12] In a 1985 survey, the proportion of respondents who said they would not invite a black guest to dinner in their homes ranged from 19 percent among the least educated whites to only 2 percent among white college graduates.[13] But such results hardly spell the end of American racism. The norms governing white-black relations have changed for the better, but the perceptions are much the same:

> There is no evidence that the virtually absolute differentiation of the American population has been reduced by any of the changes of the last four decades. Indeed, it may even have increased as a result of the growth in black consciousness and the use of racial enumeration procedures as a way of monitoring progress in civil rights. America is not much more color-blind today than it ever was ... What has changed is the normative definition of appropriate relations between blacks and whites. Whereas discrimination against, and enforced segregation of blacks was taken for granted by most white Americans as recently as 1940, today the dominant belief is that blacks deserve the same treatment and respect as whites, and that some degree of racial integration is a desirable thing.[14]

The present condition of the large and growing hispanic minority resembles that of the blacks in many ways, although their origins and prospects are quite different. Hispanics were not separately counted by the Census Bureau until 1980 so that there is no way of charting the past growth of this population. Indeed, the concept of hispanics as a single ethnic group is relatively new: as recently as 1970, Chicanos and Puerto Ricans were not grouped together by federal agencies or public opinion and there had been relatively few immigrants from Cuba or Central America. But the hispanic classification is now firmly embedded in American law and culture and the hispanic population is growing very fast, both by natural increase and by continued immigration. The 19 million hispanics of 1987 were 8 percent of the total population, but they are projected to grow to 31 million and 11 percent in the next 20 years.[15] There are currently about 3 million hispanics of Mexican origin, 2.3 million Puerto Ricans, 1.1 million Cubans, and more than 3 million others. The Mexicans are concentrated in the Southwest, the Puerto Ricans in and around New York City, and the Cubans in South Florida. The immigration amnesty act of 1986 enabled several million illegal immigrants to acquire U. S. citizenship, but illegal immigration has not abated and the number of illegal Mexican and Central American residents is still estimated in the millions, together with contract laborers who are legal but temporary residents. Puerto Ricans, by contrast, are U. S. citizens by birth and move freely back and forth between San Juan and New York. The Cuban-American population is the most recent; the original immigrants arrived as political refugees and settled in and around Miami, where their presence attracted other hispanic immigrants from Central America and the Caribbean.

Taken together, hispanics in the 1980s fall close to blacks with respect to measures of social welfare. The Census Bureau estimated that 41 percent of hispanic children were in poverty in 1985, compared to 47 percent of black children and 18 percent of white children, and that only 53 percent of hispanics were graduating from high school compared to 75 percent of blacks and 83 percent of whites, although about the same proportion of black and hispanic high school graduates went to college. The unemployment rate for hispanics in 1987 was 9 percent, midway between the white rate of 5 percent and the black rate of 13 percent.[16] In 1987, 36 percent of hispanic families with children were headed by a single mother compared to 48 percent of black families and 20 percent of white families. The median income of hispanic families at $19,900 was much closer to the $17,600 income of black families than to the $30,800 income of white families. But when Mexicans and Puerto Ricans are considered separately, the differences between them are generally greater than the differences between hispanics and blacks. For example, 48 percent of Puerto Rican families with children were headed by a single mother in 1987 compared to only 21 percent of Mexican families.[17] On balance, the differences between the situations of blacks and hispanics in the U. S. are more important than the superficial similarities. It is infinitely easier for individual hispanics than for individual blacks to shed their ethnic identities and join the white majority. Hispanics, unlike blacks, have powerful advocates abroad; Latin America as a whole is sensitive to the treatment of hispanics in this country; the national government of Mexico and the commonwealth government of Puerto Rico can bring effective pressures to bear on behalf of their citizens. The U. S. relation to Mexico is perennially delicate and grows more delicate with the headlong growth of the Mexican population; from 27 million in 1950 to 87 million in 1990.[18]

Most of the illegal immigrants and illegal drugs entering the United States come from or through Mexico. But the maintenance of good relations with Mexico has become a cardinal tenet of American foreign policy, and the maintenance of an open border with the U. S.

has become a cardinal tenet of Mexican foreign policy. As a result, the United States lost control, in the 1970s, of its long southern frontier. The effort to suppress illegal immigration became essentially ritual; tens of thousands of border-crossers are intercepted and returned unharmed to Mexico every year with the understanding that they will try again and eventually succeed. A serious attempt to reestablish border control would necessarily involve the use of force, and Mexico would regard any damage to its wandering citizens as hostile and provocative. By all accounts, the restraints imposed upon the hiring of illegal immigrants by the Immigration Act of 1986 have not much affected the steady movement across the border, although job discrimination against persons with hispanic surnames seems to have increased since its passage.

American Asians are even more diverse than hispanics, being divided into seven large contingents: Chinese, Japanese, Filipinos, Indians (from India), Koreans, Vietnamese, Polynesians, and many smaller contingents; about 6 million in all.[19] Most of them are recent arrivals; there were fewer than half a million Asians in the U. S. in 1960. This enormous influx—larger than any previous contingent of immigrants in a comparable time—has not elicited much resistance or even much comment, despite scattered incidents like the altercations between Vietnamese and Texan shrimpers and between Korean shopkeepers and Brooklyn blacks. The Asians are unusual among American minorities in having few disadvantages. Compared to the white majority, they have *higher* educational achievement, lower unemployment rates, higher incomes, a higher proportion of intact families, and lower crime rates. Although Asians are protected by civil rights legislation and affirmative action programs, they are not exposed to much discrimination. The mass immigration of Asians and their generally favorable reception reflects an extraordinary turnaround in popular attitudes and public policy. The Chinese who came to California during and after the Gold Rush were scorned and mistreated. The anti-Chinese movement that developed in California persuaded Congress to ban Chinese immigration altogether in 1882. The ban was not lifted until 1945, when Chinese began to be admitted as war brides and political refugees; it was not abandoned until 1965. The Japanese immigration which began towards the turn of the century evoked a similar reaction; it was perceived as part of a "Yellow Peril." The so-called Gentlemen's Agreement of 1907, politely negotiated between the U. S. and Japan, cut Japanese immigration sharply, and it was prohibited altogether in

1924.[20] During World War II, citizens of Japanese descent were treated, in effect, as enemy aliens and confined in prison camps. Partial restitution was not made until 1989. The virtual disappearance of anti-Oriental prejudice after World War II is a sociological mystery. Asian Americans now obtain a disproportionate share of places in the Ivy League colleges, of doctorates in science, and of opportunities in music and finance, without arousing any conspicuous resentment. American bigotry is not what it used to be.

The recent history of U. S. policy towards other immigrants shows the same abandonment of traditional prejudices. The Irish immigration of 1820–1860 was hotly opposed. The Jews, Poles, and other east Europeans who began to arrive in great numbers around 1880, and the Italians, Greeks, and Armenians who joined them a little later, aroused hostilities which culminated in the Johnson-Reed Act of 1924. It limited European immigration to fewer than 150,000 annually and set national quotas which intentionally discriminated against the immigrant groups of the previous 50 years. The quota system, although often modified, was not abandoned until the Immigration and Naturalization Amendments of 1965, followed by a series of provisions for refugees and other favored categories, launched a new era in which immigration has again become massive but is predominantly non-European.[21]

Meanwhile, the majority sector of the U. S. population, composed of the descendants of European immigrants, has been evolving by the operation of time, intermarriage, and social mobility. The notable recent trends are: (1) the crumbling of the WASP (white Anglo-Saxon Protestant) monopoly of political and social power; (2) a reversal of the long-established educational and economic advantage of Protestants over Catholics; (3) a great reduction in institutionalized anti-Semitism; (4) the decreasing homogeneity of white ethnic groups; (5) efforts to conserve disappearing ethnic cultures; and (6) the emergence of the "unhyphenated American." The general result of these trends is to reduce the clarity of ethnic group boundaries, the influence of ethnic identification on individual lives, and the intensity of ethnic conflict, as might be expected from the mingling that occurs with the passage of time.[22] Some 57 percent of the entire U. S. population is at least four generations away from an immigrant ancestor.[23] But if ethnic boundaries have faded, they have certainly not disappeared, and ethnicity is still an extremely important and consequential marker for Americans of European descent.

The WASP share of high political positions, while still impressive, has dwindled since 1960. Table 17–2, for example, lists the proportion of white cabinet members with English and Scottish names in the presidential administrations from Hoover to Reagan:

TABLE 17–2   **PRESIDENTIAL CABINET MEMBERS WITH ENGLISH AND SCOTTISH SURNAMES**

President	Percent of Cabinet
Hoover	100%
Roosevelt	82
Truman	87
Eisenhower	81
Kennedy	62
Johnson	65
Nixon	45
Ford	36
Carter	35
Reagan	38
Bush (initially)	43

SOURCE: Based on *Notable Names in American History*. I am indebted to Achsah Carrier and Louis Hicks for assistance with the tabulation. We used biographical data to clarify etymologically doubtful cases, but some errors undoubtedly remain.

Similar trends are apparent in lists of corporate executives and Pulitzer Prize winners. Such counts are not entirely reliable, because members of other ethnic groups may have names that appear British, but the trend is unmistakable.

The reversal of the Protestant advantage over Catholics with respect to education, occupation, and income cannot be precisely dated; it was first noticed around 1970, and has been confirmed by all subsequent studies. The Catholic disadvantage was created in Europe centuries ago when the Protestant countries, taken as a group, turned to commerce and industry before the Catholic countries, and Protestants took the lead in the commercial and industrial revolutions. The connection between Protestantism and industrialization was the theme of Weber's *Religion and the Protestant Ethic* and Tawney's *Religion and the Rise of Capitalism*, among other notable studies. In the United States, the Protestant advantage was created by the arrival of Protestant Yankees long before German and Irish Catholics and the low ratio of Protestants to Catholics among later immigrants. It is not entirely clear why the reversal occurred but there is no question that Catholics, on the average, now surpass Protestants in education, income, and occupational level. Greeley, using data from the *General Social Survey*, shows in Table 17-3 how rapidly this reversal occurred.

TABLE 17–3   **RATIO OF CATHOLIC TO WHITE PROTESTANT ACHIEVEMENT**

Year of Birth	Attended College	Professional Occupation
1900–09	.62	.81
1930–39	.96	1.07
1960–65	1.45	1.50

SOURCE: Based on Andrew M. Greeley, *Religious Change in America* (Cambridge, MA: Harvard University Press, 1989), Table 7–1.

It appears from the same source that in the early 1980s, the average incomes of Italian, Irish, and Polish Catholics all exceeded the incomes of Presbyterians, the most affluent white Protestants. The income of Jews was even higher.[24]

The institutionalized anti-Semitism that flourished in the United States earlier in this century reflected the special situation of Jews as a privileged but vulnerable minority. There was widespread antagonism to Jews, visualized as a separate race. But the sporadic efforts that were made to build a mass movement on an anti-Semitic platform, after European models, never got very far. The more significant component of American anti-Semitism was the systematic exclusion of Jews from elite clubs, hotels, and residential districts; a quota system that limited the number of Jewish students admitted to elite colleges; the virtual exclusion of Jews from elective office and from executive positions in many large corporations, and the segregation of law firms, hospitals, financial institutions, and department stores, so that Jews were only employable in Jewish organizations. A peculiar paranoid fear of being invaded and submerged by Jews haunted the American upper class. The attitudes and practices founded on that apprehension have not entirely disappeared but they have been greatly eroded since 1960:

> In 1959 an indignant speaker reported in a meeting of the American Jewish Committee that only one of the "top ten social clubs" in New York had Jewish members and elsewhere in the United States at that time the picture was surely similar if not worse. By the late 1970s, however, it had already changed radically. Not only had the most select Manhattan clubs such as the Knickerbocker and the Links been opened to Jewish members, but Jews had also been admitted—albeit sometimes in only token numbers to such other once "restricted sanctums" as the Meadow Club in Southampton, the Chicago Club, the Detroit

Club, Cincinnati's Queen City Club, the Minneapolis Club, Seattle's Rainier Club and San Francisco's Pacific Union and Bohemian Clubs.[25]

Jews were not the sole beneficiaries of such changes. What Robert Christopher calls "the de-WASPing of the power elite," has broken down most of the barriers that formerly barred non-WASPs, both white and nonwhite, from commensalism and connubium with the rich and powerful and from access to privileged institutions. The process continues today with undiminished momentum.

The decreasing homogeneity of white ethnic groups in the U. S. has followed inevitably from the loss of distinctive linguistic and cultural habits in each successive native-born generation, high rates of intermarriage, and the movement of the children and grandchildren of immigrants out of their original areas of settlement. Alba provides a vivid picture of the operation of these three factors among Italian-Americans, the most recently arrived of the large white ethnic groups, to bring about what he calls the twilight of ethnicity.

> Properly analyzed, the evidence on behalf of the looming ethnic twilight among Italians appears overwhelming. Despite the widely accepted image of an intense, family-centered Italian-American culture, the group's cultural distinctiveness has paled to a feeble version of its former self.[26]

Rates of intermarriage are extraordinarily high after the first generation. Of third-generation men of wholly Italian ancestry born after 1950, 71 percent married wholly non-Italian women; the comparable figure for third-generation Italian women was 73 percent.[27] The fact that women were no more endogamous than men is itself a strong indication that the traditional Italian family pattern is no longer very strong.

The signs of residential dispersal are equally plain. Of Italian-Americans living in and around New York in 1970, only 15 percent of the foreign-born first generation lived in places with fewer than 100,000 inhabitants—the suburbs—but more than half of later generations did.[28] Studies of other white ethnic groups show parallel and very similar trends.[29]

It may seem paradoxical that the twilight of ethnicity, measured by objective indicators, has been accompanied by a vast movement to conserve and celebrate the distinctive cultural heritages of the same ethnic groups—not only those of Italian, Jewish, Polish, Greek, Armenian, Scandinavian, and Balkan Americans, but also those of earlier arrivals—Scottish, Irish, German, Dutch. The movement involves the revival of distinctive languages, customs, costume, music, and cuisine, and the development of innumerable voluntary associations to foster them. These are sometimes conceived as rearguard defenses against encroaching assimilation but that does not seem to be their primary intention. Ethnicity, for Americans of European descent, is becoming elective and voluntary, like religion, and like religion, is now more commonly viewed as a calendar of enjoyable occasions than as a set of constraints.

Meanwhile, recent surveys show a large and growing population of "unhyphenated Americans,"—people of European descent whose immigrant ancestors are remote or unknown to them, or whose ancestry is so mixed that they do not identify with any descent group. Lieberson and Waters report that more than 13 million persons gave "American" as their ancestry in the 1980 census, making them the largest ethnic group after the British, German, and Irish.[30] Steinberg, reviewing their work, notes that the assessment of this response is complicated by the fact that the 1980 census, the principal source of information about ethnic identification, discouraged the "American" response by stipulating that ancestry referred to the nationality of one's forbears *before* their arrival in America.[31] It is highly probable that the increasing distance of white Americans from their immigrant ancestors and the high rates of intermarriage that now characterize virtually all white ethnic groups, will continue to swell the ranks of the unhyphenated Americans for the foreseeable future.

NOTES

1. Lawrence Fuchs, "Assimilation in the U. S.: Identities and Boundaries," *Tocqueville Review*, 9(1987–88): 181–99.
2. James P. Smith and Finis R. Welch, *Closing the Gap: Forty Years of Economic Progress for Blacks* (Santa Monica, CA: Rand Corporation, 1986), Table 13. The comparison cited is between the birth cohorts of 1906–10

and 1956–60. See also National Urban League, *The State of Black America*, 1989.

3. Based on *SAUS89*, Table 108; and 1990 press reports.

4. Smith and Welch, 12–13.

5. *Ibid.*, Table 40.

6. Commission on Minority Participation in Education and American Life, *One-Third of a Nation* (Washington, D.C.: American Council on Education, 1988). The tabular data presented in that report do not always support the gloomy assertions of the text.

7. *Washington Post*, 27 February 1990, A3. The estimate, by a group advocating reform of the criminal justice system, assumes that the number of young men on probation or parole, which is unknown, equals the number in prison.

8. Based on *SAUS89*, Tables 18 and 31.

9. For a more in-depth discussion, see Irene B. Taeuber and Conrad Taeuber, Bureau of the Census, *People of the United States in the 20th Century* (Washington, D.C.: Government Printing Office, 1971), Chapter XV; Ira Katznelson, *Black Men, White Cities* (London: Oxford University Press, 1973), 62, 86; and Robert B. Grant, *The Black Man Comes to the City* (Chicago: Nelson-Hall, 1972).

10. See Kathryn P. Nelson, "Recent Suburbanization of Blacks: How Much, Who, and Where," a report prepared for the Office of Policy Development and Research, Department of Housing and Urban Development, May 1979, HUD-PDR-378(2). The "tipping" phenomenon has been controversial as may be seen in Thomas A. Clark, *Blacks in Suburbs* (New Brunswick, NJ: Center for Urban Policy Research, Rutgers University, 1979), 108.

11. These trends may be leveling off. See Dwight L. Johnson, Bureau of the Census, "We, the Black Americans" (Washington, D.C.: Government Printing Office, 1986), 3–4.

12. Based on Public Opinion, "Opinion Roundup: The State of Intolerance," *Public Opinion* 10(1987): 22–23.

13. *Ibid.*, 24.

14. Howard Schuman, Charlotte Steeh, and Lawrence Bobo, *Racial Attitudes in America: Trends and Interpretations* (Cambridge, MA: Harvard University Press, 1985), 201–202.

15. Based on *SAUS89*, Tables 15, 16, and 45.

16. American Council on Education, *One-Third of a Nation: A Report of the Commission on Minority Participation in Education and American Life* (Washington, D.C.: Government Printing Office, 1988). Figures 3-6, based on data from the Bureau of the Census and Figure 2, based on data from the Bureau of Labor Statistics.

17. Based on *SAUS89*, Table 44.

18. Based on *SAUS59*, Table 1212; and *SAUS89*, Table 1403.

19. I have been unable to locate an official 1990 estimate of the total U. S. Asian population as of this writing. Based on *SAUS89*, Tables 7 and 45,

the 1980 census counted.3.7 million, nearly 1.9 million more were admitted from 1981 to 1987; and an unknown additional number from 1988 to 1990; my estimate is probably low.

20. A good account of the anti-Oriental movement in the U. S. is found in Chapter 10 of Samuel Eliot Morison and Henry Steele Commager, *The Growth of the American Republic* (New York: Oxford University Press, 1962), 2 vols.

21. The legislative history is nicely summarized under the heading, "Immigration," in *Encyclopedia of American History* (Pleasantville, NY: Reader's Digest 1975), 539–42. The distribution of national origins for recent immigrants is shown in *SAUS89*, Table 7.

22. For a close-up view of white ethnic equalization in a particular setting, see Joel Perlmann, *Ethnic Differences: Schooling and Social Structure Among the Irish, Italians, Jews, and Blacks in an American City, 1880-1935* (Cambridge, MA: Cambridge University Press, 1989).

23. Cited by Stanley Lieberson and Mary C. Waters, Social Science Research Council "The Rise of a New Ethnic Group: The 'Unhyphenated American,'" *Items*, 43, no. 1 (1989): 8

24. Andrew M. Greeley, *Religious Change in America* (Cambridge, MA: Harvard University Press, 1989), Table 7–2.

25. Robert C. Christopher, *Crashing the Gates: The De-WASPing of America's Power Elite* (New York: Simon and Schuster, 1989).

26. Richard D. Alba, "The Twilight of Ethnicity among Americans of European Ancestry: The Case of Italians," in Richard D. Alba, ed. *Ethnicity and Race in the U.S.A.: Towards the Twenty-First Century* (Boston: Routledge and Kegan Paul, 1985), 134–58.

27. *Ibid.*, Table 3.

28. *Ibid.*, 144.

29. See especially Steven M. Cohen, "Socioeconomic Determinants of Intra-ethnic Marriage and Friendship," *Social Forces*, 55 (1977): 997–1010; Walter P. Zenker and Econ Macer, *Children of Intermarriage* (New York: American Jewish Committee, 1983); Richard D. Alba and Mitchell B. Chamblin, "A Preliminary Examination of Ethnic Identification among Whites," *American Sociological Review*, 48 (1983) 240–47, 1983; Bureau of the Census, "Ancestry and Language in the United States, November 1979," Washington, D.C.: 1982; Stanley Lieberson and Mary C. Waters *From Many Strands: Ethnic and Racial Groups in Contemporary America* (New York: Russell Sage Foundation, 1988).

30. *Ibid.*, 1988.

31. Stephen Steinberg, Review of Lieberson and Waters, *From Many Strands*, in *Contemporary Sociology*, 19 (1990): 182–83.

18

SOCIAL MOVEMENTS

The promotion of change by social movements is as essential to political democracy as free elections. In the United States at any given moment, hundreds of social movements compete for attention. Only a few of them attract mass support but those few have enormous influence. American social movements seem to fall into three broad categories: labor movements, rights movements, and protest movements.

The purpose of a labor movement is to improve the situation of workers vis-à-vis employers. The points of contention and negotiation include wages, benefits, hours, working conditions, safety, job security, grievances, seniority rights, pensions, profit-sharing, organizational tactics, and the rules of collective bargaining. Many labor organizations have political agendas that go beyond their immediate bargaining interests.

The purpose of a rights movement is to raise the status of a disadvantaged social group. Most of the participants in a rights movement belong to the group whose status they propose to raise, but there are always a few outside sympathizers. The most conspicuous rights movements of recent decades involved blacks, women, hispanics, Native Americans, homosexuals, students, and the handicapped.

The purpose of a protest movement is to change official policy towards an activity which the protestors want to see promoted or suppressed. There are current active protest movements about abortion, drunken driving, nuclear weapons, nuclear power, South Africa, gun control, environmental pollution, product safety, capital punishment, wife abuse, school prayer, historic preservation, fur coats, animal experimentation, immigration policy, and dozens of other issues. Protest movements often come in matching pairs; there are well-organized movements both for and against abortion, gun control, and capital punishment.

Social movements of the modern type have been active in this country since early in the nineteenth century, when slavery, women's rights, and unrestricted immigration were salient issues. But the amount of activity has varied greatly from one time to another, depending upon the popular mood and the political climate. After the Civil War, labor movements and their political offshoots attracted growing attention, although working-class radicalism was more marginal in the U. S. than in any European country. Left-wing candidates in presidential elections never quite attained two-tenths of one percent of the total vote.[1] The tiny radical movements—anarchists, syndicalists, socialists, communists—that appeared on the scene between 1880 and 1930 were vigorously suppressed. But the Great Depression of the 1930s greatly broadened the base of organized labor and moved it considerably to the left, while, for the first time, many opinion leaders acquired a Marxist orientation and became strongly supportive of organized labor and vaguely committed to the idea of a proletarian revolution. The successful counterattack from the right, led by Senator Joseph McCarthy and the House Un-American Activities Committee, held the center of the political stage in the 1950s. Marxism was banished from Washington, Hollywood, and the media, although it lingered on in the universities. The industrial unions abandoned their revolutionary yearnings and became as business-like and bureaucratic as their managerial adversaries. After 1960, the war between capital and labor, with all its emotional and political baggage, seemed to fade away. The old demands for economic justice were drowned out by new demands for social justice.[2] During the 1960s, both rights and protest movements burgeoned under the stimulus of the Supreme Court's campaign against racial segregation, the legislative initiatives of the Johnson Administration (especially the Civil Rights Act of 1964 and the Voting Rights Act of 1965), and the turmoil aroused by the Vietnam war. It is axiomatic in the history of modern states that a government that loses a war will be overthrown by a revolution. The stunning defeat the United States suffered in Vietnam provoked a quasi-revolution that left the government intact but challenged all forms of authority or predominance— that of whites over nonwhites, men over women, parents over children, teachers over students, managers over workers, doctors over patients, institutions over inmates, and so forth—with varying degrees of success.

During the 1960s, old rights and protest movements revived and new ones appeared overnight. They encouraged and reinforced each other, and were supported by a large sector of the public, by the federal government, and by establishment figures caught up in the general excitement. Street demonstrations were much in vogue. Beginning with the Watts riot of 1965, hundreds of riots erupted in the black districts of large cities during several long hot summers. Beginning with the Free Speech Movement at Berkeley in 1965, theatrical confrontations between student mobs and academic administrators occurred on nearly every campus in the country until the Kent State tragedy in 1970. Violent demonstrations were staged at political conventions and scholarly conferences, in courtrooms, prisons, and on Indian reservations. The violence was real but seldom lethal. There were innumerable minor injuries and some property damage but very few fatalities. In the 1970s, the tactical emphasis shifted from confrontation to lobbying and litigation. The movements consolidated their gains with the help of friendly federal agencies and favorable court decisions. But they began to lose momentum even before the arrival of the Reagan administration in 1981 signaled a decline in official support for all the rights movements and for the liberal protest movements that had been encouraged by previous administrations. Nevertheless, the goals of the rights movements were by then so deeply embedded in law and regulatory practice that they continued to gain ground through the 1980s.

The liberal protest movements had mixed outcomes in the 1980s. The environmental and gun control movements were effectively blocked, but the movement against nuclear power helped put a stop to the development of that industry, and the pro-immigration forces repeatedly prevailed. At the same time, there was a sharp growth in conservative protest movements centered on such issues as abortion, pornography, and school prayer.

In this chapter, we consider in some detail those recent social movements that have attracted the most support: the civil rights movement, the women's movement, the various environmental movements, and the paired movements that favor and oppose abortion. The great number and diversity of social movements requires any account of them to be selective.

Although the principal goal of the civil rights movement was to influence public policy, it is inaccurate to visualize the actions of the government as reactions to the movement's initiatives. There was a complex interplay between the several branches of the movement and the several branches of government; the directions taken by civil rights leaders were as frequently the results as the causes of government actions.

The modern development of civil rights began with President Roosevelt's Executive Order 8802 in June 1941, forbidding racial discrimination by defense contractors, followed by the Supreme Court's 1948 *Shelley* v. *Kraemer* decision that made restrictive covenants unenforceable and its unanimous 1954 vote against segregated schools in *Brown v. Topeka*, and then by President Eisenhower's despatch of troops to Little Rock, Arkansas, in 1955 to desegregate the public schools of that city. The successful brief in *Brown v. Topeka* was presented by Thurgood Marshall on behalf of the National Association for the Advancement of Colored People, founded nearly half a century before. He argued for the prohibition of "all state action based on race or color."[3]

The dramatic phase of the civil rights movement began with the Montgomery bus boycott of 1955 and the emergence of Martin Luther King as the movement's leader and strategist. The same period witnessed the rise of new figures within the civil rights movement who rejected the goal of integration in favor of black separatism and offered visions of armed struggle in place of King's nonviolence.[4] The same split between those working for change within the existing order and factions urging revolutionary solutions, would appear a little later in the Native American, Chicano, and Puerto Rican civil rights movements and in the student rights and antinuclear movements.

After the assassination of King in 1968, the majority faction that succeeded him became a permanent political lobby, while the black separatists staged compelling episodes of political theatre and attempted to form alliances with colonial liberation movements in Africa and Asia. The urban riots of the 1960s and the antiwhite rhetoric of the black separatists did not lessen the political influence of the civil rights lobby, and may have enhanced it. In 1964, Congress, silent on civil rights since 1868, reentered the lists with the Civil Rights Act of 1964, which authorized federal agencies to oppose discrimination by litigation, negotiation, and active enforcement, and followed it up with the Voting Rights Act of 1965, designed to reenfranchise black voters in the South and by the Civil Rights Acts of 1968 and 1972, which broadened the federal government's powers to deal with housing and job discrimination. A stream of executive orders beginning in 1961 and continuing to the present day amplified and enlarged the antidiscrimination umbrella and brought more groups—women, the elderly, veterans, homosexuals and the handicapped—under it. Affirmative action was introduced into federal employment policy by an executive order issued by President Nixon in August 1969; it developed a large regulatory apparatus over the next 20 years. Even the Reagan administration, pointedly unenthusiastic about civil rights, continued to expand federal powers in this field. The number of job discrimination cases investigated by the government increased from 14,000 in 1970 to 77,000 in 1986. The number of federal employees engaged full-time in civil rights enforcement increased from fewer than 2,000 in 1970 to more than 11,000 during the Reagan years.[5]

The goal of the civil rights movement shifted abruptly around 1965 from achieving the color-blind society preached by Martin Luther King to securing restitution for past exploitation and injuries. The new doctrine emphasized equality of outcome rather than equality of opportunity—it was embraced by most civil rights activists and bitterly criticized by a few.[6] Beginning around 1967, it became obligatory for government agencies, educational institutions, and private employers, to classify applicants for benefits, schooling, or employment by "race," and to modify their treatment of individuals according to that criterion. People whose racial classification entitled them to affirmative action routinely received some degree of preference in hiring and promotion, dismissal and layoff, admission to colleges and professional schools, access to public housing, and bidding on government contracts. Although originally intended for blacks, the preference system was soon extended to include all other "nonwhites": hispanics, Native Americans, Asians, Eskimos, and Aleuts, and in some respects, women, homosexuals, veterans, and handicapped persons. In legal theory, the various nonwhite categories have equal claims to preference; in practice, a rough degree of proportional representation is expected. But a nonwhite individual who falls into more than one preference category—a handicapped hispanic woman, for example—can be counted more than once in assessing an organization's compliance with affirmative action goals. The Supreme Court has wavered unpredictably from case to case on two issues raised by this system: whether groups as well as individuals have constitutional rights, and whether a person who is denied some advantage which he or she would otherwise obtain in order to make room for someone with a group preference has been treated inequitably. In the 1978 *Bakke* case, a divided court ruled that a university could not assign an exact quota of places to minority applicants but could take account of race in weighing their qualifications. In the following few years, lower courts approved, and sometimes imposed, racial quotas for hiring and promotion. In the *Stotts*, *Wygant*, and *March* cases, decided between 1984 and 1986, the Court struck down various affirmative action plans that seemed to deprive whites of promotion or job opportunities on the sole basis of race but in the 1987 *Johnson* case, it upheld a plan by a California county that required county officials to pass over more qualified job candidates in order to produce a work force that reflected the racial and gender composition of the county's population.[7] For the time being, nobody can be sure what the law permits or forbids with respect to affirmative action.

The women's liberation movement of the 1960s resembled the civil rights movement in many ways and women were eventually bracketed with racial minorities in civil rights legislation and equal opportunity regulations. But there were profound differences between the disabilities nonwhites suffered because of their pariah status and the disabilities women began to discover in their traditional roles. Unlike blacks, women had full voting rights and ample wealth; their living standards were no lower than men's, and they were not barred from good residential districts or segregated on common carriers. The discrimination about which women complained was primarily occupational. In the family system that prevailed in the U. S. before 1960, women were expected to work for a few years before marriage and might work intermittently during marriage to supplement their husbands' earnings. They were concentrated in underpaid female occupations—secretaries, waitresses, schoolteachers, maids, nurses, social workers, salesclerks, and machine operators. Women were virtually excluded from positions of power and responsibility in large organizations. They had only token representation in the major professions, politics, journalism, and finance. The conventional arrangements reserved most of the public sphere for men and most of the private sphere for women, placed the primary responsibility for the support of women and children on men, and the primary responsibility for childraising on women, and assigned psychological traits and mannerisms to each gender that fit these assignments. In order to overcome women's occupational disadvantages, it was necessary to challenge all the assumptions and values that supported the conventional division of gender roles. "Consciousness-raising" became a central activity of the women's movement. A rough measure of its success may be seen in the percentages of women who put the following items among "the two or three most enjoyable things about being a woman today" in two New York Times surveys[8] only 13 years apart:

	1970	1983
Being a mother; raising a family	53%	26%
Being a homemaker	43	8
Being a wife	22	6

The ideologists of the women's movement went far beyond criticism of occupational discrimination against women to question aspects of nature and culture that had always been taken for granted. At the height of the women's movement in 1970, one of its leaders wrote:

> Feminists have to question not just all of Western culture, but the organization of culture itself and further, even the very organization of nature. For we are dealing with an oppression that goes back beyond recorded history to the animal kingdom itself.[9]

Some opposed sex, marriage and childbearing altogether.

> Sex is not part of a relationship; on the contrary, it is a solitary experience, noncreative, a gross waste of time. The female can easily—far more easily than she may think—condition away her sex drive, leaving her completely cool and cerebral and free to pursue truly worth-while relationships and activities . . .[10]

Others demonstrated against brassieres, the Miss America contest, cosmetics, childcare centers, and the idea of a male Savior. Such extreme opinions were never widely accepted, but they helped to convince a large part of the general public that conventional gender roles are not natural or necessary and that the sentiments associated with them are not obligatory. These new views accompanied and encouraged the decline of fertility, the rise of the single-parent family, the full-time employment of mothers, and other recent trends in the family and the workplace.

The major political goal of the women's movement was the ratification of the Equal Rights Amendment to the Constitution. That measure, passed by Congress in 1972, came within three votes of ratification in 1979 and then receded, as some of the ratifying states reversed their votes. The failure of ERA reflected the waning political influence of the women's movement but had little practical importance; most of the announced objectives of the amendment had already been attained as the Supreme Court extended the equal protection clause of the Fourteenth Amendment to cover gender discrimination. By 1975, nearly every important institution of higher education formerly segregated by sex had begun to admit students of the opposite sex; women were being appointed to the service academies; the first female general officers were named; and the Navy began to send women to sea. All-male private clubs, taverns, locker rooms, and labor unions were compelled by judicial or legislative order to admit women. The two major political parties revised their rules to give women more representation.[11] Large enterprises were required to demonstrate to federal agencies that they did not discriminate against women in hiring and promotion. A few women became war correspondents, airline captains, and jockeys. A great many more became firefighters and police officers. Women were as free as men to use obscene language in private and public. As with ethnic discrimination, the formal structure of gender discrimination was swept away, and much of the informal structure also. Women acquired essentially the same sexual privileges as men and could choose alternatives to marriage—consensual unions, single parenthood, lesbian relationships—as freely.

The practical results of women's liberation were mixed. As we noted in Chapter 9 on work trends, the average earnings of employed women are still much lower than the average earnings of employed men, partly because of lingering discrimination, partly because women entering new occupations have not had time to acquire much seniority, but mostly because women's careers continue to be hampered by domestic obligations. The abandonment of conventional gender roles involved costs as well as benefits for women. The obligations of married men to support their wives and children were much reduced, along with the obligations of unmarried men to women they impregnated and the obligations of divorced men to their former wives. As a result, more women and children lived in poverty in 1990 than in 1960. For women at the higher income levels, the tension between career and family goals is much more severe today than it was a generation ago. But despite these drawbacks, most American women strongly favor the continuing trend of gender equalization and most American men accept it with equanimity.

In contrast to the civil rights and women's liberation movements, which peaked in the 1960s and achieved their major objectives by 1975, the environmental movement slowly gathered force between 1965 and 1990 but could claim only limited success. The problems are more complex, their ramifications are worldwide, and solutions are not easy to devise. Indeed, it may be misleading to speak of *the* environmental movement since most activists focus on one or two environmental issues and are only marginally concerned with the others.[12] The list is formidable and includes: wilderness areas and endangered species; habitat preservation; energy, fuel and water conservation; water pollution; oil spills; smog; acid rain; strip mining; the thinning of the ozone layer by fluorocarbons; the rising concentration of greenhouse gases in the atmosphere; deforestation in the Amazon basin, Africa, and Asia; radon gas in homes and public buildings; nuclear waste disposal; the cleanup of chemical waste; garbage and trash disposal; residues of fertilizers, pesticides and hormones in food products and drinking water; and the risks associated with nuclear power and nuclear weapons.

Each of these problems is a separate facet of a fundamental tension between population growth and technological progress on the one hand and the delicate self-adjusting balances of the earth's natural ecology on the other. On a practical level, most environmental problems take the form of short-term benefits that carry deferred long-term costs. The short-term benefits accrue to well-organized users—real estate developers, chemical companies, automobile manufacturers, commercial fishermen, logging companies, municipalities, farmers, pipeline operators, highway builders. The long-term costs are imposed on everyone.

The goal of most environmental activity in the U. S. is to bring about regulatory or remedial action by the federal government. With the exception of the national park system and a weak 1948 measure on water pollution, environmental legislation by Congress began with the Air Quality Act of 1960; in the ensuing 30 years, more than 30 major statutes were enacted to improve air and water quality, protect endangered species and habitats, control automotive emissions, abate noise, prohibit dangerous pesticides, remove hazardous wastes, and pursue other environmental goals. Some of these measures have been very effective; rivers like the Hudson and the Potomac, which had become open sewers, are again clean and sparkling. The extinction of bird, animal, and plant species has been slowed in American territory, although it proceeds recklessly elsewhere. Some species that were almost gone, like the bald eagle and the timber wolf, have been partially restored. Automotive emissions were effectively reduced for a while; the ravages of strip-mining were checked; and thousands of acres of wetlands were rescued from development. Despite these notable accomplishments, there is a consensus that the environmental situation is less favorable today than in 1960, partly because new and intractable problems like acid rain and the exhaustion of aquifers have appeared, partly because some of the gravest environmental problems—ozone depletion, atmospheric pollution, tropical deforestation, species extinction—are global and possibly uncontrollable, partly because some federal programs—nuclear waste disposal, the Superfund cleanup of toxic sites, and the improvement of air quality—have been dismal failures. For example, the U. S. has thousands of tons of high-level nuclear waste—spent fuel rods from power plants and the hazardous by-products of nuclear weapons manufacture—in temporary and insecure storage. In 1982 Congress ordered the Department of Energy to find a site for a permanent underground repository and to open it by 1998; the date has since been pushed back to 2010 and even that seems excessively optimistic.[13]

The global problems are particularly challenging because the hazards involved in ozone depletion, the increasing levels of carbon dioxide and methane in the atmosphere, and the destruction of the Amazon rain forest, cannot be precisely assessed at the present state of knowledge. No one can accurately predict the future reaction of the ozone layer to given amounts of fluorocarbon; no one knows what the eventual effects of atmospheric pollution will be or how tropical deforestation will eventually affect the weather of the northern hemisphere.[14] What does seem certain is that each of these assaults on nature will eventually exact a price. Although the environmental movement is highly fragmented, the number of activists and the amount of political pressure they exert have been rising steadily. The growth of the Sierra Club, one of the oldest and most influential of the environmental advocacy groups, has accelerated sharply in the past few years:

TABLE 18–1   SIERRA CLUB MEMBERSHIP

1960	16,066
1970	114,376
1980	181,773
1988	502,503

SOURCE: I am indebted to John W. Herrmann and Scott M. Barretta for these figures.

The other large organizations in this field—the National Wildlife Federation, the National Audubon Society, and the Wilderness Society have grown in parallel. Newer groups, such as the Environmental Fund, the Defenders of Wildlife, and the National Resources Defense Council, have been growing even faster.

Environmental activists are not distinctive in income or occupation, but they are likely to be independent in politics and to have graduated from college. Although environmental themes figured largely in the 1988 presidential campaign and in current political rhetoric, mass support has been slow to develop.

Roper's annual surveys of the personal concerns of the general public from 1974 to 1986 showed air and water pollution close to the bottom of the list and not gaining during that period while the public concern about energy resources slid from close to the top of the list, just behind inflation, in 1974 to the very bottom in 1986.[15] The environmental public is about the same size as the audience for classical music. But there are signs of widening interest today.

In the 1980s, rights movements receded and many of the protest movements that occupied the center of the national stage were focussed on symbolic issues—capital punishment, abortion, gun control, school prayer, flag-burning—which had fewer practical consequences than they seemed to have.

The capital punishment issue in its present form dates from 1972, when the Supreme Court's decision in *Furman v. Georgia* declared all existing death penalty statutes unconstitutional—a bold piece of judicial legislation that lacked majority support. In 1976, the court bowed grudgingly to public opinion and reinstated the death penalty, but with numerous restrictions. Since then Congress and the legislatures of most states have enacted new statutes imposing the death penalty for murder with aggravating circumstances— mass murder, murder of a rape victim, murder of a law officer, and so forth. Public support for the death penalty has risen from 53 percent in 1972 to nearly 70 percent today.[16]

But although 2,655 offenders were sentenced to death under the new statutes in the 11 years following 1976, fewer than 4 percent of them were executed.[17] Being sentenced to death in the United States became less life-threatening than mountain climbing, because of the tenacious rearguard resistance of the courts. The rules for imposing capital sentences are so full of traps that only a tiny fraction of them stand up on appeal, and the appeals can be almost interminable. The result of this standoff would not be tolerated in any country less law-struck than the United States. In the rare cases in which a capital sentence is carried out, the average delay between sentencing and execution is more than seven years and the average cost of the legal proceedings is about $5 million. Although there were active and well-organized social movements on both sides of the capital punishment issue, they have little real effect.

The same might be said of the confrontation between the "right-to-life" and "pro-choice" movements that has played such a large part in electoral politics. The 1973 Supreme Court decision in *Roe v. Wade* nullified the statutes that made abortion a criminal offense in nearly all of the states and substituted a plan whereby first trimester abortions were exempt from state regulation, second-trimester abortions might be regulated and third-trimester abortions, except in medical emergencies, might be prohibited. At first, most of the states made no attempt to rewrite their statutes to conform to the new formula; the legalization of abortion was a *fait accompli*. But in the 1980s, a powerful antiabortion movement developed, based on two new doctrines—that life begins when the ovum is fertilized and that a fetus has the same civil rights as any other person—and was supported by an unusual coalition of Protestant fundamentalists and Roman Catholics. Although it copied the street demonstrations and civil disobedience tactics of the liberal protest movements, the pro-life movement relied principally on bloc voting and intensive lobbying. Its influence reached a peak in 1988 when the winning candidates for the presidency and vice presidency and for many congressional seats and state offices ran on antiabortion platforms. But the tide began to turn after the *Webster* case of 1989, in which the Supreme Court upheld a state law restricting second and third trimester abortions and seemed to be leaning towards the eventual reversal of *Roe* v. *Wade*. The *Webster* decision galvanized the formerly silent majority of abortion proponents into vigorous activity. Pro-choice Democrats found abortion rights to be an unexpectedly powerful weapon against their Republican opponents in state and local elections. Before the end of 1989, politicians of all parties were in full retreat from pro-life positions while both movements continued their intensive lobbying.

But again the issue was largely symbolic and the practical consequences were minimal and likely to remain so. The data on legal abortions in 1987 published in 1990 by the National Center for Health Statistics indicate that 92 percent of abortions were performed in the first trimester of pregnancy, and 99 percent of them before 21 weeks, the point at which the statute upheld in *Webster* requires a test for the viability of the fetus. Four out of five abortions involve unmarried women, many of them very young. The most common method of abortion, suction curettage, carries almost no risk.[18]

First-trimester abortions, especially when the "woman" is age 12 or 13, are not likely ever to be banned again and even if they were, a pharmaceutical product that safely accomplishes the same purpose (RU-486) is already on the market in Europe and will inevitably become available in the U. S. Second-trimester abortions are restricted by physicians and hospitals even when not regulated by law because of the potential malpractice liability. Third-trimester abortions are virtually unknown. The much-debated question of whether abortions should be publicly funded is wholly symbolic: the cost of the current procedure is so low that public funding is irrelevant.

However the abortion issue is ultimately resolved in the legislatures and the courts, large numbers of women will continue to obtain prompt and safe abortions when they discover themselves to be pregnant, and smaller numbers of women in the same predicament will refuse that option on religious or moral grounds. The fervor is intense on both sides of the great abortion debate but the likelihood of any major change from the current situation is low.

NOTES

1. Based on Richard A. Scammon and Alice V. McGillray, *America Votes 17: 1986* (Washington, D.C.: Congressional Quarterly, 1986), and *Congressional Quarterly Weekly Report 47*, 21 January 1989.
2. There were close connections at the outset between the "old left" and the "new left." For example, Students for a Democratic Society, which played such a conspicuous part in the student movement after 1965, was founded in 1960 as the youth group of the League for Industrial Democracy, an old left social democratic organization. But the connections soon weakened. This sequence of events is described in detail in Irvin D. Solomon, *Feminism and Black Activism in Contemporary America: An Ideological Assessment* (Westport, CT: Greenwood Press, 1989).
3. *Brown* v. *Board of Education of Topeka*, 347 U. S. 483, 493 (1954), Brief for Appellants, 16.
4. Malcolm X, *The Autobiography of Malcolm X*, with the assistance of Alex Haley (New York: Grove Press, 1965).
5. Steven A. Shull, *The President and Civil Rights Policy: Leadership and Change* (Westport, CT: Greenwood Press, 1989), Appendix Tables C1, C2, D3.
6. A partisan but informative account of this controversy is provided by Clint Bolich, *Changing Course: Civil Rights at the Crossroads* (New Brunswick, NJ: Transaction Books, 1988).
7. *Johnson* v. *Transportation Agency*, no. 85-1129 U.S. 17 (1987).
8. Beth B. Hess, *Women and the Family: Two Decades of Change* (New York: Haworth Press, 1984), 251.
9. Shulamith Firestone, *The Dialectic of Sex* (New York: William Morrow, 1970).

10. Valerie Solanas, 1968, quoted by Alice Echols, *Daring to Be Bad: Radical Feminism in America 1967-1975* (Minneapolis: University of Minnesota Press, 1989), 174.

11. By 1984, 50 percent of the members of the Democratic National Committee, Democratic state chairs, and convention delegates were women; the corresponding figures for the Republican party, which had no set quota, were 37 percent and 44 percent. See Denise I. Baer and David A. Bositis, *Elite Cadres and Party Politics: Representing the Public in Party Politics* (Westport, CT: Greenwood Press, 1988), Appendix A.

12. A Green Party on the European model, concerned with environmental issues across the board, has not yet appeared in the United States, although there has been talk about it. For an account of the rise of the Greens in western Europe see Herbert Kitschelt, *The Logic of Party Formation: Ecological Politics in Belgium and West Germany* (Ithaca, NY: Cornell University Press), 1987.

13. John Horgan, "Indecent Burial," *Scientific American*, February 1990, 24D.

14. For a pessimistic assessment of all these dangers see Bill McKibben, *The End of Nature* (New York: Random House, 1989). "Managing Planet Earth," a special issue of *Scientific American*, September 1989, takes a more hopeful view of the same facts.

15. James P. Lester, *Environmental Politics and Policy* (Durham, NC: Duke University Press, 1989), especially Tables 4.3 and 4.4. For a comparable foreign study, see Mario Diari and Giovanni Lodi, "Three in One: Currents in the Milan Ecology Movement," in B. Klandermans, H. Kriesi, and S. Tarrow, eds., *International Social Movement Research* (Greenwich, CT: JAI Press, 1988), vol. 1., 103–124.

16. *GSS72*, Item 72; and *GSS87*, Item 86.

17. Katherine M. Jamieson and Timothy J. Flanagan, ed., *Sourcebook of Criminal Justice Statistics 1988* (Washington, D.C.: Government Printing Office, 1989), 666.

18. Kenneth D. Kochanek, "Induced Terminations of Pregnancy: Reporting States, 1987," National Center for Health Statistics, *Monthly Vital Statistics Report*, 38 (January 1990): 9.

19

FUTURE TRENDS

Every purposive social activity from courtship to space travel is based on images of the future—which may turn out to be mistaken when the future arrives. Scientific research improves the quality of such images but cannot free them from error, and the predictive value of social science is further restricted by the ability of human subjects to modify their own behavior in order to avoid a predicted event or condition.[1] Thus, any serious discussion of future trends must be modest and hesitant. We know that we cannot chart future trends with much precision and that some future conditions are unimaginable today. Not one of the sociologists who studied race relations around 1950 foresaw the rise and success of the civil rights movement. No student of American culture imagined the counter-culture before it happened. Not a single political analyst of the mid-1980s predicted the imminent end of the Cold War. We will always be amazed as the future unrolls.

But although comprehensive social prediction is impossible, the extrapolation of ongoing social trends can often carry us some distance into the future with reasonable confidence. Both the distance and the confidence vary from one trend to another. In general, the longer a trend has been running, the further out it can be projected, and the greater the probability that the projection will be accurate. Long-term trends that have been interrupted or reversed in the past, like the decline of poverty, are harder to extrapolate than unbroken trends, like the increase of telephones, and long-term trends that approach a numerical limit, like high school enrollment, cease to be useful for prediction. Of the various elements that enter into social change, the easiest to predict are new technologies, the hardest are new ideologies.

Because so many prophets fail, it is instructive to study the methods of those who prophesy successfully. In the entire literature of social thought, the best prophet has been Alexis de Tocqueville, whose *Democracy in America*, published in two separate volumes in

1830 and 1835, accurately describes the growth of American population and territory through 1930 and the eventual domination of Europe by two superpowers, America and Russia, among many other things. Tocqueville was not always right, but even when he was wrong, as in his guess that the Union would be unable to prevent the secession of the South, he had a clear grasp of the essential issues many years before anyone else.[2] He was fully aware of his abilities: "I have not undertaken to see differently than others," he wrote, "but to see further."[3] When Tocqueville speaks to us from the early nineteenth century about the future of Europe or the future of America, he seems to be talking about the world as we know it now. How did he do it? The secret seems to lie in certain assumptions that guided his reading of the future. They can be summarized as follows.[4]

- The persistence of major social institutions is taken for granted. Unlike many of his contemporaries, and many of ours, Tocqueville did not expect the family, religion, or the state to disappear or to be rapidly transformed.

- The stability of human nature is taken for granted. He did not expect men and women to become much better or worse or different than history had shown them to be.

- Two very powerful, long-term trends are expected to continue: a trend towards equality and a trend towards administrative centralization.

- Social change is always channeled and circumscribed by the limited availability of material resources.

- The future is not fully determined by the past. The future, viewed from the present, is an amalgam of probabilities based on past experience and of contingencies arising from accident and free will.

- There are no social forces aside from human actions. "I detest," Tocqueville wrote, "those absolute systems which represent all events of history as depending upon great causes linked by the chain of fatality . . . "[5]

These assumptions, taken together, exclude both the unbounded optimism of some modern futurists and the bleak pessimism of others.[6] Tocqueville visualized a continuous tension between the gradual progress of equality, which enlarges freedom and administrative centralization, which extinguishes it. He did not see an easy resolution of the dilemma. It is proof of his prescience that the reduction of inequality and the expansion of government are so conspicuous among the major trends in American society between 1960 and 1990. I count 90 of those trends, as follows:

1. Continued technological progress, especially in information technology.
2. Continued economic growth, at a slowing rate.
3. Moderate population growth, attributable to immigration.
4. Continued preparation for a nuclear war.
5. A sharp decline in the social and economic advantages of the United States over other industrial nations.
6. The aging and deterioration of the nation's infrastructure.
7. A great increase in public and private debt.
8. A dramatic decline of fertility.
9. A great increase in nonmarital sexual activity.
10. A great increase in illegitimate births and single-parent families.
11. A great increase in the number of dual-earner families.
12. The adoption of no-fault divorce and a slow increase in the divorce rate.
13. The increasing divergence of white and black family patterns.
14. Approximate stability in the general level of religious observance and belief.
15. A shift of membership from mainline Protestant denominations to Fundamentalist and Pentecostal churches.
16. A shift of the mainline Protestant, Catholic, and Jewish clergy towards liberal positions on doctrine, morality, and social issues.
17. A marked decline in religious bigotry.
18. An increase in the political activity of religious leaders and organizations.
19. The virtual cessation of educational progress, except by minorities, around 1970.
20. The continued escalation of educational costs.
21. A great expansion of the nonacademic functions of educational institutions.
22. A spectacular increase in the employment of women, especially married women with young children.
23. A great increase in the ratio of white-collar to blue-collar jobs.
24. A decline in the membership and influence of labor unions.

25. The increasing prevalence of bureaucratic employment systems.

26. An interruption of the long-term trend of rising real wages.

27. A great expansion of fringe benefits.

28. A rapid reduction in the number of dangerous and physically punishing jobs and a corresponding reduction of industrial accidents.

29. A general improvement in workplace conditions.

30. A spectacular increase in the number of American enterprises owned by foreigners.

31. Increased participation in nearly all leisure activities, both active and passive.

32. The expansion, elaboration, and diversification of leisure domains.

33. The reduced differentiation of leisure patterns by social class, gender, ethnicity, and age.

34. A slow decline in the length of the work year.

35. A vast expansion of federal authority in matters formerly reserved to state, local, and private authorities.

36. A vast increase in federal outlays for welfare purposes—health, education, pensions, housing.

37. A vast increase of aggregate expenditures at all levels of government.

38. A vast increase in the power of the judiciary and in the volume and scope of litigation.

39. A steady decline in voter participation.

40. A sharp decline of public confidence in government.

41. The commercialization of electoral politics.

42. A spectacular increase of corrupt practices in the federal government.

43. The development of serious operating problems in the welfare system, the political system, and the armed forces.

44. A continuous inflationary trend that quadrupled the prices of basic commodities between 1960 and 1990.

45. A rise of per capita personal income that outstripped inflation by more than two to one during the same period.

46. An increase of the money supply that outstripped the rise of personal income by more than two to one during the same period.

47. The superinflation of prices for real estate, specialized services, and scarce goods, enriching some groups and impoverishing others.

48. The legalization and superinflation of gambling.

49. A massive shift of wealth from the young to the old.

50. An interruption of the long-term trend towards the elimination of poverty.

51. The deregulation of sexual relations with mutual consent.

52. The increasing regulation of sexual relations without mutual consent.

53. A dramatic equalization of male and female sexual attitudes and practices.

54. The slow equalization of sexual attitudes and practices by social class, ethnicity, and age.

55. An enormous increase in the commercial production of sexual imagery.

56. A rapid increase of life expectancy, especially at later ages.

57. A slow but steady decline of infant mortality.

58. The reversal of the American advantage over other industrial countries in infant mortality and life expectancy.

59. The virtual disappearance of infectious childhood diseases.

60. A great increase of health awareness among the public.

61. The spread of the HIV epidemic after 1980.

62. Enormous technological progress in health care, without a proportional improvement in the general health of the population.

63. A dramatic escalation of health care costs.

64. A great increase in the incidence of malpractice claims and in the size of malpractice awards.

65. A sharp rise in the number of health care providers.

66. The invention and diffusion of new patterns of health care.

67. A slow decline in cigarette consumption.

68. A slow decline in the consumption of hard liquor, offset by increases in the consumption of beer and wine.

69. Vast increases in the consumption of legal mood-changing drugs, and sharp fluctuations in the consumption of illegal mood-changing drugs.

70. A vast increase of law enforcement personnel and facilities in the attempt to suppress the consumption of illegal mood-changing drugs.

71. The increasingly elective character of American ethnicity.

72. The abandonment of official discrimination against nonwhites.

73. A dramatic improvement of the educational opportunities and achievements of minorities, interrupted in the 1980s.

74. The rise of black athletes to predominance in the major spectator sports.

75. A narrowing of the gap between whites and nonwhites with regard to education, income, and health.

76. The development of affirmative action in favor of nonwhites.

77. The increasing concentration of the black population in metropolitan cities.

78. A marked decline in private expressions of ethnic hostility.

79. A vast and continuing increase in illegal immigration from Mexico, Central America, and the Caribbean.

80. A vast and continuing increase in legal immigration from Asia.

81. A rapid erosion of the political and social power of white Protestants of Anglo-Saxon descent.

82. A reversal of the long-standing educational and economic advantage of Protestants over Catholics.

83. A great reduction in institutionalized anti-Semitism.

84. An increasing effort by ethnic groups to conserve their cultural heritages.

85. A steady increase in the number of white Americans without a well-defined ethnic identity.

86. The rise of movements claiming expanded rights for blacks, hispanics, Native Americans, women, homosexuals, the elderly, and the handicapped, and the incorporation of those claims into public policy.

87. A partial shift from the goal of equal opportunity to the goal of equal outcome as the rights movements gained strength.

88. A tendency for social movements to move from confrontation to lobbying and litigation.

89. The rapid but fragmented growth of environmental protest movements to match a growing list of environmental threats.

90. A sharp increase in the number and importance of social movements with primarily symbolic goals.

Many of the foregoing trends testify to the continuation of that very long-term trend that Tocqueville called: "the gradual progress of equality,"[7] between men and women, the old and the young, whites and blacks, Anglos and hispanics, blue collars and white collars, natives and immigrants, Christians and Jews, Protestants and Catholics, farmers and city-dwellers, heterosexuals and homosexuals, normal and handicapped, the United States and other countries. Much of this progress resulted from deliberate actions by government that were intended to reduce social inequality and did so. Nearly as many of the trends in the list[8] reflect administrative centralization—the greatly expanded role of the federal government as the initiator and manager of social change. That role has been expanding, in one way and another, since the earliest days of the Republic, but the enlargement of federal functions that began in the 1960s, and continues to this day, turned the U. S. government, which had been the least centralized of the industrial democracies, into one of the most centralized. The transition has been uncomfortable, partly because administrative centralization is naturally inimical to other democratic values, partly because the U. S. Constitution was originally designed to thwart administrative centralization and is not easily adapted to the opposite purpose.

As of 1960, the federal government was responsible for defense, foreign relations, and the postal service; the regulation of interstate common carriers, financial markets, and banking; antitrust enforcement; immigration and citizenship, patents and copyrights; social security; and jointly with the states for roads and bridges, unemployment insurance, public housing and aid to dependent children. But, unlike European welfare states, the federal government was not responsible for education, health care, workplace conditions, criminal justice, family relationships, the regulation of sexuality, crime control, child care, product safety, historic preservation, industrial personnel policy, insurance, handicapped care, nutritional standards, or linguistic usage. As it reached out to take on responsibilities for these matters, the government's problem-solving capability visibly diminished and the adverse effects of its programs multiplied, as many of the above listed trends show.[9]

The adverse effects include the superinflation of costs in health care and education. The result of the badly designed federal programs in these fields is that the government's costs continuously spiral upward without lifting the burden of heavy costs from individuals and families and without providing adequate health care or education for the entire population.

Another important effect is the superinflation of defense costs. As the prices of new weapons became sheerly poetic—close to $1 billion for each Stealth bomber—the guiding strategy of military preparation became incoherent. With the cold war won, nobody could explain what the bombers were for.

Another adverse effect has been the institutionalization of poverty. The alabaster cities of America, unlike their European and Canadian counterparts, contain slum districts of medieval squalor where life is nasty, brutish, and short. The expensive programs designed to improve this situation serve in practice to enrich speculators who have political connections.

The two federal programs most visible in the urban ghettos, Aid to Families with Dependent Children and the War on Drugs, are both counterproductive. The former forces families into the single-parent mold without relieving their poverty. The latter subsidizes and encourages the habits it intends to suppress, while multiplying the number of policemen and prison cells out of all reason.

These foolish programs, and others too numerous to mention, are so costly that the national debt has been doubling every six years. Meanwhile the routine operations of federal agencies are slow, cumbersome, and uncertain. Congress contributes to the problem by endlessly piling up laws. The smallest federal contractor must certify compliance with more than 50 separate statutes. The executive branch emits its own unending stream of regulations, often contradictory or inscrutable. It surprises no one when the agents delegated by the Internal Revenue Service to answer questions from taxpayers give wrong answers nearly half the time. The judiciary continually amends or nullifies the actions of the other two branches by decisions that often seem capricious. The authority of the courts has grown steadily and almost without challenge in recent decades, together with the number of lawyers, the price of legal services, the scale of damage awards, and the lengthiness of proceedings. By a wide margin, the United States is the most litigious country in the world.[10]

The courts have used their expanded powers to encourage the gradual progress of equality. They have, for example, imposed desegregation plans on reluctant school districts, ordered redistricting to ensure equality in voter representation, awarded spousal rights to unmarried lovers and inheritance rights to illegitimate children, checked the authority of professionals over patients by encouraging malpractice suits, and lessened the disparity between manufacturers and consumers by broadening the concept of product liability. But the courts, working within a framework of rights, have been generally indifferent to the costs of the benefits they confer. The dollar costs of litigation and insurance against litigation are passed on to the public, which also must bear such nonmonetary costs as the withholding of useful products, the curtailment of essential services, and the abandonment of all sorts of worthwhile projects, from love affairs to municipal skating rinks, because of the risk of being sued.

Thus, as Tocqueville showed long ago, the progress of equality continues to be accompanied and undermined by administrative centralization. The various trends of equalization can be extrapolated with some confidence. The short remainder of the twentieth century and the beginning of the twenty-first are almost sure to see the continued convergence of the career patterns of men and women; continued gender equalization in business and politics; an additional decline in fertility; a further narrowing of the gaps between whites and nonwhites in income, education, and health; continued large-scale hispanic and Asian immigration; and a further blurring of the boundaries among ethnic groups and social classes.

It is a much more chancy matter to extrapolate the trends that represent administrative centralization in the federal government. The time is long past when the states could claim a measure of sovereignty and resist encroachment. The expansion of federal prerogatives has not provoked much resistance from the general public, who are largely unaware of it, or from organized interest groups, which have discovered ways to profit from it. And modern technology favors administrative centralization in two special ways: computers enable the government to strive for omniscience while the most advanced technological projects become too gigantic for private sponsorship.

Nevertheless, the tendency towards administrative centralization in the United States cannot be extrapolated with as much confidence as the general movement towards equality. The expansion of the federal government is likely to be checked, and perhaps reversed, by the operating ineffiencies reflected in the escalation of health, education, and justice expenditures and the increase of the public debt at rates that cannot continue indefinitely, and by a growing inventory of intractable problems that includes:

- The aging and nonreplacement of the infrastructure—roads, railroads, bridges, airports, and urban transit.
- The persistence of poverty and the increase of single-parent families.
- The practical failure of school desegregation and the partial collapse of the public schools.
- The self-defeating war on drugs.
- The continued decline of industrial competitiveness.
- The continued decline of educational competitiveness.
- The savings and loans catastrophe.
- The many forms of political corruption whereby money buys favorable treatment from public agencies.
- The government's inability to control illegal immigration.
- The government's inability to clean up toxic wastes or ensure nuclear safety.

With the possible exception of the decline of industrial competitiveness, each of these intractable problems is attributable to the failure of government programs and policies. Taken together, they foreshadow a constitutional crisis whose exact outline is difficult to foresee but which will probably result in some curtailment of federal welfare functions and some limitation of the jurisdiction of the federal courts.

If the debit side of the ledger is crowded, so is the credit side. We remain, for the time being, the strongest and richest nation in the world, the main source of its popular culture, and the principal custodian of its scientific knowledge. There is more equality, in law and in fact, than ever before, and more millionaires as well. Labor-management conflict, religious bigotry, and ethnic hostility have largely subsided. The boundaries between social classes are fading. The institution of the family has been shaken, but not shattered, by recent trends. Religion flourishes. Patriotism is fervent. The two-party system is universally accepted; the extreme left and the extreme right of the political spectrum are almost uninhabited. And technological progress gives no sign of flagging.

Technological progress is much the easiest part of social change to forecast. In 1887, Edward Bellamy attempted to describe American society in the year 2000. On the technological side, he was able to foresee closed-circuit television, credit cards, computerized accounting, interstate highways, community colleges, disposable clothing, natural childbirth, giant earth-moving machinery, telephone answering machines, and the availability of rental cars at airports. By contrast, his picture of family, work, education, leisure, religion, and government in the year 2000 was wrong in every detail.[11] When another flurry of interest in the year 2000 developed in the 1960s, the forecasts of new technology were again remarkably accurate. A panel of 150 experts who were questioned about the future in 1963 predicted that the following technological innovations would appear by the year 2000: economically useful desalination of sea water, effective oral contraception, new synthetic materials for ultra-light construction, automated language translators, organ transplants and artificial organs, reliable weather forecasts, large-scale data storage and retrieval, new mood-changing drugs, lasers, controlled thermonuclear power, creation of a primitive form of artificial life, and mining of the ocean bottom.[12] The same panel's forecasts of institutional change were sparse and uninformative. Another set of forecasts for the last third of the century, published by Kahn and Wiener in 1967, follows the same pattern. The first 15 technological innovations they predicted are already in general use; but at least 8 of their 15 predictions of social and economic change were wrong.[13]

Many of the unrealized technological innovations predicted by these experts a generation ago remain on the agenda today. They include chemical control of the aging process, the production of electricity from nuclear fusion, interplanetary travel, ocean agriculture, accurate weather prediction, and antigravity devices.

Social forecasts are not only less reliable than technological forecasts; they are intrinsically more complex. In the Middletown III study, we tested a proposition, derived from Vilfredo Pareto, that in a social system over time, motives are much more stable than the social acts that express them, and social acts are much more stable than the explanations given for them. When we traced social trends in Middletown from 1924 to 1984, it appeared that the motivational signature of the community had remained almost unchanged. Between 1924 and 1984, Middletown showed remarkably little change in the motivational structure of its family, religious, political, and educational institutions. The motive-expressing rituals performed at basketball games, revival meetings, company picnics, weddings, and graduations remained the same. Action patterns in Middletown between 1924 and 1984 were much less stable. Many types of action, like women's work, sexual practices, interracial transactions, and leisure activities were transformed. The stereotyped explanations that people in Middletown gave for their own actions were more volatile still. Very few of the explanations of social relationships that they gave in 1924 (for example that women are better and purer than men, but that men are more practical and efficient) command agreement today.[14]

The volatility of popular social theories is so great that, for all practical purposes, future variations in them are unpredictable. We can form no concept of how Americans 30 years hence will view environmental issues or how they will theorize about childbearing. But we can predict with some confidence that the relationships between husbands and wives, parents and children, employers and employees, clergy and laity, officials and citizens, will not be greatly modified in the near future and we can prophesy with even more confidence that the distinctive American character, which has somehow persisted since the dawn of our national history, will not change appreciably from this generation to the next.

That character has been shaped by two main influences—the ideal of freedom and the fact of ethnic stratification.

American history is still taught in school as a morality play—the continuous perfecting of freedom from the Mayflower Compact through the Cold War. Freedom in this context refers not only to free speech, fair elections, representative government, and religious tolerance, but also to private property, due process, ethnic equality, educational opportunity, and the possibility of starting one's own business. The concept is flexible enough to accommodate any value shared by a large number of citizens. And it is linked to a claim of moral superiority over other nations that has been remarkably resistant to the humiliating national experiences of the past three decades—the political assassinations, the Vietnam defeat, the Watergate scandals, the hostage-takings, the loss of industrial supremacy to Japan, the Iran-Contra affair, the successive drug epidemics, and the plunge towards national insolvency. Fervent displays of patriotism on public occasions have been customary in the U. S. since the earliest days of the Republic and they continue to this day. The celebrations of the successive bicentennials of the Declaration of Independence, the Constitution, and the Bill of Rights, and the centennial of the Statue of Liberty, were as enthusiastic as anything before, and the theme of moral superiority was sounded as strongly as ever.

The fact of ethnic stratification is the other side of the coin. More than any other large nation, the United States is a mosaic of diverse ethnic groups stratified by wealth, education, occupation, and self-esteem. The cultural distance between the country club and the inner-city street corner is too great to be bridged by patriotic sentiments. The tension between the promise of freedom and the reality of hereditary advantage lies close to the heart of the American character. It is particularly acute for black citizens, to whom boasts about American freedom still have a hollow ring.

The tension is accommodated but not resolved by the attribution of dangerous and immoral behavior to outgroups, which justifies hostility towards them. The continual effort of the American polity to legislate and enforce moral improvement seem to be grounded on intergroup hostility, the disapproved behavior being generally attributed to outgroups: nineteenth-century drunkenness to Irishmen, twentieth-century drug addiction to blacks, insider trading to Jews, organized crime to Italians. There are always Indians lurking in the woods, and new people, with uncouth habits, moving into town. People like *us*, whoever that is, are always outnumbered or about to be outnumbered, by *them*.

The uneasiness generated by this ethnic pressure may help to explain the importance of anticommunism as a unifying influence in American public life for most of this century. The communists were the ultimate outgroup—an enemy that all ethnic groups could share. The Cold War, like other wars, unified the country, and coincidentally or not, it was accompanied by a striking decline in the general level of intergroup hostility, marked by the disestablishment of racial segregation, the broad prohibition of ethnic discrimination, and a spectacular decline of ethnic and religious intolerance.[15]

The end of the Cold War and the evaporation of the communist threat leaves a vacuum to be filled in the motivational framework of American society. If past experience is a guide, the vacuum will be filled by moral crusades against newly defined outgroups. There are fashions, of course, in the stigmatization of behavior. With the decline of intergroup hostility, the forms of behavior selected for public concern and official response are less often associated with disadvantaged minorities than formerly. Among recently fashionable subjects of moral crusades, pedophilia, influence-peddling, industrial pollution, animal rights, drunk driving, abortion, and homelessness are ethnically neutral. But drug abuse, the leading subject of popular and official intolerance, does have thinly veiled ethnic connotations; the war on drugs is directed principally against blacks and hispanics. On the other hand, the AIDS epidemic, which might have been expected to provoke a moral crusade against homosexuality, led instead to a public relations campaign for safe sex. And it is notable that the recent waves of immigration from Asia and Latin America are the first large-scale immigrations in American history that have not aroused much organized resistance.

Will future American trends sustain the gradual progress of equality and enlarge the promise of freedom? The question cannot be answered with the data in hand. There are portents of trouble in the deterioration of the federal government, the erosion of natural resources, the rising burden of debt, the superinflation of essential services, the byzantine complexity of the legal system, the interruption of educational progress, the persistence of poverty, the growing number of single-parent families, the expansion of police forces and prisons, and the decay of the infrastructure. But there are signs of hope in our continued economic and technological progress, the reduction of ethnic discrimination, the blurring of class divisions, the equalization of the sexes, the vitality of family and religious values, and the large consensus that supports the vague but powerful idea of freedom.

Let Tocqueville have the last word. Towards the end of his life he wrote to a friend that, "In my view, societies, like individuals, become worthwhile only by the exercise of freedom. I have always said that freedom might be more difficult to establish and maintain in our democratic societies than in some aristocratic societies of the past. But I will never be so rash as to think it impossible."[16]

NOTES

1. The limits of social science prediction have been admirably described by Wendell Bell and Jeffrey K. Olick, "An Epistemology for the Futures Field: Problems and Possibilities of Prediction," *Futures*, April 1989, 115–35; and Richard L. Henshel, *On the Future of Social Prediction* (Indianapolis, IN: Bobbs-Merrill, 1976).
2. Alexis de Tocqueville, *Democracy in America*, vol. 1, (1930; New York: Knopf, 1945) 377–94.
3. Alexis de Tocqueville, *The European Revolution and Correspondence with Gobineau*, ed. John Lukacs (Gloucester, MA: Peter Smith, 1968), 44.

4. For a fuller account of Tocqueville's model of social change, see Theodore Caplow, "The Current Relevance of Democracy in America," *The Tocqueville Review*, 7(1986): 137–47.

5. Tocqueville, *The European Revolution*, 54.

6. For unbounded optimism see John Naisbitt and Patricia Aburdene, *Megatrends 2000: Ten New Directions for the 1990's* (New York: William Morrow, 1990). For bleak pessimism try Michel Crozier, *The Trouble with America: Why the System Is Breaking Down* (Berkeley: University of California Press, 1984).

7. Including numbers 5,11,12,22,23,33,53,54,71,72,73,74,75,76,78,81,83,85,86,87.

8. Including numbers 4,7,21,25,35,36,37,38,49,52,63,64,70,72,76,86,87,88.

9. Including numbers 4,6,7,10,13,19,20,26,30,39,40,41,42,43,49,50,58,63,70,79.

10. For the conceptual background of this development, see Macklin Fleming, *The Price of Perfect Justice: The Adverse Consequences of Current Legal Doctrine in the American Courtroom* (New York: Basic Books, 1974).

11. Edward Bellamy, *Looking Backward* (New York: D. Appleton Company, 1888).

12. Olaf Helmer, *Social Technology* (New York: Basic Books, 1966), 56–57.

13. John Horgan, "Indecent Burial," *Scientific American*, February 1990, 24D.

14. This analysis is more fully reported in Theodore Caplow, "Paretian Theory Applied to the Findings of the Middletown III Research," *Revue Européene des Sciences Sociales*, 25(1987): 55–78.

15. Between 1948 and 1987, the proportion of U. S. survey respondents objecting to black neighbors declined from 63 percent to 13 percent; the proportion objecting to Jewish neighbors from 22 percent to 3 percent. "Opinion Roundup: The State of Intolerance," *Public Opinion* 10(1987): 22–23.

16. From a letter to A. de Gobineau, 25 January 1857. Alexis de Tocqueville, *Oeuvres Complètes* (Paris: Gallimard, 1959), 280.

INDEX

B 1
C 2
D 3
E 4
F 5
G 6
H 7
I 8
J 9